I Swear I'll Make It Up to You

A LIFE ON THE LOW ROAD

Mishka Shubaly

PUBLICAFFAIRS
New York

PublicAffairs books are available at special discounts for bulk purchases in the U.S. by corporations, institutions, and other organizations. For more information, please contact the Special Markets Department at the Perseus Books Group, 2300 Chestnut Street, Suite 200, Philadelphia, PA 19103, call (800) 810-4145, ext. 5000, or e-mail special.markets@perseus books.com.

Book design by Jeff Williams

Library of Congress Cataloging-in-Publication Data

Names: Shubaly, Mishka, author.
Title: I swear I'll make it up to you : a life on the low road / Mishka Shubaly.
Description: New York, New York : PublicAffairs, 2016.
Identifiers: LCCN 2015040867| ISBN 9781610395588 (hardback) | ISBN 9781610395595 (ebook)
Subjects: LCSH: Shubaly, Mishka. | Rock musicians—United States—Biography.
| BISAC: BIOGRAPHY & AUTOBIOGRAPHY / Personal Memoirs. | SELF-HELP / Substance Abuse & Addictions / Alcoholism. | SPORTS & RECREATION / Running & Jogging.
Classification: LCC ML420.S542 A3 2016 | DDC 782.42166092—dc23 LC record available at http://lccn.loc.gov/2015040867

First Edition

10 9 8 7 6 5 4 3 2 1

For my sisters, Tashina and Tatyana

Contents

Oh my God, what have I gotten myself into?
I'm a human corkscrew and all my wine is blood
They're gonna kill me, Mama
They don't like me, bud.

—JOHN PRINE

Prologue

People misremember things. Even if I remember it
wrong, this is how I remember it.
　　　　　　　—MURRAY SHUBALY

O ne Sunday morning when I was twenty-two, I was working my way home from a Saturday night out—badly
hungover, a trail of orange vomit descending from the
collar of my Salvation Army T-shirt all the way down across my
Salvation Army pants to the tops of my Salvation Army shoes.
When the No. 2 train pulled up at 14th Street, Anne, a girl I had
gone to school with, was standing on the train directly in front of
me. I hadn't seen her since I was seventeen, when I'd cheated on
my then girlfriend, Riley, with her. As the doors opened, I gave
Anne my most winning smile. She surveyed me wistfully.

"Oh, Mishka," she said as she brushed past with a grimace,
"you haven't changed a bit."

I boarded the train and rode uptown in silence. I had moved
to the city less than a year earlier in order to claim the fame I was
sure awaited me. Instead, I'd had to prostrate myself just to find a
job I felt beneath my unique gifts, a job I loathed: data entry in the

Women's Apparel Department at Bergdorf Goodman, New York's most ostentatious department store. I shared a one-room apartment with my stepbrother, Jesse, the most cramped living conditions I'd ever endured for the highest rent I had ever paid. My mother and my younger sister lived in the Virgin Islands, and I saw them one week a year at most. I hadn't spoken to my older sister or my father in years. I was badly heartbroken, still madly in love with Riley, who had disappeared without a word when I was twenty.

When I emerged onto the 96th Street subway platform to transfer to a local train, a man was playing steel drums. The song was at once light and droning, uplifting and plaintive, foreign and intimately familiar, defiant and inexpressibly sad. I was so light-headed and woozy that I couldn't make out the tune at first. It was "Amazing Grace." The song's lyrics rattled into my dehydrated brain without even being sung, and with them, a terrible epiphany.

In the airless cloister of the subway platform, I wept: suddenly, copiously, uncontrollably, in the same manner I had upchucked my malt liquor and Nacho Cheese Doritos the night before. I didn't know how to live—anywhere, but especially in the big city. My greatest comfort—my alcohol—had begun to terrify me. My teenage arrogance had been beaten out of me. I had been humbled. I was lost.

As a child, I had learned from my mother's Arlo Guthrie cassette that "Amazing Grace" had been written by a slave trader. The story goes that this slave trader picked up his human cargo on the coast of western Africa and set sail for America. But when he reached the middle of the ocean, he had an epiphany—I have made a *horrible* mistake—and he turned the ship around. He returned to Africa, set the people he had abducted free, and devoted his life to fighting against slavery.

Envision this majestic and baffling spectacle: a massive, ancient, handmade wooden ship, under full sail on an ocean bare of land or any sign of humanity, gradually slowing down, then hesitating for a moment, as if in deep contemplation. Then the cumbersome mast swings about, and the mammoth vessel ascribes a slow, wide circle and returns back the way it came, as if under the pull of a bigger force.

Sadly, the slave trader narrative behind "Amazing Grace" is untrue. The song was indeed written by a slave trader named John Newton, but he had no crisis of conscience at sea involving the ethics of slavery. John Newton did experience a spiritual conversion in 1748 during a fierce storm, but no ship turned around, and no one was freed. In fact, Newton was a hellion with a well-documented pattern of coming close to death, swearing to change his life, then enthusiastically plunging back into debauchery, blasphemy, and a level of creative profanity that made even his fellow sailors cringe.

After Newton's conversion, he continued to work as a slave trader and continued to mistreat his slaves until 1754, when he became physically unable to do so following a stroke. Even then, he continued to invest in slave trading operations for many years. Newton wrote "Amazing Grace" in 1773, and he did *finally* speak out against slavery . . . but only after he had made his fortune enslaving his fellow human beings.

Still, grace exists. You flail around, you stumble, you weep in public on subway platforms, the cries of trains in your ears, knifing pains in your gut, and orange vomit on your shirt. You get it wrong and you get it wrong and you get it wrong . . . and then one day, somehow, you find your way.

CHAPTER I

Sucker Punch

One of those swampy, hollowed-out nights in August when anyone with a means of escape has fled New York City and everyone left behind is ready to kill or die, anything to interrupt the boredom and the heat. I was behind the bar making change for Eddie the bartender when we heard the unmistakable sound of Something Going Wrong in a Bar—chairs scraping, the clatter of something falling over, grunts of exertion, the heavy, meaty sound of blows, women squawking. I whipped around and saw the arm of a man in a white long-sleeve shirt rising and falling over someone flat on the ground.

Eddie and I sprinted from behind the bar. Eddie grabbed the guy's arm, and I got him in a choke hold and dragged him toward the door. I'd lost control of a bar I was managing once before, and the entire room turned on me. I got put through a wall and was lucky to come out of it with just a black eye. My old friend Javad was working the door, and we'd been hanging out all night—where the hell was he now that we needed him?

I heaved the guy outside and shoved him away from me into the street so I'd have warning if he charged me. I was surprised by how preppy he looked—somewhere between Dave Eggers and

Timothy Bottoms from *The Last Picture Show*. He shot me a black look and walked off. These guys fighting were probably just day traders blowing off steam about something I didn't understand, points and percentages and percentages of points. So make up an ice pack for the bump on the chin of the other dude, buy him a drink or two, and just get through the night.

When I went back inside, I found Javad. He was lying on the floor, eyes closed, body motionless, face flat and lifeless. Javad was one of the first friends I'd made when I'd moved to New York twelve years earlier. I dropped to my knees. Eddie cradled Javad's head and called his name. There was blood in his mouth and an egg on the back of his head from where he'd hit the floor. Someone touched a piece of ice to his forehead. Slowly, Javad opened his eyes.

After we'd turned the lights on for the paramedics and they had taken Javad off in an ambulance, we watched the incident on the security cameras. The man in the white button-down had been bothering a woman with curly hair in the back. She came and talked to Javad at the front door—an Australian man was bothering her, she'd told him. Javad had politely asked the Australian to leave. As Javad was escorting the man to the door, the curly-haired woman started talking trash to her antagonist. Javad turned his head to tell her to shut it, and the Aussie sucker-punched him, knocking him out, then continued wailing on him after he'd fallen to the floor, unconscious.

At the end of my shift, I was still too rattled to bike home to Brooklyn. I couldn't even decompress with a couple of drinks. After nearly twenty years of drinking, I'd made it sober for a couple of months, and I knew that even one beer would be my complete undoing. I left my bike chained to a light post and took a cab home, my heart still racing.

My cell phone rang in the cab. Javad was calling me from the ER. He'd just realized he was chewing the same piece of gum he'd been chewing when he got coldcocked—should he hang on to it for forensic evidence? I could hear him grinning on the other end of the phone. At least the blow hadn't knocked any sense into him.

———

I awoke the next morning in a black rage. This Australian asshole, this amateur, this poorly tipping *tourist* had attacked my friend without provocation and gotten off scot-free. I'd had him in my hands, and I'd let him go. I should have pulped his face.

I had to get my bike. I threw on the clothes that were on my floor and an ancient pair of Adidas indoor soccer shoes, the leather stiff and cracked from a job pouring concrete. I walked out into the stifling heat.

When I'd moved into this apartment, I was determined to insulate my neighbors from the chaos of my life, not something I'd excelled at in the past. My previous living situation, I'd woken up once on the sidewalk a block from my apartment, once directly in front of it, and once on the landing outside my door. My landlord grilled me: "I can never tell if you're running on blood or alcohol." I should have pointed out to him that I was narrowing the margin of error, at least.

But I'd failed early and flamboyantly at this apartment, coming home at 5 a.m. covered in blood the day after I moved in. I'd had to knock on the landlady's first-floor window because I couldn't get my key to work.

There were three or four people standing at the bus stop, fanning themselves with newspapers. Between the heat radiating off the pavement, the exhaust from passing trucks, and the everyday Brooklyn stench of hot, wet garbage, it was like standing in front of a trash fire. Fuck waiting on a bus. I would run all the way into the city to get my bike.

I had never been a runner. I couldn't be bothered to run to catch a train. For as long as I could remember, "going on a run" meant I was going to the corner to buy beer or, if I was feeling particularly ambitious, across the street to the liquor store.

Even as a kid, running was only punishment, something you were forced to do for goofing off in PE class: "Shubaly. Shut your mouth and take a lap." As an adult, the only time I engaged in running—that idiotic behavior where you flail your arms and legs around like you're drowning in the air—was when addressed directly by a police officer. But that blazing August afternoon, something broke in me. I began to run.

My shoes scuffed the pavement awkwardly or slapped down too hard. My tummy jiggled shamefully with each step. I passed the apartment of Shilpa, my former best friend and current nemesis. Our band had gotten right to the edge of doing something memorable, only to shit the bed at the very last second. In our last communication, she had challenged me to a fistfight. I later got a letter from her lawyer, threatening to sue me for over a million dollars.

I crossed McGuinness Avenue into Williamsburg and over a decade's worth of shitty memories. Brooklyn was a map of my disappointment, a city built of my failures. The bars I'd been fired from, the bars I'd been tossed out of, the bars I could never, ever return to. The ex-roommate whose last words for me had been a text that just read, "You are a speck of shit." My oldest and most trusted friend, James, whom I hadn't spoken to in five years. The ex-friend who I knew was going to take a swing at me the next time he saw me for going home with his girl the night after they broke up. I feared the physical confrontation, not because I might lose—in which case I'd be getting the beating I deserved—but because I might snap on him and win. I'd caused enough injury.

Then, of course, there were the women. Women I'd spent a night or a couple of weeks or a couple of months with before retreating, women I'd stolen drugs from and who had stolen drugs from me, women I'd stormed out on in the middle of dates after pounding both our drinks, women who were mostly justified in hating my guts but who had only made sad eyes at me when they'd seen me staggering around at night or crawling home in the morning.

McCarren Park was the heart of Williamsburg. Summer week-ends, it was the neighborhood's backyard, and everyone convened there: African American, Latino, Polish, Jewish, Italian families barbecuing or picnicking and playing softball or soccer or just hanging out. When I moved to New York in 1998, there had been a small number of kids from Ohio or Michigan or Montreal in black punk and heavy metal T-shirts who hung out in the southwest cor-ner, close enough to conveniently nab a tall, powerful margarita in a Styrofoam cup from the Turkey's Nest. Each year, we grew more numerous and more dilute, no longer just rocker kids escap-ing dead-end towns but club kids, DJs, white dudes with dreads, "Internet entrepreneurs," hacky sackers. Six years later, Young, White, and Not From Here seemed to have reached critical mass. Still, each year the infestation worsened, till the entire park was overrun, till the whole neighborhood became an open-air dormi-tory for adult children with platinum credit cards, pursuing their MDMA from Red Bull Academy.

The lone corner of resistance was the northern point of McCar-ren Park, devoted to older Polish men showcasing the four phases of alcohol's orbit. Some drank slyly out of bottles in brown paper or black plastic bags; some were openly shitfaced; some, already blacked out and snoring; some, freshly awoken, wincing at the sun-shine, in grievous pain and eager to move into the next quarter.

Ten years ago, I had been one of those kids at the southwest end of the park in the rock T-shirts, scrambling and starving, look-ing to get loud and weird and fucked-up and maybe even write for a magazine. Ten years later, the only progress I'd made was a glacial migration of maybe eight hundred feet north—eight hun-dred feet removed from "hipster" and eight hundred feet closer to "homeless."

Only minutes into my run, still an unthinkable distance from my bike, I could already feel things going wrong with my body. My T-shirt had cinched up in my armpits, and my floppy upper arms made wet clapping sounds against my torso. I could feel each heartbeat reverberating throughout my body, trying to hammer down the walls of my skull. My face felt so hot it hurt. I kept running.

I had moved to the city at twenty-one with $300 and the naked ambition of becoming a famous writer and musician. In over a decade of hustling in the city, I had worked as an order-entry clerk, furniture mover, audio engineer, editor, customer service rep, ghostwriter, caterer, doorguy, trash picker, barback, bartender, talent buyer, envelope stuffer, night manager, ship's mate, carpenter, laborer, and office bitch. I had stopped short of gay-for-pay, but just barely. I'd learned to bitterly envy my friends with health insurance the way I once bitterly envied people in love.

The gigs I hadn't been fired from, I'd quit in a huff. Months or only weeks later, I'd move on in desperation to something even baser. And each one of those depressing, humiliating gigs had earned me more money than I'd made as a writer or musician. But then, everything had come a distant second to my true calling: waster.

For someone who had moved to NYC with the bald intention of getting famous, my anonymity remained so pristinely intact that one would think I'd been fighting to preserve it. (A reporter I knew once told me, "Man . . . you never miss an opportunity to miss an opportunity.") So many dreams I had neglected and then forgotten, like a child's old stuffed animals in a wet basement, their bodies filling with humidity, then mildew, then bugs, blossoming only in decay.

Some asshole pedaled by on a ridiculous bike built of three frames welded together, so he towered over cars, as high as a second-story window. He gave me a practiced "What are you staring at?" look.

I was staring at your dangerous, idiotic bike, you fucking imbecile, a bike you went to great lengths to construct not for its practical applications but so people would stare at you. And now I stare, and you're unhappy with that? Fuck you, I hate you, take your unicycle and your devil sticks and your FREE TIBET and just get the fuck out of here, run back to the affluent DC suburb that spawned you. Fuck your boringly easy life, so vacuous that you must fill it with custom-built bike frames.

The aperture had narrowed to the point where my most reliable source of income was working off Craigslist, picking up stuff from the "free" section, then reposting it and selling it for $60 or $40 or hell, just give me $20, man, and get it out of here. I'd sold the contents of abandoned storage units and even worked a couple of days cleaning out the apartments of people who'd died. I kept any open bottles of liquor I found.

My friends had put in their time and pulled down six-figure salaries as admen or graphic designers or fashion whatevers. They were buying houses or apartments; they were getting married; they were having children. A few had hit it really big. I watched them on TV or read about them in *Rolling Stone* or the *New York Times* or the *New Yorker*. They'd written best sellers, or their bands had blown up, or they'd gotten their own show on HBO. One guy had even won a MacArthur "genius" grant. Fucking hell.

I was thirty-two and getting smaller every day. I didn't have a house or apartment or wife or girlfriend or child or even a real job. I worked off the books, I didn't have a lease, I was in the US on temporary status I'd been renewing since I was eight. My last name isn't a real name, just a bastardization of "Chevalier" that an illiterate French ancestor got stuck with by a hurried immigration official in the Ukraine. My first name isn't a real name but a child's nickname I never outgrew. I didn't have a 401(k), I didn't have a couch, I didn't have fucking ice cube trays. I owed $90,000 in student loans. One wall of my room was made up of two sheets. It wasn't just that I hadn't made it—I had nearly ceased to exist. Not dying, just slowly bleaching out, like old newsprint in the sunshine.

I had the music I'd written, songs about drinking with leitmotifs of heartbreak and despair to, you know, jazz it up a bit. I hadn't been some refined, secret binge drinker or guilty closet drunk with nips of vodka squirreled away in a locked drawer of my desk; I *was* alcohol, the word made flesh. I had a tattoo of Drinky Crow in the center of my chest, *X*'s on his eyes and a nameless bottle of poison tipped upright, draining into his craw. "Shubaly is a chronicler of mankind's darkest impulses and failures, a guy with a ticket to hell and back," said one critic. "One listen will send an AA meeting into complete disarray," said another. And my favorite, from comedian Doug Stanhope: "If you've ever considered suicide at happy hour, this is the songwriter for you." I had lived with one foot in the gutter and the other in the grave, face down on the bar with both middle fingers in the air.

But now, I was not who I was. I had been sober for three months. Whenever I bumped into people I knew, they commented on how good I looked or asked what was different about me. It was nice, but it was meaningless. We were all waiting for the other shoe to drop. I'd made it three months before, showered and gotten my hair cut, found a new job . . . then turned around and cannonballed right back into the pool of filth I'd crawled out of.

I was in agony by the time I hit the ramp up the Williamsburg Bridge. I was gushing sweat and could feel my chubby thighs chafing against each other, my boxer shorts so soaked it felt like I was wearing a wet diaper. My T-shirt was drenched, binding and rubbing in my armpits. Every couple of steps, a fresh drop of salty sweat trickled onto the abraded flesh, searing like a bite from a fire ant. I slowed but refused to allow myself to walk.

My father had been a runner. Didn't that mean I should have the genes for it? But then, I also lacked my dad's mechanical aptitude, his math brain, his intuitive understanding of physics, his diligence, his focus, everything.

My dad had done a near infinite number of things that I would never do. At fourteen, having already read the Bible, the encyclopedia, and every other book in the house, he read the dictionary. I didn't make it through the *A*'s. At eighteen, Dad tore a 1936 Ford Coupe completely apart—every nut, every bolt—cleaned every single part, and then put it back together. Even now, I could barely muddle through an oil change. My father's university added a wing so that he could continue his physics experiments. I had to plead with my college not to kick me out days before I was to graduate. Dad could crack walnuts with his bare hands; Dad had had his pocket picked and caught the thief; Dad had been spied on and caught the spy; Dad had shot top-secret things into outer space and blown them up with motherfucking laser beams for the government, for Christ's sake. As my father had mastered doing cool things, I had mastered doing nothing.

I could remember watching him come home from a run when I was only four. He ran up our driveway, his massive chest heaving, his white T-shirt soaked, his dark hair, mustache, and eyebrows a dramatic black from perspiration. He peeled off his headband and wrung it out, his sweat splattering noisily on the blacktop. What a magnificent creature he was, his huge, strong, hairy hands, his bristly mustache . . . I even marveled at the way the bathroom stank after he had used it. Dad was something between a human being and an animal, greater than either, greater than both: a mythological beast. My father sweat so much, you could wring his headband and T-shirt into a glass and drink it! My tiny body didn't sweat at all. Even as a child, I understood running was only one of the many things he did that I would never be able to do. I was the mortal offspring of an immortal.

As I crested the Williamsburg Bridge, there it was: The City. Even after 9/11, the primacy of the Manhattan skyline was unchallenged. I recalled an old Soul Coughing line: "You can stand on the arms of the Williamsburg Bridge, crying 'hey man, this is Babylon.'" When I moved to New York, I was convinced the city held some special destiny for me, that I was destined to do something . . . well, at least something memorable if not brilliant or amazing. Now it was over.

The City wasn't over: *I* was over. New York was *possibility*. I could have done anything. Then, almost imperceptibly, my prospects had faded, my options had dwindled. I'd moved seamlessly from promising to failed. New York still shone; it was still the city where dreams became real—but only if you pursued them. I'd had trouble keeping sheets on the bed.

My conviction at twenty-one—that I was special—hadn't been just bland or commonplace but utterly banal, the most mundane and flawed conviction ever. Sure, we were all special, every one of us: the hunchbacked old man working at Kinko's, the fat girl at the pet store, the weed delivery guys on battered ten-speeds, the people selling term papers or Adderall or worn panties on Craig's List, the guys pushing stolen shopping carts overburdened with scrap metal, the tired illegals selling water or Gatorade at stoplights, the barbacks, the servers, the escorts, the doormen, the janitors, the cleaning ladies, every junkie, every addict, every alcoholic, every single one of us.

Another song lyric crawled unbidden into my head, from the Pogues's "Fairytale of New York": "I could have been someone. / Well, so could anyone." I had scored two free tickets to the Pogues on St. Patrick's Day. The tickets weren't just free, I was to write about the band. I was getting paid to go and see the Pogues! I brought my friend Fisher, another struggling musician. We snuck in coke and whiskey, got shitfaced, then bailed during the last song to dodge the thick scrum that would soon form at the exits, off-duty cops who'd been drinking all day and meathead Jersey amateurs in plastic green top hats and shamrock beads.

We'd spilled out into the street together, arms around each other's necks, crowing with pleasure. Free tickets! Cheap whiskey! Fuck the cops! We were gaming the system! We were making it!

Fisher overdosed a couple of years later in a tiny, overpriced Williamsburg apartment. We hadn't even been able to scrape together a benefit show for him.

—

My shoulders prickled like someone was drawing tiny shards of broken glass out through my pores. My mouth was so dry it felt like it had been stuffed with pink fiberglass insulation. A sticky white film coated my tongue, and when my sweat dripped into my mouth, it mixed with the film and tasted like bile. I wheezed, and my lungs stung as if I'd inhaled some poisonous vapor. My thighs throbbed, then burned till I prayed for them to just seize so I would be forced to stop.

The only logical thing to do was give up. Quit my job—if there was one word to describe my professional life in New York, it was "replaceable"—give my landlord notice, sell my shit, and then . . . what? After years of silence, I'd exchanged a few tentative emails with my father, but I knew I wasn't welcome there. My mother had lost her house in the California real estate bubble of 2008 and was crashing on my older sister Tatyana's floor. My little sister Tashina was barely scraping by. I had failed so badly, I couldn't even give up.

Something catastrophic was coming—a heart attack, a stroke, a brain aneurysm. Had I finally complained myself to death? Bring it on, then. Let's get this over with. My skull filled with the white noise of my spasming heart and my whistling breath.

But the bridge was now sloping down into Manhattan. That yammering voice in my head went abruptly silent. I relaxed a little as gravity pulled me forward. As I plodded up First Avenue toward 14th Street, I felt nauseous and lightheaded and sore, but also giddy, as if someone had strangled me nearly to death and then, at the last second, loosened his grip and spared my life.

My heart soared when I saw my bike chained to the light pole outside Beauty Bar. I had said I was going to run to get my bike. I had actually done it. I bought a bottle of water at the closest bodega and quickly sucked it down, squatting in the shade, then slowly biked home.

I was stepping out of the shower before I noticed that the rage that had woken me had disappeared completely, like it had been surgically removed.

As an adult, I avoided looking at my body. Now, I forced myself to look.

Shoulders scattered with bad or unfinished tattoos. My torso crisscrossed with scars, most concealed or nearly concealed by the tattoos. Beer belly and love rungs hanging off my front and sides, but less than before. I wasn't just fooling myself. A couple of months of biking to work, doing some push-ups and not drinking, and my alcoholic tubbiness had gone down considerably. Under that receding layer of blubber, maybe muscles were growing? It wasn't even approaching good . . . but I looked better than I had before.

I stared at myself in the mirror. Dark, unkempt hair like a drowned crow lying on my head. My face blotchy red and white from the effort of my run. Though I'd dried my face three times, sweat still poured out of me. But I no longer had that "cornered animal" look I had gotten used to. My body was still in a blind panic, fervently trying to recover from the exertion, but my eyes looked almost serene. As torturous as the run had been, I felt strangely at peace.

People had been accusing me of wanting to kill myself since I was a kid. I only ever wanted to kill half of myself—the good half, the half that, against logic, kept hoping, kept trying, kept caring. I'd gotten everything else wrong—maybe I'd just picked the wrong side?

In exhaustion and wonder, I looked up the distance from my house to Beauty Bar. I had run nearly five miles without stopping.

I had run that far once before, when I was thirteen. I tried to remember it. It felt like a lifetime ago. But almost twenty years later, it had mysteriously happened again. My life seemed to shift a few degrees. New possibilities had only been negative for a long time—it was possible that I would wind up in rehab; it was possible that I would wind up in jail. On my run, some invisible divider had cracked and then shattered. It was now possible that I could do good things too.

CHAPTER 2

Chemical Youth

Alcohol is written into my family's genetic code. My parents were poor farm kids from Saskatchewan, Canada. Three of my four grandparents died from alcoholism. I don't remember my first drink. Apparently, my folks got a giggle out of watching me slurp down the last drops of my dad's beer when I was a toddler. "It was a cultural norm then," my mom said when I quizzed her about it. "We all had pictures of our kids with beer cans to their lips. God, I can't tell you how many times I've thought back to that and wondered if we weren't making a huge mistake."

My parents sometimes put a little wine in our apple juice at dinner. I couldn't have been seven then. Uncle Albert, my mother's youngest brother, slipped me a couple of rum-and-Cokes on the sly at a family reunion when I was nine, a trespass for which I think my mom is still mad at him. But my first drunk was on seven Budweiser tall boys when I was thirteen. That's where it all began.

We moved to New Hampshire from New Mexico in the winter of my eighth-grade year. We had followed my father, a nuclear physicist and our sole provider, to Kingston, New Hampshire, as we had followed him from Ontario, Canada, to Los Alamos, New Mexico, five years earlier. He was the eldest child and only son, fawned over by his mother, grilled relentlessly by his father. Whether doted on or cut down, he was the center of the universe, and his sister, Marilyn, came a distant second. When he returned to his father's farm with his PhD from the University of Saskatchewan, his father said, "Don't think this makes you any better than us."

The second of seventeen children, my mother had always been a mother, minding the children under her, practically raising the youngest as her own. She was independent, the first in her family to get a college degree. She created a small stir in our tiny town by keeping her maiden name when she married, but she had always known she would have children. She had wanted to have "only six," she told us. She seemed to have her hands full with half that.

Tatyana maintained a hurt silence nearly the entire, days-long December drive to our new life in Kingston. Two years older than I, she'd been popular in Los Alamos, got good grades, and had a boyfriend who skated and drove a pickup with oversize tires. She'd always been getting picked up or dropped off, swapping clothes with her friends, GUESS and Vuarnet and JIMMY'Z, and talking on her Swatch phone for hours. She was distraught about being plucked from her high school clique in the middle of her sophomore year. Not that I cared. Tatyana and I had been embroiled in a cold war for years.

Our grueling cross-country move was just another road trip adventure for my sister Tashina. She was eight, four years younger than I, my mother's brother's child. She'd come to live with us when she was four because her parents couldn't afford to look after her. She was Native American, adopted, and wore hearing aids, which made her unforgivably bizarre to other kids her age. I worried for her.

I worried for me too. My transition from Canada to New Mexico had not gone smoothly. My first day, my teacher made a big production of stopping the Pledge of Allegiance because I wasn't standing up with my hand over my heart. No one had told me! I stood up, but I didn't say anything, because I knew she couldn't make me. Instantly, I became that weird kid from that weird country that had something to do with hockey. Did I speak Canadian? Did we still have dirt floors?

I had skipped a grade and was in the gifted program, a freak even among the freaks. "Potential" was a word frustrated teachers often deposited on my report cards, a word I came to hate: "Mishka has such potential, it's a shame that his performance is marred by behavioral issues and lack of focus." Such a bullshit word. Finally, I looked it up: "showing the capacity to develop into something in the future." Something good? Something bad? It just meant that, right now, I was nothing. When I was nine, I started having panic attacks. When I was ten, I started cutting myself.

By seventh grade, my awkward entry had compounded into genuine alienation. I couldn't skate, and I sucked at sports despite my size. I didn't have the confidence to wear clothes I thought were cool, so I wore my dad's old clothes or clothes from the thrift store. I thought I looked tough. I probably looked like an aspiring hobo.

I was the tallest in my class, but I'd become a target for bullies who recognized I lacked the sense of self to fight back. I got beat up on the bus to school or between classes. My lunch got stolen so frequently that I started bringing two. They just took them both. During one lunch break, I was held down, and my shoes were stolen off my feet. I got jumped by a ninth grader after school, and he cracked my new glasses. I'd broken down in tears, which only made it worse.

By eighth grade, I felt I deserved to be alone. When the possibility of leaving New Mexico came up, I was all for it. I knew nothing of New Hampshire, but anywhere was better than here. I didn't tell anyone we were moving, just downgraded myself one notch from "ignored" to altogether absent.

Mom had always been my first and best friend. It wasn't unusual for her to draw open the curtains while we were eating breakfast before school and say, "You know what? It's far too nice a day for you kids to go to school. Run and get ready, we're going cross-country skiing." Or to the beach. Or berry picking, us kids just eating what we picked, my mom taking off her halter top ("So I can get some sun," she said) in the privacy of the berry patch and filling pails with blueberries for muffins and pies. Mom had always been my protector: dragging me out of an apple tree I'd climbed when I was six while she was photographing the mother bear and cubs in the next tree for the town paper; standing up for me when I got kicked out of Cub Scouts for fighting; stunning us kids into silence and then hysterical laughter when she told the lady at the gas station to "fuck off" for calling me a retard when I was nine; standing up for me when I got kicked off the swim team; taking me to get my ear pierced at the mall in sixth grade when I got suspended from school; driving me to school each morning when the bullying on the bus got out of control.

But even this had soured. The summer before we left New Mexico, my mother took off her shoe to whack me for some vile thing I had said to Tatyana. We struggled, and I took the shoe away. I was 5'10" and already towered over her. We stood there in the hallway to my bedroom, staring at each other, neither of us knowing what to do, a pair of actors who had gone off script and had no idea what to say or who to be.

The lone ray of light that bleak winter was Chuong.

≡

A new kid had appeared in my sixth-grade class one morning. He was Asian, a couple of inches shorter than me, well muscled but with a finer structure. Chuong was from Vietnam, our teacher explained, and he had just arrived in America. He had endured a dangerous boat ride and then spent two years in a refugee camp in Malaysia. He was fourteen, a couple of years older than us, but he spoke little English, so he would study with our class. We were to make him feel welcome.

When we all stood for the Pledge of Allegiance, he stayed seated, his head down.

"Chuong," I said under my breath.

He looked at me.

I gestured for him to stand, and he did. While the rest of the class said the Pledge of Allegiance, Chuong stood there silently, not speaking. Like me.

My teacher pulled me aside at lunch. The new boy had moved in across the street from me with an uncle he didn't know. Could I try to befriend him? That night, after dinner, I went over to call on him.

A tall, thin, stern Vietnamese man answered the door. Chuong had run away, he told me. That quick, huh? Well, which way did he go? Chuong's uncle pointed to his left, up the street.

It was dark by the time I caught up with Chuong, walking stiffly upright in Bugle Boy pants, a long-sleeve plaid shirt, a green baseball hat perched high on his head, and flip-flops. I fell into step with him.

He spoke almost no English, and I spoke no Vietnamese, but he was able to communicate to me that he had a friend in Houston. He was going to walk there. The moon was already high in the sky, and it was starting to get chilly.

I stopped him and went down on one knee on the sidewalk. Chuong dropped to his haunches next to me. I put one little stone down.

"Uncle. Yes?" I said.

He nodded his head.

I took another little rock and held it up for him to see.

"Chuong. Yes?"

Again he nodded.

I made a walking gesture with the fingers on one hand to signify walking for a long time and then put the stone down about a quarter of an inch away from the Uncle stone. I grabbed a third, larger stone and held it up for him.

"Houston. Yes?"

Again, Chuong nodded, cocking one eyebrow at me, curious.

I stood up and threw the rock as far as I could down the street. We watched it bounce once and then disappear into the darkness. Chuong looked at me, his eyes wide.

"Ahhh," he said, crestfallen.

"It's *really* far," I said. "Really, really, *really* far."

He let out a deep sigh. We turned around and headed home.

Chuong was a marvel. He could outrun anyone, and in flip-flops. He could fart on command. He'd grown up on the streets of Saigon, and his body was covered in scars, a slash across his chest where he'd been cut with a sharpened key and an ugly star on his forehead where he'd been hit with a bottle. My mother told me that people had committed suicide on the boat to Malaysia by throwing themselves overboard because the conditions had been so bad. It was whispered that Chuong had only been sent on to America because he and some friends had ganged up on and killed a guard in the refugee camp who had been abusing them. His life was so cool, vastly superior to my boring life of spelling homework and cleaning the cat litter.

Chuong's uncle had little patience for the nephew he didn't know, so Chuong slept at our house more than at his home, cooking mountains of egg rolls for us on the weekends. Chuong taught me how to make weapons out of scrap metal, how to shift your center of gravity when running so no one could catch you, and how to tattoo yourself with a pencil, a sewing needle, and ashes. I taught him how to speak English by explaining heavy metal songs on the radio, sitcoms on TV, and *Police Academy* movies. When we left for school in the morning, he echoed my farewell to my mother: "Bye, Mom!"

In seventh grade, his uncle finally threw him out, and he was assigned to foster care in Albuquerque. My mom and I were heartbroken. Each time we went to visit him, his situation was worse.

He had dropped out of school; then his foster family had kicked him out; then he had run away from the group home. Our last visit, it had taken hours to track him down through his friends. He was thin and gray from smoking more than he ate. He had cut the tip off a finger making jewelry in a sweatshop, then stuck it back on with a Band-Aid.

Our last Christmas in New Mexico, Chuong came to spend a week with us. I spent the entire time lobbying for him to come to New Hampshire with us. My parents finally assented. It only took one visit to his social worker to get permission. Nobody else wanted him.

I could not believe my parents had agreed. Chuong, my hilarious best friend, singing filthy made-up lyrics to Skid Row songs while dancing with the dogs . . . Every night would be like a sleepover.

Still, getting out of the car in New Hampshire to those oppressive clots of wet snow, I couldn't shake the feeling that, by leaving New Mexico, we had made a terrible mistake.

≡

Our house in New Hampshire was a ramshackle five-bedroom on a swampy one-acre lot off a minor highway. It was an old farmhouse that had been extended twice, first on one side, then the other. The basement leaked and stank of black mold and cat piss. There was no air-conditioning, and the ground floor was only heated by a small woodstove. Los Alamos had been subject to extreme weather, with summer days that regularly broke a hundred degrees and massive snowstorms that buried our vehicles, but it was dry heat that disappeared each night, and the sun shone brightly between dumps of snow. New Hampshire was a hot, wet, inescapable jungle all summer, an icy and sunless gulag all winter, and gray for weeks in between.

Our house was surrounded on three sides by woods that quickly devolved into swamp. Our lone neighbor across the highway was an old farmer who had more than eighty cats. He was hunched with age, long past working. The only thing his farm produced was more cats. He fed them each morning but declined to neuter/spay them or to provide veterinary care. Virtually all of them developed huge, crusty scabs in the corners of their eyes, eventually creeping off to the woods to die or getting run over by the heavy trucks that barreled down the highway in front of our house.

"White trash" was not a phrase I'd heard in Canada or New Mexico. In Canada, nearly everyone had gardened, hunted, and fished and knew how to stretch a dollar. Everyone wore hand-me-downs without shame. In fact, a hand-me-down shirt was almost preferable to a "new" shirt from the Whistle Stop Thrift Store—a hand-me-down was something of Tatyana's I had coveted for months, maybe even a year. That it now fit me proved that I had grown into it, which meant I was becoming like my older sister, whom I envied, and had also won a victory over her by getting something away from her. In New Mexico, I was vaguely aware of us having more money than some of my friends' families and less than others, but poverty was not something I was keenly aware of.

In New Hampshire, poverty was everywhere. According to the 1990 census, New Hampshire was more than 98 percent white at the time. I recall there being a total of three black kids in our school—one set of twins and their cousin—and one Puerto Rican. Our school district was the poorest in the state. In our town, poverty and white trash Yankee pride had curdled into something toxic, a specific decaying northeastern despair.

The locals gave my mother the cold shoulder because we were "from away," and unless your grandparents had been born in Kingston, you would always be "from away." And wasn't it a little suspicious that the wife still went by her maiden name and that the dad was never around? And they had that teenager, Chinese or whatever, who barely spoke English and wasn't in school, and then the little girl with the hearing aids, who was also some kind of colored person?

Tatyana was heartbroken for her teenage love. Chuong missed his unsupervised, chaotic life among the other Vietnamese immigrants in the city. Tashina missed her friends and, young as she was, understood she didn't fit in here as she had in New Mexico with her black, Asian, and Native American friends. I didn't miss New Mexico or anyone there. I had been wretched there. But this? We were bored, we were lonely, we were uncomfortable. We suffered. We complained. We turned on my father for once again dragging us across the continent. He retreated—into his work, into his travel, into his workshop and a six-pack of Budweiser.

My father had always been a cypher. Our mother made sure we were well versed in his folklore: the drunken antics of his college rugby team, his beloved MG convertible that had been stolen out of their driveway, how he had been building his own remote-controlled airplanes since he was a boy. As little kids, we laughed at his foibles: He had thought that he didn't want kids! He was so absent-minded that our mother had been the one to propose! But who was he? We knew we adored him. Tatyana and I were allowed to crawl into bed with him one Easter morning, and I had been thrilled to be allowed to be that close to him. His feelings toward us were less clear. We weren't allowed to jump on him—remember, his bad back from the rugby injury. We weren't to pester him when he was working in his shop at night or on the weekends. He was Dad; he was inside the very core of who we were, but somehow he remained a stranger. I remember trying to make sense of it, even before we left Canada. Kids, for my father, were like sugar—too much, and he got cranky. No, that wasn't quite right, because we never got sick of sugar.

Resentful as I was about the move, I was still desperate to impress him. One night, I lugged his Seagull acoustic guitar downstairs to play for him some new song I'd learned, "Stairway to Heaven" or maybe "Sweet Child o' Mine." Dad sat down at the dining room table, a simple but flawless pine affair he'd designed and built by hand. He listened patiently while I hacked my way through the song. Then he took off his glasses, rubbed his face hard with both hands, and fixed me with a sad stare.

"Mishka," he said, looking deep into my eyes, "if I had it all to do over again . . . I would be the lead guitar player in a hard rock band."

His reaction baffled me. If he wanted to be a guitar player, why had he never learned to play the guitar he'd bought, the guitar that had sat in the closet so many years, the guitar that I had learned to play on? If he knew what he really wanted to do, why hadn't he taken one single step to purse that dream? I turned it over and over in my mind, and over and over I came to the same conclusion: my father was pathetic.

≡

One day Chuong and I were kicking around in the front yard. Lon, an older kid with shiny black hair and a sharp, maniacal laugh, came by in his tiny beat-up pickup. Lon had graduated the year before but hadn't gone to college. He and Chuong had become friends.

"Hey," he said, grinning, not getting out of the truck, "what are you two homos doing?"

"What it look like, man?" Chuong said. "No-thing."

"Grab your bikinis and get in the truck."

Chuong hopped in the back.

"Where are we going?" I said.

"Just grab some towels and get in."

I ran into the house and changed into my swim trunks as fast as I could. I had no idea where we were going, but I didn't want them to leave without me. I grabbed two towels and ran back out.

"Chuong, where's your bikini?" Lon said when I hopped in the back.

"Under my pants, man," Chuong said, blowing smoke at him and grinning. "White bikini. No top."

Lon backed out of the driveway, then peeled out, the bald rear tires of the little truck smoking. That day he led us to the lone good thing I ever found in New Hampshire: the rope swing.

The rest of that summer, Chuong and I went to the rope swing almost every day. We'd beg a ride from my mom, ride our bikes, or even walk the couple of miles to it. The highway wound through the woods, past a swampy finger of Powwow Pond and several houses set back from the road, to an old arched bridge spanning some railroad tracks. Walking down the railroad tracks, hopping from railroad tie to railroad tie that oozed tar and stank of creosote because the sharp rocks were hard on bare feet, you came to a tiny concrete culvert spanning a deep, brisk current connecting the two halves of Powwow Pond. To the left was the rope swing—a long cotton rope descending from the top of one scraggly pine leaning out over the water with tiny wooden steps built onto it.

The first kid had the unenviable task of entering the water with no fanfare and swinging the rope up to the second kid, waiting at the top of the tree. For maximum swing, you jumped out to the right and the rope whipped you in a delicious arc down and around and then up, up, up, and that was where you let go, at the apogee of your trajectory. Chuong was smaller than me, but he was muscled like an acrobat. He was fearless: cannonballing headfirst, executing perfect, unlikely swan dives, doing spins and flips and backflips that terminated in tidy, poetic dives. Lon was daring and athletic, and I got better with practice, but neither of us could rival Chuong for hang time. Each of us jumped, each of us swung, each of us splashed into the water. But only Chuong had a fourth phase between the arc and the impact when time slowed to a crawl, when his wet, black hair spun off his head like spikes and the setting sun sparkled off his tightly muscled limbs, when no one was misunderstanding his broken English or making fun of his accent or kicking

29

him out or telling him to go back to China. For a long, honeyed moment, he was flying.

—

One night at the end of the summer, after my mom picked Chuong up from his dishwashing job, we crawled out his window onto the roof to smoke cigarettes. We had often stayed up late together in New Mexico, talking. Chuong told me about his mother, his brother, Chin, and his father, a convicted murderer who had abandoned them when Chuong was just eight. Occasionally, he cried. His voice didn't quaver and his face didn't move, but tears fell from his eyes, his only concession to sadness as he sucked on his cigarette.

Chuong didn't cry that night on the roof or even talk much, just stared grimly off into the night. We sat and smoked in silence. I didn't push him. I knew he missed his family, missed his friends in Albuquerque. He hated his job. He hated New Hampshire. I knew he was getting sick of me.

—

My dad found a couple of lukewarm beers in Chuong's room. When he tried to take them, Chuong pushed him or maybe took a halfhearted swing at him. It was a big deal.

That night, there was a serious discussion on the back deck. My father hectored Chuong. My mother defended him. Tatyana, Tashina, and I were even asked to weigh in. I was annoyed at Chuong, but only because he'd outgrown me and because we now had to sit through this whole ordeal.

Everyone took a turn speaking except the accused. He kept his head down, never looked up, only spoke when addressed directly, and then just uttered a barely audible yes or no. Finally, my father called him out.

"Okay, okay, enough. Everyone has spoken here except the one person we really need to hear from. Chuong, what have you got to say for yourself?"

There was a long, pained silence. Chuong sniffed. More silence. "Chuong?" my dad said.

"Don even wanna live here anymore!" Chuong blurted out, then jumped up and ran off.

He didn't come back that night. Or the next. Or the next.

Finally, Chuong called my mom one day while I was at school. He had taken a bus back to Albuquerque, as my mom had guessed he would. He called her the day he arrived, as my mom had guessed he would. He wanted to tell her that he was safe, that it had been a very long ride, and "I'm sorry, Mom." He asked her to hang on to his Vietnamese-English dictionary, that he would get it from her one day.

I didn't say anything to anyone at school. But each day, when I came home from class and went out to the chopping block to split and stack the wood for the woodstove for the winter, I cried.

Chuong called me once. He wanted me to sell his leather jacket and send him the money, along with some stuff he'd left behind. I did. One letter came for me, dated September 29, 1990, in Chuong's careful, almost feminine hand: "If you guys don't understand, some day I'll call you guys, ok? I don't know what to say, well, I'm miss you guys very much. Love, Chuong."

We never heard from him again.

———

That fall was a wasteland. I felt like someone had reached inside me with a pair of vise-grips and torn something out. The hole was too ragged to heal, just kept bleeding and bleeding. I was lost without Chuong. I hated him. I was sick with worry for him. And I was angry as hell.

We'd been had. My mother had made New Hampshire seem exciting, exotic even. We'd leave the cold wars—between my mother and father, between Tatyana and me—behind. New Hampshire would be a fresh start, not just for me but for our entire family.

It was a sham. We'd found a filthy, impoverished dump where everyone acted like they were better than us. We were as shitty to each other as we'd ever been, or worse. Now my only friend, the brother I'd never had, had been driven off. New Mexico had been hell for me, and I had been eager to escape, but New Hampshire was just a fresh hell.

Everyone had lied to me—my mother, my father, my teachers. Life wasn't some grand adventure, as my mother would have us believe. It was just fleeing from one shithole to the next, each one worse than the last.

≡

After hounding him about it all summer, Lon let me drink with him in the fall of my freshman year. He bought a couple of six-packs of Budweiser tall boys, and we lit a fire out by the railroad tracks with some of his friends. That first sixteen-ounce can felt heavy in my hand and, by extension, dangerous, like a brick or a gun. I had sipped from my dad's beer occasionally, but having my own felt wild, exhilarating. Putting the frosty can to my lips, I drank as long and as fast as I could, relishing the grown-up, un-sweet taste, the coolness pooling in my belly. Then I was laughing and stumbling, wrestling with Lon, peeing in the bushes, falling in the bushes, lying down next to the fire. This was hilarious, he was hilarious, everything was hilarious.

When I awoke the next morning, I laid in my bed for a mo-ment. I knew from reading what hangovers were, but I didn't have a hangover at all. I felt great, better than great.

What a night I'd had! Some older girl—a junior!—had put me in her car and driven me around. We had been smoking cigarettes together and listening to the radio. When I had hung my head out the window to barf, there had been two moons! Then we had been lying down together for some indeterminate time, and I had felt her up, or we had kissed or maybe just hugged? The police had been called. The police had been out looking for me!

32

Alcohol was miraculous. Like in *Harold and the Purple Crayon*, I had drawn an escape hatch in a wall and plunged into another world. Drunk, I'd finally felt comfortable in my own skin. I'd had wild adventures. For a minute, I had been cool. Then I had woken up in bed as if transported by faerie magic. This was an earth-shattering discovery.

As a child, I had pinwheeled through various imagined futures: I would be a knife thrower, I would be an undersea explorer like Jacques Cousteau, I would wail on guitar like Slash. Now I had found it. My father was a nuclear physicist. My mother was a mom. *Alcohol* was what I was supposed to be. I would do this again as soon as possible. I would do this all the time!

After Lon got a solid chewing out from my mother, my main connections for alcohol were Bernie, a homeless schizophrenic Vietnam vet who occasionally tried to grope me, and Pinhead, an ex-Marine who had been kicked out of the military. He had a tattoo on his stomach of a flying penis and testicles ejaculating a winged drop of semen with a single blue eyeball.

I pounded a liter of white zinfandel and fell down a flight of stairs. I chugged a magnum of champagne, swallowing the cigarette butt someone had tossed into it. I got drunk on vodka and came home covered head-to-toe in poison ivy. I climbed one of our neighbor's apple trees with a bottle of Sambuca and drank until I fell out. I lost my virginity later that year on the floor of Lon's bedroom with four other people passed out around us. I remember the dark fake wood paneling and the orange shag rug and not much else.

By the time I was fourteen, my mother had given up trying to control me. She tried to ground me, but what could she do—stop me as I was walking out the door? I was over six feet tall and strong, powerful as I was naive, juvenile and hardheaded, abrasive and arrogant. My dad was rarely around, traveling constantly for business. I got in daily screaming matches with my mom and Tatyana and got shitfaced at every opportunity.

I breezed through my classes with minimal effort, squeaking by at just above C level. I had finally learned to fight back when picked on and had been suspended from school for fighting so often that I faced expulsion for my next offense. My hairy legs sprawled out from under my desk into the aisles, my gangly arms hung over the front. Once, I stood up, and the desk-and-chair came with me. I almost made it out the door wearing it before the study hall teacher stopped me.

High school's arbitrary social codes were as meaningless as they were constricting. Champion sweatshirts, button-down shirts, and lettermen jackets? I felt like I had walked into an *Archie* comic book. Why the hell must you roll the cuffs of your jeans? I wore the same clothes two or three days in a row, sleeping in them so I could sleep later. My classmates' dreams were hollow, their concerns pointless. The girl I liked wanted to be a dental hygienist! It was all beneath contempt. I had two friends, a couple of guys in my grade who shared my passion for alcohol and my distaste for everything else, and that was enough for me. I carefully set about mocking, offending, and alienating everyone else.

There was nothing I couldn't overpower or outsmart, no game I couldn't cheat or manipulate, no system I couldn't beat. Childhood was claustrophobic and demeaning, a truncated, dependent existence. I was so done with all this. I had nothing else to learn from my parents. I was ready to go out into the world. Okay, I had to learn how to drive, but that was it.

In the beginning of my sophomore year, my two friends suddenly stopped talking to me. A week later, our house was vandalized: "GET OUT COMMIE" and a huge swastika in fluorescent orange spray paint. It was as baffling as it was hurtful. We were not Jewish, or Russian, or communist, or socialist. Was it a response to the immigrant last name I hated so much, the token remnant of my father's Ukrainian heritage?

Surprise, surprise, the vandals were my ex–best friends. What had I done to alienate my only allies? I never found out. I wanted them dead. My mother declined to press charges.

Overnight, I went from cocksure to persecuted. Before, we had been outnumbered. Now I was alone. My mom tried to throw me a surprise birthday party at the Kingston House of Pizza a couple of months later, in the depths of winter. Two large pizzas, one cheese and one pepperoni. We waited there for an hour together before packing them up and bringing them home.

———

A bulk mailing came one day, addressed to me. I turned it over. "Attend college early!" it said. I tore open the slim pamphlet and read with mounting interest. Simon's Rock College was an accredited university in Massachusetts that accepted students after just two years of high school. Their specific focus was teaching a college curriculum to "bright, motivated adolescents." "Bright" was a word often tossed my way. "Motivated" wasn't. But if escaping both high school and my parents two years early couldn't motivate me, nothing could. I walked into the house and said, "Hey, Mom, can I borrow twenty-three thousand dollars?"

My parents talked it over when my dad got home from his latest business trip. There was no way they'd be able to afford it in the same year they were footing the bill for Tatyana's out-of-state tuition to the University of Colorado . . . but what was the harm in getting a little more information?

It was decided that I would be allowed to send away for an application. My mom made it clear that the B-minuses I had been pulling down in everything except weight training wouldn't impress anyone. Overnight, I dug in at school.

The application required what amounted to extra homework. Such bullshit! But the faraway school seemed to shimmer with possibility. Simon's Rock didn't just promise escape. It made me reconsider all the lectures I'd gotten about the potential I was wasting.

That thin booklet had sought me out for a reason. I was supposed to do Some Great Thing.

I tackled the application with immediate and sustained effort. For the first time I could remember, I gave an essay my full attention, writing it not with the minimum amount of effort necessary but with everything I had. This work counted for something.

When my next report card came, it was straight As.

After I sent off my application with my latest report card, I began checking the mailbox every day. Finally, I got an envelope with the seal and return address of Simon's Rock. Without bothering to close the mailbox, I tore the envelope open. I hadn't just gotten in—they had given me a big scholarship.

Every cell in my body felt alive. My entire life was about to change. The sky seemed to open. I would not drop out and get a job driving a forklift. I could do anything. I would do everything. I sat down on the grass in the summer sun to treasure the moment for a minute. Then I ran in to tell my mom.

———

Somehow my parents found a way to cover college tuition for not one but two kids in the same year. There had been many heated discussions, and it was made clear that all of us would have to make sacrifices in order for this to happen. The school had strict rules. Two infractions for drugs or alcohol, and you were out. One fight, and you were out. And no refunds. Even as an infant, I had recognized the duality of my nature. Like the nursery rhyme, when I was good, I was very, very good, but when I was bad, I was rotten. Could I control myself? I would have to.

The tiny school of Simon's Rock was tucked away behind the small town of Great Barrington in western Massachusetts. The other kids . . . it was like every high school across the country had sent its weirdest, smartest, funniest kids there for quarantine. My roommate, James, had blue hair and a pierced nose. He wore a beret constantly, even to bed. Each morning, he carefully pulled his pants on both legs simultaneously just so no one could say, "Oh, James, he's a regular guy, he puts his pants on one leg at a time like everyone else." Zack, the lanky smartass across the hall, owned every Beastie Boys album, even the early punk shit, and had played drums in his high school band, Fuck You, Punk Rock. Ben Bertocci was a local kid, a handsome goblin obsessed with Tolkien, a great chunky scar over his left lip from blowing up aerosol cans. He drove a lurching 1970s Chevy Nova, always blasting Gwar or Metallica, and enjoyed making weapons and terrifying masks and creepy sculptures out of the bones of roadkill. Ben White, a skinny Florida redneck in a Skinny Puppy T-shirt, was quiet but cuttingly funny whenever he spoke. Sure, there were nerds and jocks and even a few normals, but for once, freaks were in the majority. After a month, Simon's Rock felt more like home than any of the five houses I'd lived in, my friends closer than my family.

My easiest course was more challenging than anything I'd encountered in my life. We were treated like adults in class and expected to respond as such. My classmates were up to it—was I? For the first time, I couldn't phone it in. I was no longer the smartest kid in the class; I had to bust my ass just to keep up.

Still, to be a rebellious fifteen-year-old, liberated from your parents, treated with respect by your professors, living in a coed dormitory with your best friends, three meals prepared for you each day, surrounded by woods, a creek running through campus . . . it was heaven. I had been allowed to spit out my pacifier. I was living my real life.

But you can't be good all the time. We drank vodka, we drank cough syrup, we smoked pot, we screwed, we stayed up all night, talking endlessly about music: Big Black, the Velvet Underground, the Stooges, Nick Cave, Bauhaus, Daniel Johnston, John Zorn, Einstürzende Neubauten, Bikini Kill.

I lived in terror of getting caught drinking. One night, I stumbled home drunk to find myself locked out. James was in his girlfriend's room, not to be disturbed. I wobbled out to the atrium, where people often hung out till the sun rose. A couple of second-years were in the kitchen. One sat on top of the fridge, loudly singing Frank Sinatra, tripping on acid. The other, Galen, sat at the table, smoking a Camel, laughing at his friend. He had a wooly head of thick brown hair tied into a loose ponytail at the base of his neck, scruff on his face and neck.

When I explained my problem, Galen grinned and rolled his eyes, then hopped up from his chair.

"You," he said, pointing to his friend giggling on top the fridge, "stay here. I'll be right back."

Galen followed me to my room.

"I can't believe no one's showed you this. This is one of the fundamentals."

He knelt down by my door, pulled out his student ID, and pushed it into the crack between my door and the doorjamb. There was a soft click. My door swung open. Galen stood up, bowed grandly, and gestured at my open door. I shuffled in. When I turned around to thank him, he was already gone.

———

I spent all of Monday, December 14, cramming for my physics final the next morning. The class had seemed an obvious choice, but I soon realized my father's gifts for physics had passed me over. I was in my room with a friend from class, struggling desperately to understand the concepts that were so immediately logical to him. I heard a thin, explosive sound, a feeble *pap*, then another, then a flurry. Firecrackers? No, firecrackers didn't sound like firecrackers; they split the air, they made your ears ring. Firecrackers sounded like guns. That firecracker sound I heard, it was a gun. It could only be Wayne Lo.

Under the spikes and Mohawks and combat boots, Simon's Rockers were just goofy kids. Many of us had been ridden hard in the outside world and carried baggage from it, but under that, there was a sensitive, open humanity, an intelligent caring to Simon's Rockers, almost every one of us. Even Zack, bitter and caustic before he even got out of bed, had a wicked sense of fun. Wayne was different.

Wayne was one of an elitist group we called "the hardcore kids" because they listened exclusively to hardcore punk. Everyone listened to some strain of punk/noise/metal/experimental/unlistenable music, and lots of us listened to hardcore. But the hardcore kids had a deeper investment in it; hardcore music was a vehicle through which they held themselves above the rest of the student body and the rest of humanity. At meals, they sat at the same table in the corner closest to the cafeteria entrance, with Wayne at the head, facing the entrance. You could see him clocking and judging every person who walked through the door.

Of the hardcore kids, Wayne was the darkest, the most intense, the most extreme. He was openly misogynistic, racist, and bigoted. Wayne had turned in papers arguing that African Americans, Jews, and gays were inferior, that the Holocaust had never happened, that HIV-positive people should be quarantined or executed.

Wayne and I were on the basketball team together. He was eerily intense on the court, even just running drills. One night after practice, I had talked about shooting cans with my .22 rifle. Wayne asked me if I could get him a gun.

"Maybe over winter break," I had said, stalling.

"No," he had said, "I need it now."

—

In my dorm room, my mind put the pieces together so fast I felt nauseous.

"Those are gunshots," I said. "It's gotta be Wayne."

I'd run into him earlier that night. I always said hi to him, not because I wanted to befriend him but because I wanted him to know not everyone was intimidated by him. He never responded, not even a grunt or a nod. But that night he had.

"How's it going?" I said as I passed him on the stairs, not expecting a response.

"Good, man," he had said with a small smile. "See you later."

I told my friend to stay put and ran out of my room, headed in the direction of the gunshots. I didn't know if I could stop Wayne, but I would try. When I burst out of our hall into the atrium, one of the resident assistants was coming up the stairs. He was the all-American kid, always wearing a baseball hat and an I-dare-you grin. Tonight, for the first time, he wasn't smiling.

"Mishka, get back in your room. Wayne's got a gun."

I kept running toward the door.

"I heard it. He's down by the library."

"Mishka! Get back in your room right fucking now. Turn the lights off, lock the door, and lay on the floor away from the windows. *Right fucking now.*"

I went back to my room, turned the lights off, and locked the door. I looked out the window toward the library. I could hear screams, and I saw silhouettes of students running away from the library, students I knew. My friend grabbed my physics notebook and started writing frantically. I looked over his shoulder. He was writing out his will.

After a while, the screams stopped. There were sirens, then cop cars and flashing lights. Then, as we watched, Wayne Lo was led down the path from upper campus toward a waiting cop car. He was handcuffed, and two cops held his arms tightly.

I ran out into the atrium, then outside and into Dolliver, the boys' dormitory. I didn't know what else to do. There was blood on the stairs and blood on one of the landings, more blood than I had ever seen, a thick pool of blood, just starting to congeal at the edges.

Students were crying and saying that people had been shot, that Galen was dead. But rumors were insane at Simon's Rock—people just repeated shit they'd heard without a thought.

"Are you sure?" I said. "Did you see him?"

No, no one had seen him.

"He's not dead. He's fine," I said. "Maybe he's been shot and he's hurt, but he's not dead. Don't say it unless you know it's true."

I saw one of the residence directors for Dolliver.

"Is Galen okay?" I said. "I guess he got shot?"

"Mishka," the residence director said, "Galen's dead."

≡

We were ushered into the dining hall. Six people had been shot. Galen and Nacunan, a teacher, were dead. Wayne had only surrendered because his cheap Chinese SKS assault rifle had jammed. He had been carrying enough ammunition to kill us all.

My friends were stone-faced. A lot of girls were crying, but I'd seen girls cry before. I had never seen my teachers cry. I didn't cry. I took Wayne's seat at the head of the hardcore table, a move that creeped out my friends. I refused to leave that seat open, to grant him any kind of legacy out of fear.

We stayed awake the entire night. My mom arrived in the morning to bring me home to New Hampshire. The campus had been locked down, so my mother had to park beyond the front gate, then check in with police before she was allowed to come and get me. As we were walking off campus to her minivan, a cluster of reporters was waiting just beyond the gates. It was 1992, a long time before Columbine or Virginia Tech or Newtown; the media arrived in droves.

"You don't have to say anything if you don't want to," my mom said. "And we don't need to be polite. We can just walk right through them."

The minute we stepped off campus, we were surrounded. My mom tried to pull me through, but I stopped her. We had to make some good come of this.

I told the reporters that everything Wayne had done, right up until he pulled the trigger, was perfectly legal, and that that was wrong. A kid shouldn't be able to buy an assault weapon, a weapon designed to kill the most human beings in the smallest amount of time possible. Hit with a barrage of questions, I let it slip that I had known it was Wayne the instant I had heard the shots, then climbed into the back of my mom's Ford Aerostar for the long drive home.

I couldn't talk. I couldn't cry. But as we drove further and further from Simon's Rock, my body began to realize that I was safe. My heart slowed. The shooting was no longer *happening*; it was something that had happened. I tried to sleep. But as the terror of the night before began to dissipate and I began to process what had taken place, horror rose up in its place. My mind raced.

I had known Wayne was violent. I had known he was looking for a gun. I had even seen him early the night of the shooting. I could have stopped him. I should have stopped him. Why hadn't I stopped him? I had nearly died. Had I nearly died? I should have died.

Earlier that semester, we had joked about what we wanted our last words to be. Something juvenile and frustrating, like "The money is buried under . . ." then trailing off. What about just the cryptic and classic "knock knock"? What got the biggest laugh was when someone suggested that the perfect sign-off would be "I'm dying." As Galen bled out in the library atrium, those had been his final words.

One day at lunch, we had gotten into a conversation about Charles Whitman, the disaffected college student who had climbed the bell tower at his university, killing sixteen people and wounding thirty-two others before he was killed. Whitman had been a punk, we decided. The way to maximize the body count would be to wait till everyone was gathered in one place—the dining hall at lunch, say—then seal off the exits and kill them all. (Seven years later, this would be the exact approach Eric Harris and Dylan Klebold took at Columbine.)

Even if I put all that on the irreverent friends I'd made at Simon's Rock, I'd fantasized about violence on my own. Tashina is First Nation, descended from the Cree Tribe on the Big River Reserve in Saskatchewan. The mascot at our high school, Sanborn Regional High, was the Indian. Our school was too poor to field a football team, but the windbreakers of our soccer and field hockey teams were emblazoned with the grim face of a cartoon Indian in a stereotypical Lakota Sioux eagle-feather warbonnet.

Even at thirteen, I had understood that Indian Festival, our fall spirit rally of war whooping and face painting and toy tomahawks, was disrespectful white trash bullshit. By my sophomore year, I had alienated enough classmates that Indian Festival became the backdrop for a colorful fantasy.

I conjured a scenario in which I had been put in charge of our class's float for the parade. The final day of Indian Festival, the float was revealed to hold only a small teepee, out of which emerged Tashina, in the traditional war dress of her people. She muttered an ancient incantation, a song to "free the blood" that slowly and painfully burst the veins of all the kids in my high school. I, of course, would be spared, and I had envisioned the two of us gleefully bathing in the blood of our dying classmates.

It's not just that I could or should have stopped Wayne or should have died. I had basically willed the shooting to happen. My mother had wept over me when she picked me up. Galen's parents must have gone insane with grief. How could I have been so stupid, so selfish, so horrible? I was as guilty of Galen's and Nacunan's murders as Wayne Lo. I wanted to tell my mom, to confess my sins, to get that sickening knowledge out of my heart, but I couldn't yet speak. It was okay—we had time. Tomorrow I would be able to talk. I would tell her, and she would listen.

Each winter, my mother wrote a Christmas letter to her sixteen brothers and sisters and all her faraway friends, updating them on the events of the year and wishing them happy holidays. That night, still not having slept, I noticed my mother's annual family Christmas letter printed out on the pine dining room table my father had built. I picked it up and, walking into the living room, began to read it.

My father had been working out in Vancouver since the spring. It had been our understanding that we would be joining him there.

In the letter, my mother revealed that she and my father were getting a divorce.

I could not breathe. I fell to the floor. Now the tears came, so hard and so fast that I felt like I was drowning.

The next night, I pulled on my hat and coat and stepped out into the winter night. I exhaled a big, steamy breath and watched it swirl in the moonlight for a second before it disappeared. I felt the best I had since the shooting, the best I'd felt in a long time. I didn't yet feel relief, as such, but anticipation of relief, like I'd finally got an appointment to have the dentist pull a rotten tooth that had been causing me pain for years. I started walking.

I hiked the couple of miles out to the stone bridge that arched over the railway tracks on the way to the rope swing, the highest point within walking distance. I climbed up on the low retaining wall. It wasn't that far to the train tracks below. I'd have to go down head first in order to actually die and not just fuck myself up.

It was curiously cosmic when you thought about it. It took twenty-four hours for the world to spin on its axis, and it had taken twenty-four hours for my world to turn on its head. I waited for the sound of a car approaching, which would be my cue to jump. Just one quick, brave swan dive to end my life. I closed my eyes. In my mind, I could see Chuong, flying off the end of the rope swing, floating through the air, and then disappearing forever.

No car came. I waited. Still, no car.

I looked down into the darkness and saw nothing.

My father was a coward, abandoning us the minute he saw his chance. To give up now, to tap out, to submit, would be to admit that I was a coward like him.

That was no way to live and a worse way to die. Things were terrible now, this was true. This was the absolute worst. Things could never again be as hard or as painful as they were on this desolate night. But if I could get through this . . .

Galen hadn't wanted to die. He had wanted very much to live. He had fought to hang on to his life, fought to the very end. He had been seventeen, a whole life of late-night smoking and pontificating and gently mocking idiots like me ahead of him. Gifted as he had been at math and physics, Galen had wanted to be a poet. If he were here, standing on this ledge with me, he would roll his eyes, ask me what kind of asshole I was, then turn around and go home.

Carefully, I got back down off the low rock wall at the edge of the bridge. Then I turned around and started walking. You had to always keep trying, keep fighting; you had to never ever, ever, *ever* give up. I pulled my hat on tighter and hunched my jacket up around my ears. It was cold out, and I had a long way to go to get back home.

⇐

Despite Wayne Lo's killing spree, despite the impending divorce, against all reason, my parents elected to proceed with our planned family Christmas vacation at a WASP-y little ski resort in Pagosa Springs, Colorado. The tickets were bought and paid for, and we didn't waste anything in our family.

I understood from the movies that if you punched a guy with a roll of quarters in your hand, you would break his jaw. Days before the flight to Denver, I got my mother to drive me downtown, and I dutifully got a roll of quarters out of the bank while she waited in the Aerostar minivan. "For the video games," I told her. I intended to knock my father out.

I once asked my mother why my father, who had tried unsuccessfully to prevent us from getting each of our four dogs, didn't like them. She looked puzzled for a second, then explained that it wasn't because he didn't like dogs. When Dad had been a boy, maybe eight or nine, he'd had a dog he loved dearly, a cocker spaniel named Mickey. One day, another dog attacked and killed Mickey. The man who owned the other dog came over to Dad's house with his dog to apologize to Dad's father. Dad ran into the house, got a rifle, pointed it out the window, and shot and killed the other man's dog.

The story had blown my mind. Gleaning a moral from it had been impossible. My entire life, my parents had told us that if someone hit you, you weren't supposed to hit back; you were supposed to tell a teacher so the person wouldn't do it again. Didn't my father's actions run completely counter to this? But in the days after I got the news of my father's betrayal, I finally figured it out: If someone hurt you, you took it. But if that person hurt someone you loved, you summoned up all the destructive power in your reach, and you took bloody revenge.

When Tashina spied my dad and Tatyana waiting glumly for us at baggage claim in Denver, I wrapped the fingers of my right hand tightly around the roll of quarters. Dad looked grievously tired and beaten down. When he reached out to hug me, I stepped back and clenched my fist. In that instant, he looked so wounded that I froze.

I couldn't bring myself to punch him. I loved him. It made me hate myself. I wasn't man enough to swing on the coward who had been my hero. So I was a coward too.

Incredibly, my parents slept in the same room. My mother was constantly on the verge of tears, as clingy as my father was distant. I retreated into my music, listened to Dinosaur Jr. and Fugazi and Bob Dylan obsessively, fruitlessly searching obtuse rock lyrics for some explanation.

I called my father out at dinner one night, accusing him of competing with me for everything my entire life, telling him the contest he had wanted so badly was over, that he was an old man and that I had won. I could outrun him, outswim him, and if he wanted to step outside, he would find out that I could outfight him. Tatyana yelled at me to shut up. She was his favorite, she always had been, but backing him up on this? I hated her for it, as I hated the old man for not responding, for just standing there with his arms folded, like I had when I was getting taunted in grade school.

Tashina, who'd now had three parents completely flake out on her, fled the dinner table. When things settled down, Tatyana and I found her sitting on the bed in the girls' shared room. Tashina asked us if we ever thought about just walking out to the middle of a snowy field and lying down there and never moving again. In a rare moment of accord, Tatyana and I both instantly swore that we would never abandon Tashina, that she would always have us.

At my mother's insistence, we devoted one evening to watching *The Prince of Tides*. Sitting there in the darkness, the movie flickering before us, the silence only broken by my mother's sniffling, I didn't want to cry or scream or howl but merely to flick a switch, like turning off the TV: the world would fade, then dwindle down to a tiny white dot, then finally disappear.

No one in my family said a word to me about the shooting.

When I was a baby, I woke up every couple of hours during the night, crying for my mom. My mother's friends told her that at some point, you have to let babies cry until they learn to comfort themselves. At nine months, I caught whooping cough. She lost thirty pounds while caring for me, terrified that I would die. After that, my mother couldn't bear to hear me cry. Despite my father's protestations, my mother always came for me.

I was scared of the dark. On the nights that my mother didn't sit with me until I fell asleep, I hid under the covers, breathing through only the tiniest gap in my blankets, drenched in fearful sweat until I finally succumbed to sleep.

When I awoke in the night, I automatically ran to my parents' bed. I remember my father's wide, hairy, freckled back in the night. He was so much bigger than me, too big to be human, like an elephant, part wild animal and part geologic formation. I was twelve before I made it through one night in my bed.

Having an oversized boy come into your marital bed in the middle of the night, each and every night . . . that must have been a huge barrier to intimacy. When I got news of the divorce, this much was clear: I had destroyed their marriage. My father was abandoning my mother because I was weak.

≡

The next year unfolded like a slow-motion film of a train derailment: the moment of hesitation from some minute anomaly, then the hurtling mass of metal slipping horribly sideways, the wrinkling of great sheets of steel, the folding of box cars, huge torn hunks of metal arcing dreamily through the air. Mentioning to reporters that I knew it was Wayne when I heard shots was enough to get me served with a subpoena as soon as I returned to campus. I was sequestered as a witness for the prosecution, which meant I could not talk to my friends or anyone else about what had happened. I found myself both mired in and deeply alienated from the most traumatic experience of my life.

My personal tragedy of the dissolution of my family—the worst thing I had ever encountered—was eclipsed, even in its inception, not just by the shooting but also by the experiences of my classmates. A friend's mother had dropped dead one Christmas, and her father had placed her with a foster family and signed over his guardianship of her. Another friend's father was a career drunk who occasionally worked as a carpenter and dipped in and out of homelessness without complaint or even comment. Another friend's father had been a government agent poisoned in prison by the CIA. Another friend's stepfather had caught him looking at his *Penthouse* magazines the day before Thanksgiving and with a "You *really* want to know what a woman is like?" had dragged him to the kitchen and plunged his hand deep into the semifrozen cavity of the Thanksgiving turkey defrosting in the sink. My story was so banal it hardly merited mentioning.

Zack took a little pity on me, and though he wouldn't allow me to compromise my sequestration, he shared with me one tidbit of happy news: Wayne Lo had been getting the shit kicked out of him with such regularity while he awaited trial that they had put him in solitary confinement for his own safety.

My roommate, James, was clever and insightful but not particularly touchy-feely. His parents were happily married and, like most parents of Simon's Rockers, very well-off. He couldn't understand what I was going through as money got tighter and tighter. He extended bland sympathies when I told him, but that was about it.

Still, he was a comfort to me. At night, we'd climb into our beds at the same time, put the slow version of the Pixies "Wave of Mutilation" quietly on repeat, watch the star field screensaver, and talk—about girls, about music, about Galen—till we fell asleep.

One night while I was on the phone with my father, trying to figure out where I would go for the summer, he ventured that I would be welcome to come and live with him.

"Yeah? That might be cool," I said.

His job in Vancouver had soured, as all his jobs seemed to sour, and now he was in California. I was still unsure about our relationship, but California sounded appealing, especially during the nadir of a Massachusetts winter. Just the two guys . . . it might be really cool.

"It's an option. There's room here for you. Of course, you would have to pay rent."

"Rent? Dad . . . I just turned sixteen."

"You're out on your own now, which is what you wanted. I think it's appropriate for you to contribute. We'll work out something fair."

"Dad . . . I'm your kid. Aren't you legally obligated to, like, feed me and stuff until I'm eighteen?"

"Mishka, you have always made the argument that you're a special case and that ordinary rules shouldn't apply to you. You're out of the house, you come and go as you please, you drink alcohol, you smoke cigarettes. I pay rent—why shouldn't you?"

I got off the phone as quickly as I could and fell back on my bed. I had been using the word "unfair" to describe my relationship

49

with my parents for so long that, though entirely accurate here, it seemed completely inadequate to describe the situation. It was insane. He was insane. And to invite me in just to push me out like that . . . it was making *me* insane.

I made the mistake of voicing my displeasure to my friends. Zack told me, once and for all, to shut up. Zack had grown up a clumsy, skinny weakling utterly dependent on his glasses and his comic books in Pittsfield, Massachusetts, a town enamored with its history of backbreaking industrial and agricultural labor. His childhood experiences hadn't exactly bred sympathy or a high tolerance for whining. When Zack's father came out of the closet and split with Zack's mother while Zack was in high school, he had endured public humiliation beyond all imagining, he informed me, and I was to never bitch about my parents' divorce again. It hurt, but he was right, I told myself. My troubles, troubles that were ruining me, in the grand scheme of things, well, they were nothing. Life is hard. Harden the fuck up, soft boy.

$\Longleftarrow$

I hated my father that winter, but by then I had hated him for years. I hated him because I loved him and he ignored me. When my father wasn't away on business trips for Atomic Energy of Canada and then the Los Alamos National Laboratory, he had only been a token presence, returning from long hours at work just to disappear after dinner into his basement wood shop and a six-pack of Budweiser tall boys. I missed him, and I expressed it by constantly pestering him when he was around.

I couldn't have been more than six, shadowing him around his basement workshop, when he finally tried to engage me. He plopped me in an office chair in front of a computer. I still remember the green flashing cursor on screen and the built-in keyboard, a cutting-edge machine at the time. My father explained to me that a computer was so smart that it could solve any problem.

Okay, fine, I had a problem for it. I laboriously typed into the computer "How do you work?"

My father saw it coming and began hemming and hawing before I'd written my third word. Then, when I'd finally finished, he began trying to explain himself out of the corner I'd painted him into, telling me I hadn't asked the computer the question in a language it could understand.

I burst into tears. I had beaten his challenge and found a question the computer couldn't answer. My father couldn't stand that I had outwitted him, so he'd changed the rules. He had cheated.

When I was in second grade, I asked my father to help me design a trap to kill Jason Frederick, the class bully. On my instructions, he drew a deep pit full of jagged blades concealed by a thin camouflage covering. Then he drew Jason Frederick approaching, holding an ice cream cone. Then he drew a little holder on the side of the pit to catch Jason's ice cream cone when he fell in. I decided then and there that my dad was an asshole. This was a serious situation, Jason had to be dealt with, and my father was mocking me, his only son! On that day, I wrote him off, and I held fast to my disappointment in him.

———

As the winter wore on, it became clear that my father intended not just to shuck off his wife of nineteen years like an ill-fitting coat but to ditch the children too. Had he ever liked me? My father clearly preferred Tatyana over me—she was quieter, tidier, more orderly, less wild. Tashina had only come to live with us at the age of four, when it had become clear that her father, my mother's brother, couldn't afford to take good care of her. Though my father didn't have the disdain for Tashina that he had for me, they had never really bonded. It occurred to me that when Chuong moved out to New Hampshire with us, my father stopped trying to connect with his wife's extended brood and resigned himself to being a stranger in his own home. Had he felt anything other than relief when Chuong had run away?

My father's exit had been so convenient, so seamless for him that it seemed impossible he hadn't planned it. He'd walked into a new life in which his family didn't exist, had never existed. He didn't even need to flee us. We had been unwritten.

Months out of a marriage of nearly twenty years, he already had a new woman. Who, we didn't know, and of course he played dumb. But we had proof of his betrayal. My mother showed me a letter she found in the back of a book he had been reading. It wasn't addressed to anyone, and it wasn't signed, but it was written in his hand, so loving, so tender that he could not have been writing to my mother. I was dying to confront him about it, but Mom swore me to secrecy—he could not know that I knew.

My parents struggled to keep the bills paid with two kids in college as they sorted out the divorce. My mother had been out of the workforce for eighteen years, raising us kids: she had no resume, no professional references, no marketable skills. Still, nothing was going to stand in the way of taking care of her children. "You do what must be done," she had told us as children, and we'd seen her live those words, time and again.

"Well, if there's one thing I know how to do after raising you kids, it's baking. Cookies, muffins, bread . . . just point me to the eggs, flour, butter, and sugar and stand back!" She got a job working in the bakery department at Albertsons for minimum wage, sneaking the stale cookies home in her purse for her and Tashina to eat. She never let it get her down. My parents had both been poor farm kids so we weren't indoctrinated in social stratification. A job was a job, and any job had dignity. Still, I burned inside to think of her in her Albertsons uniform and hairnet, bagging bagels in clear plastic gloves, a servant to the sneering locals.

That spring, at my father's insistence, my mother tried to re-finance our house. The bank told her that, as a matter of course, there was no reason to refinance their mortgage because my parents hadn't missed a single payment. Though they had the money in their account, she didn't make the house payment one month. The bank immediately initiated foreclosure proceedings. It wasn't enough that my father had abandoned us; the bank had played us for fools, and we were now to be driven from our home.

We unceremoniously disposed of our pets. Tasha, our gorgeous, airhead Afghan hound—she had knocked herself out by running into not just a sliding glass door but also a tree—was given to a snooty but kindhearted old lady. Zeke, Tatyana's gregarious golden retriever, who spoke to us and wagged his tail so hard his rear legs skittered back and forth across the hardwood floor, went to a group that brought animals to visit old folks' homes and the terminally ill. Our three cats, too, were handed off like old clothes.

Katie was my dog, a black lab born on my mother's birthday, whom we got from an animal shelter. As a puppy, she used to fall asleep inside my shirt. When she got bigger, she slept on my bed every night. She wasn't a particularly obedient dog, but I taught her a trick much better than heeling or doing something so banal as sitting on command. When I tapped my chest, Katie would jump up, put her front paws on my shoulders, kiss my face, then put her head next to mine and draw me in for a hug. God, I loved her. Katie would go to a fussy young family my mother had found, a family I had zero feeling for. There was nothing to be done about it.

Our oldest dog, Princess, an abused Afghan hound mix we had adopted from the pound when I was six, did not have to be given away. My father owned a La-Z-Boy recliner my mother had given him for Christmas before they had us kids, before they had any money. She had saved up her earnings from taking pictures for the local newspaper, bought the La-Z-Boy from Sears, and hid it at a friend's house. On Christmas Day, she had brought my father over there to surprise him. Princess crawled into my father's easy chair one night, a chair that had always been off-limits to her, and quietly died.

My mother found Princess the next morning and was allowed the rare pleasure of burying her dog in the backyard before our house was repossessed. It seemed like a good, lasting fuck-you to my father from the dog he'd never wanted.

We sold everything we could at a garage sale that stretched on interminably. My father's Ford Taurus, our Aerostar mini-van, our furniture and TV, my Atari, my Nintendo, board games, toys, dishes, clothes: everything must go. We had so much useless crap—a jogging trampoline? Nightmare, the VCR board game? Garbage bags full of stuffed animals, Popples and Pound Puppies and Cabbage Patch Kids. Literally tons of cheap plastic molded into GI Joes and Barbies and Ninja Turtles and My Little Ponies. Had we really needed this? My vast crates of Lego, my library of Choose Your Own Adventure books . . . how much of this self-indulgent garbage would we have to un-buy in order to have enough money to keep our home? How much, or how agonizingly little?

It was crap, undoubtedly crap, literally crap, just plastic and wood pulp offal . . . but also somehow meaningful, drenched as it was in the nostalgic sweetness of my childhood, our life together, perfect in the rearview mirror. And now the whole town parading through the detritus of our life? Our condescending neighbors who had sneered at us because we were "from away," because Tashina and Chuong were brown, leaving muddy footprints on my mother's carpet, haggling us down to the last dime on everything, a death of nickels, of pennies. First the hyenas, then the vultures, then the maggots. Fifty cents was forty cents too much for my mother's old Neil Diamond tape that she had played in the car on the way to the grocery store for how many years now? I couldn't remember a time in my life before I knew the words to "Brother Love's Traveling Show."

Only once did I see my mother lose it. During spring break, while other collegians were pouring Smirnoff vodka into bottles of Sprite in Daytona Beach, grinding, flashing, and sunburning under the blue Florida skies, while my more affluent fellow Simon's

Rockers were in Europe or Mexico or South America, I nursed lukewarm Budweisers with my mom while people trickled into our driveway, poking through our crap. I didn't bother to hide my beer. Fuck what they thought. We were never coming back.

Finally, the rain came. My mother and I, groggy from the shitty beer, scrambled to drag everything back into the garage, out of the drizzling rain. Then it started to pour. We were fucked. The couches, the carpets, the books, the jigsaw puzzles turning slowly into gray mush . . . my mother started to curse on the front drive.

"Shit, shit, shit! God damn it! God *damn* it! I . . . why? Oh, God, *why?*"

Tears filled her eyes, and the words hung up in her throat. Her knees went, but I caught her before she hit the ground and carried her into the front room, the same place where she had had to scrape me off the floor only months earlier, when I had collapsed after reading about the divorce. I got her up to her bed, sobbing so hard she couldn't speak. "Shit" was pretty common for her, elicited by a banged thumb or a parking ticket. "God damn" was a much bigger deal for our mother, raised Catholic. She cried so infrequently that it was still traumatic to witness. None of us had *ever* seen her break down like this, even when her father died.

I moved what I could and covered what I couldn't move. Then I walked out to the mailbox in the rain and opened it. There was nothing inside. I closed it and sat down where I had when I'd gotten my acceptance letter from Simon's Rock almost exactly a year before. How optimistic I'd been, how eager to leave this place behind. I'd hated my father, hated my family, hated this house.

Suddenly, it didn't seem so bad. I had loved my mother. And Tashina. I had loved Tatyana too, listening to the Doors and playing cards together in the camper. And my dad, especially my dad. More than any one of us, I had loved all of us, our family, the thing we became when we were all together.

I looked back at the house, at the big dining room bay window. The lights were off inside—to save money—and I couldn't see in, but I remembered that window glowing. Every night, we had gathered there in the dining room. It was my job to set the table and Tatyana's job to clear it. Dad sat at the head. We all sat down together, each of us in our specific spots. No hats at the table, no books at the table, and certainly no TV. We ate together and laughed together and talked about the day we'd had. And now this, an abrupt betrayal, and then the slow, cold, public humiliation. I wished we had just burst into flames, sitting there around the family dinner table, hiding our broccoli under the chicken bones on our plates, sneaking scraps to the dogs. At least in death, we would have been together.

I walked into the garage and fell into my father's La-Z-Boy, the chair Princess had died in. Drenched to the bone, I grimly forced down the rest of the warm beer, watching the rain rattling off the tarps and folding tables, the last yard sale slowly dying on the lawn in front of me.

It hadn't been any of our crap that had bankrupted us at all, I realized. The hammock chairs, the cross-country skis, the mini pool table, the weight bench I had never used . . . they were all innocent. It was Simon's Rock. It was my fancy overpriced college for "sensitive" kids who couldn't hack it in high school—$23,000 a year my parents hadn't prepared for. It was the kid who'd never been able to manage a night's sleep on his own, who'd depended on his parents even to go to school to get away from them. It was me.

Tears came, but I choked them back down. I had cried enough. Tears wouldn't help. I had to be strong.

I stared out at the rain falling on the shrapnel of our exploded family and made a solemn vow: I swear to you, Mom, I will take your revenge. I will make it up to you, I will make this right. Not justice, because how fucking naive can you be? This couldn't be undone. But you will get the good things you deserve. And our traitorous father, he will get what he deserves. I will make a mark on this world. I will take the pain you put on the person I love above all others, magnify it a thousand times, and then turn it back on you motherfuckers.

═

At the end of the school year, spending the last night in our old house was like crawling into bed with a corpse. Tatyana had stayed in Boulder for the entire, drawn-out death rattle of the last six months. Tashina was staying the night at a friend's house. Without ever discussing it, Tatyana, my mother, and I did our best to shield her from the worst as the poor kid had seemed lost even before the divorce. My father was long gone, in California with his sports car and his secretary, but then, he'd been gone for years, hadn't he?

Mom and I slept on the floor of my bedroom because it was carpeted. The beds had been packed or sold or just given away. We drank whiskey out of a plastic bottle, covered ourselves with our coats, and cuddled up with Katie for warmth. In the morning, my mother would drop Katie at her new home, then head to Colorado to join Tatyana. Tashina and I would catch a Greyhound bus to Saskatchewan, where she would crash with family and I would pump gas at our uncle's general store.

"Think of it as one grand adventure," Mom had told us.

Even Tashina knew that was bullshit. Adults were so full of shit. We knew adventures—hiking the Grand Canyon, descending to the bottom of Carlsbad Caverns, and, the queen mother of them all, driving from New Mexico to Alaska with Mom one summer. This wasn't an adventure. This was exile.

When the sun rose, my family scattered to the winds. The bank took our house. Everything else was already gone.

CHAPTER 3

Working-Class Zero

Five days before graduation from Simon's Rock, I got an alcohol infraction. As the entire student body was underage (some as young as fourteen), Simon's Rock had a strict alcohol policy. One infraction landed you on social probation; two infractions in a year were grounds for expulsion. This was my third alcohol violation of the semester. I was summoned before the Judicial Committee, our disciplinary panel composed of fellow students, nearly every one of whom had seen me wasted, high, or visibly hungover.

I just wanted out of Simon's Rock's affluent, self-congratulatory freak show. Many of my friends had elected to stay for all four years. Even if we could have afforded it, nothing could have made me stay.

I had testified at Wayne Lo's trial. I'd answered a few mundane questions and related the story about him trying to get a gun. When they asked me to identify the defendant, I made eye contact with Wayne, pointed straight at him, and said, "There. The short guy in the cheap green suit." I had done my part. When Wayne was sentenced a month later to life in prison without the possibility of parole, we were cheered and relieved. Finally, I could find out what had happened, what had been going on, what everyone else had known for a year. But it was all the kids on campus had been talking about for the last fourteen months, and they were sick of it. The sentencing had finally freed them, and the subject was never to be brought up again. I never talked to anyone about it, never even found out exactly what had gone on before that dark night, on the night itself, or during the many sad days that followed.

My roommate James had been kicked out. Ben White, always a dark soul, had gone much darker. He was perpetually high on cough syrup, pale and gaunt, cultivating a desolate squalor in his dorm room. Zack had been charmed by him, and then the whole school seemed to have fallen in line around these two arbiters of taste, a liberal northeastern cult built around cough syrup and gangsta rap and mockery, some kids going so far as to ape Ben White's tics, his awkward gait, his made-up words. He'd called my girlfriend a disgusting slut in front of me, and I'd been too intimidated to respond. Finally, I had taken on both Ben White and Zack one wasted night and came away with a broken nose and two black eyes for my trouble.

I groveled before the Judicial Committee. They reminded me of my infractions over the years: the half gallon of whiskey, the half gallon of vodka, the shoplifting, the many curfew violations . . . I swore that if they would only let me walk, I would be meek as a lamb, quiet as a mouse, a humble, gracious monk of a student until graduation, then slip away and never return. Alternately, I offered that if they tossed me now, I would make such a ruckus that they would tear their hair and rend their clothes, despairing that they hadn't had the wisdom to let me leave quietly.

They made me wait out in the hall while they deliberated. I had been accepted into the film program at the University of Colorado at Boulder, a cheap school now that Tatyana and I qualified for in-state tuition, and all we could afford. Fuck this cloistered, fussy faux-intellectual utopia. I looked forward to disappearing into the crowd at a huge state school, deep undercover in my jeans, T-shirt, and baseball hat . . . if I was allowed to graduate. They couldn't throw me out. My grades were excellent. They wouldn't throw me out. Would they?

Finally, I was summoned back in. I would be allowed to walk on the condition that I never return. I could hardly contain my glee. Anyone could make dean's list, but it took a special type of student to graduate on triple-secret social probation. And putting the two together as I had, being allowed to walk only on the condition that I never return, the excellent exile? I imagined a fat French chef kissing his fingers: *c'est magnifique!*

It was who I was: the up arrow and the down arrow in the same seventeen-year-old mannish boy. I'd read a tabloid about Elvis in a bus station that spring, about how his twin brother was stillborn. Many cultures believe that, in a set of twins, one is good and the other evil. If one of them dies, the other takes on the burden of being both good and evil. More than *The Stranger*, more than *The Catcher in the Rye*, more than any book that supposedly spoke to troubled adolescents, that tabloid told me who I was and who I would be.

———

We graduated. We celebrated. We annihilated and destroyed. We made a "wine machine" by hanging a box of wine from the ceiling in one of the dorms. My mom flew in from Colorado for graduation (she and Tashina had moved there so Tatyana could get in-state tuition). She drank from the wine machine to cheers from my pals. I slept in a bathtub. The next morning, when I couldn't stop throwing up, she helped me box my stuff up to ship to Colorado.

While my mother gathered my dirty laundry and I lay on the floor dying, my girlfriend, Riley, perched on my desk, chatting with my mom and taunting me. My mom had a pile of whites and a pile of darks, and then, before I could stop her, "These sheets will finish off the dark load." She pulled my mattress away from the wall, unearthing a treasure trove of a million glittering silver condom wrappers. Riley went red.

Without even looking up, my mom said, "Well, at least you're not doing drugs," and continued her work.

My classmates got cars or summer vacations to Europe for graduation. My mom gave me a tent. My father didn't call.

I'd become close friends with Punk Rock Gabe, a misanthropic chain smoker with a green Mohawk stuck up with Elmer's glue and a tattoo that said "HATE." We planned to hitchhike across the country to Ellensburg, Washington, so I could see Riley, then up to Alaska to find work in the canneries for the summer.

We partied at upperclassmen's houses in town. I made love to Riley one final time, on the roof of the hardware store. The next day, my mother drove Gabe and me out to my art teacher's house. My art teacher's son Manu, a massive New Zealander with dreads down to the middle of his back, more mountain man freak than hippie, was going to give us a lift as far as Ohio. His ride was packed and ready when we got there: a Toyota pickup that had been used as a pace truck for off-road races, its battered body emblazoned with huge Miller High Life logos, Manu's teepee poles arched over the cab like a bow, bent and lashed to the front and rear bumpers. The bed of the truck was full of his gear, including a tiny fridge that plugged into the cigarette lighter to keep his homebrewed beer cold.

Gabe and I tucked our backpacks snugly in the back of the truck, leaving just enough space for one person to curl up into a ball. My pack had been a gift from Errol, a man my mother had befriended in Colorado. It wasn't enough for her to work full-time answering phones in a call center in addition to looking after us kids, so she volunteered with an outreach organization that worked with recovering alcoholics and drug addicts. Errol was an aspiring writer and a recovering cokehead. He had dreamed of writing a book called "Jonesing Around Boulder" about being a ski bum with a head full of snow, but instead he just spent his life jonesing around Boulder. He and I had become friends over the winter break, so he'd given me his old external-frame backpack. "I don't know if I'll ever be well enough to use it again," he had said. A couple of months later, Errol shot himself in the face with a shotgun.

"I want to say 'be careful,'" my mom said with tears in her eyes, "but I feel like that'll just annoy you. So . . . stay out of jail and stay out of the army and you'll be alright. And *don't die*! Just don't die."

I hugged and kissed my mother and hopped into the cab. Gabe hopped into the bed of the truck. Manu and I each ate two hits of acid, and we hit the road.

By the time we got to Washington, Gabe and I were barely speaking. Too many days walking backward on the side of the road with our thumbs out, baking in the sun, covered in dust as cars roared by; too many hours making polite conversation with strangers who wanted us to come to Jesus or recognize the primacy of truck drivers in the American economy or sell us Amway; too many close calls. We'd covered the largest part of our journey in great time—only five days—but we knew there were still long miles ahead of us, miles made longer now that we couldn't stand each other. We dragged our feet in Washington, gathering our courage for the big push to Alaska—doing yard work for cash, getting drunk, getting high—while I made time with Riley. That only made things worse.

Riley was petite with violently red hair, pale skin, and green eyes. She'd been born in South Africa and had never quite lost her accent, never quite fit in. The first time I saw her, she was wearing a red sweater and short white shorts, picking her way through the grass between the girls' dormitory and the path to the dining hall like a prey animal warily crossing an unsheltered space. She had a low tolerance for bullshit, so we had clashed early and gone our separate ways.

We wound up in an environmental studies class together my final semester. She was outspoken and insightful in class, and, well, she had always been beautiful. I noticed her thin, freckled arm resting on the table one day and wondered if she had freckles everywhere. We began studying together, and then we were "studying together," and then I was trying to get her to be my girlfriend. We made out ferociously a couple of times, but then she refused.

"It's just that . . . I feel like you treat me as a woman first and as a person second. I want to be a person."

I couldn't get my head around what she was saying. I liked her, she liked me, what was the problem? Finally, I gave up. I wanted her in my life, and I wanted her in my room, hanging out with me while we did our homework. If she wouldn't deign to be my girlfriend, I would force myself to endure that humiliation.

The next night I told her, okay, no funny business; we would just be friends. She seemed surprised, but then she settled in. We worked late into the night. I had taken ephedrine to study, as I often did, but something went wrong that night, and it just made me feel feverish and tired. I felt like I was going to pass out. I told her to go ahead and keep studying, that I was just going to lie down for a minute.

Riley woke me up later. All the lights were off. She was crawling into my bed naked. Afterward, we fell asleep in each other's arms. The next morning, I had her sit on the couch while I played "What a Wonderful World" for her, the Nick Cave/Shane McGowan version. It began to snow, and we sat on the couch together and watched the snow come down in impossibly huge flakes.

After that, we spent every free minute together in my room. Riley was intelligent and caring, but cruelty was only ever one word away. When she was on top, I imagined her spine as a finely detailed poisonous millipede under my fingers, delicate as it was dangerous. I talked down about her to my friends, but I was crazy about her. She kept me on my toes.

"You make me feel like I'm in a movie," she said one day.

"Like I'm Indiana Jones and you're Willie, that dancer girl?"

"Why do you always get to be Indy?" she said.

We fought. My high school experience was a wound that hadn't healed; hers had been a rosy crescendo. Riley had been one of the popular girls, a member of the court at the senior prom when she was just a sophomore. She had lost her virginity to her boyfriend Randy, three years older than she, on Valentine's Day, after the Valentine's Day Dance. "It was just *perfectly* romantic," she told me with faraway eyes.

Randy was older, stronger, cooler, just all-round *better*, the boyfriend I could never be. His primacy in her heart was unquestionable as, shortly after he had joined the Marine Corps, he had been found dead. They declared it suicide, but Riley was convinced it was foul play. She spoke of him constantly, lovingly, and chastened me for sulking: I had nothing to worry about from him, he was *dead*, couldn't I just appreciate what a great guy he had been?

One night, she related to me how she had been sexually abused as a child and then date-raped by one of Randy's friends after a drunken campfire party after Randy had enlisted. If that weren't hard enough for her sheltered, seventeen-year-old boyfriend to process, she then detailed how she had gone back home on her first break after entering Simon's Rock and fucked her rapist.

"I just went in and took what *I* wanted. I raped *him*," she told me, lying there in the dark.

I suspected that he didn't see it that way, but I was quickly learning not to give voice to every thought I had around Riley.

<hr>

I awoke one morning a couple of months into our relationship, dying for a piss. I heaved myself out of my bed and lurched to the bathroom in my boxer shorts. I stumbled to a stall, pulled my shorts down, put a hand up to steady myself over the toilet, then closed my eyes and let go.

I tried to reconstruct the events of the day before. I had started drinking at noon when I got out of class, then dropped two hits of acid, then drank a bottle of cough syrup, then smoked pot. I recalled not seeing double but seeing the world refracted many times over, as if I had the eyes of a dragonfly.

I felt that gratifying sense of relief you get when you pee, and I sensed warmth but I didn't hear any sound. I opened my eyes. I was wearing a condom that had already ballooned to the size of a small cantaloupe with hot urine. I gasped and grabbed for it, and at that precious moment, it slipped off and hit the edge of the toilet with a splash.

Why had I been wearing a condom? I racked my brain while I tried lamely to clean myself up, then walked back into my room. Asleep in my bed was Anne, a girl from my acting class.

I lived my life in opposition to my father's. Yet here I was, a weak, shitty man, cheating on my girlfriend as my dad had cheated on my mother. I had inherited all of his flaws and none of his strengths.

Riley took me back without forgiving me. After my infidelity, she seemed to love me more, or at least to want me more. But after a couple of drinks, she took great pleasure in twisting the blade. I took it: I had betrayed her.

Riley's "come closer/stay back" froze me between what I felt was real love for her and my refusal to play the game. During the bickering before the divorce was finalized, my father had told my mother that he had never loved her. He had only said that he did because it was "appropriate." For how many years and how many millions of times had he told that lie? Love had been tainted and abused, definitively ruined by my father, so the word was no good to me. I never said the words to Riley: I love you.

≡

Finally, Gabe had enough. He caught a bus south to visit friends. We had failed. I hitched down to California to drop in unannounced on my father at his new home in Pleasanton, an idyllic inland city even the name of which I found despicable. I'd visited him a couple of times in different apartments over the last eighteen months, usually at my mother's urging. Sometimes it was okay. I had apparently inherited his genetic aptitude for not talking about shit. He let me drink, and we ate a hell of a lot better than we did when I visited my mom.

But his new place was in a gated community. I knew the security guard wasn't about to let me walk in with my pack, so I called and called from a payphone across the street: no answer. Hours after the sun went down, Dad still wasn't home. I bought a bottle of generic NyQuil, slipped over the wall into his wealthy colony, chugged the cough syrup, and blacked out in the cedar chips between two carefully manicured hedges.

The sprinklers woke me the next morning. I started throwing up before I could even get out of my sleeping bag. Still, I took comfort in the thought that while all these pathetic drones around me were eating their breakfasts, I was losing mine.

I packed up my bedroll, shouldered my pack, and located my dad's condo. The look of alarm on his sleepy face when he answered the door was priceless. Hey, Dad, it's the prodigal son! Ya miss me?

When I landed in Colorado ten days later, I moved into the unheated, unfinished basement of the rundown duplex my mother was renting next to Tashina's high school in Lafayette, a small town an hour's bus ride away from the university in Boulder. The carpet smelled like cat piss. We didn't have a cat.

I wasted a couple of days wandering around the lifeless town: a couple of subdivisions behind strip malls and big box stores on either side of the state highway connecting Longmont and Broomfield; a high school with a football field; a neglected old concrete-lined "reservoir" that had become solely a repository for goose shit. I'd told Riley in no uncertain terms that we weren't going to carry on a long-distance relationship. I mean, look at what had happened to my mom and dad. But I missed her terribly. I demanded that my mother procure alcohol for me, then drank alone in my room, listening to Gallon Drunk and mooning over her.

I got a job as a fry cook at the local Sonic Burger drive-in for minimum wage, $4.25 an hour. I had to spend money on a pair of black polyester pants and a Sonic T-shirt before I even clocked in. What a scam. And the work, standing over a blazing hot grill, frantically flipping burgers for hours and hours while getting screamed at by the servers, till my hair was gritty with dried sweat, my hands, wrists, and forearms flecked with burns, my clothes saturated with grease, my feet swollen and aching, my back screaming. I remember shuffling the mile home after work, shell-shocked, then stripping off my clothes, too filthy to even bring inside, on the back deck. During dinner, I was so tired, I could barely talk. I fell asleep immediately after eating, without even taking a drink. Good thing—I had to wake up the next morning, pull my greasy clothes back on, and drag my tired ass back in for another day of the same.

I'd done hard labor before, chopping firewood and hanging sheetrock and carrying sixty-pound bales of hay up a ladder into a hayloft. I'd dug holes for underground water tanks so broad and deep that I'd had to yell for someone to pull me out. In those days, I slept well and rose early. My muscles would be sore but in a satisfied way, like our dogs after a hard run, grinning with their tongues hanging out of their mouths. The fatigue from cooking burgers eight hours a day was different. My whole body felt swollen, even my eyelids and lips. Shoveling dirt tore up your back and hands and arms, but it would make you bigger and stronger. Cooking would just wear me down like water pounding interminably on stones, my shoulders curling in, my back hunching, my chin descending slowly toward my chest.

Yes, I had drunk as much as humanly possible at Simon's Rock, till my closet filled up with empties and my trash can stank continually of vomit, but I had also worked my ass off, waking up early to write papers or finish the assigned reading, drunk or high or coming down from the night before, my foul trash can always within reach. Had I endured all that just to get to *this*?

All our furniture had been sold, so I had nowhere to keep my clothes. On a day off, my mother and I cruised garage sales, looking for a dresser and a desk. The cheapest pieces we could find—dusty white particle-board units held together with plastic screws— were twenty or thirty bucks. Screw that—fifty bucks bought a lot of wine. I did my homework at the kitchen table and used pickle buckets from work as a dresser, which made my clothes reek. Fuck it, it's not like my many friends were going to notice and taunt me.

I got promoted to night manager at Sonic Burger and began work- ing six nights a week. Time off? For what? So I could lean on the chain-link fence behind our house and watch other boys my age— the Centaurus High football team—tackle and high-five each other, worried only about making varsity and getting laid? Thanks, but no. God, I had been so eager to escape the oppressive environment of my high school. I should have just faked it, or even capitulated entirely, played the game, submitted to the American dream of high school rah rah rah, a job at the auto body shop, then gradual acquiescence to sloth, despair, obesity, obscurity, alcoholism.

We had read *Night* at Simon's Rock, Elie Wiesel's harrowing account of survival in Auschwitz during World War II. I recalled the sign mounted over the gates of Auschwitz, capital letters cut out of metal by imprisoned Jews: "ARBEIT MACHT FREI." Its English translation, "Freedom Through Work," became my per- sonal motto. I repeated it daily while scrubbing the hot, filthy grill with a wire brush, cleaning out the grease trap on the roof, or walk- ing home, stinking and exhausted, in the middle of the night. Did I understand it was idiotic to dangerous to adopt a Nazi slogan as a mantra? Maybe. But the few things I enjoyed fell into the gray area between idiotic and dangerous.

In the fall, I started at the University of Colorado, "Ski U," a party school known for its athletics, the criminal misbehavior of its fraternity brothers, its patchouli-and-blonde-dreadlocks poseur hippie vibe, and the egregious wealth of its mostly out-of-state student body. Classes were a joke. Many of my credits from Simon's Rock—expensive credits, premium credits, blue-chip credits!—didn't transfer, so I was stuck taking core curriculum classes in huge lecture halls where the greatest challenge was not falling asleep. All the film classes I wanted to take were held in the afternoon or evening hours when I had to work. I grudgingly changed my major to writing so I could keep my job.

Though Riley and I were officially broken up, we talked on the phone nearly every day and wrote each other long letters whenever time permitted. Her roommate was annoying, she adored her professors, it was sad being at Simon's Rock without me. Ben White was getting weirder, getting worse. One night at a party at his house, a filthy squat with no heat or working plumbing, he told her a story about his friend in Florida who had set a girl on fire and buried her body in a swamp but never gotten caught. I felt the skin on my back prickle. I'd heard this story before. Ben trotted out this dark tale each time he was seducing a girl or just a new friend.

Was Ben after her? There had been revulsion in her voice when describing their encounter, but I knew that darkness fascinated her. I tried to warn her. I had nothing to worry about, she said; she would die before she'd let that creep touch her.

I loathed my new life. On a rare night off, I walked past a group of young men on my way to a punk show. They were talking and laughing, great teeth, great posture, their shoulders square under the high-thread-count cotton of their Oxford blues. They were America's bounty, the future senators, the torch in Liberty's hand, the power and the glory, amen. This, all of this, not just energy drinks and Natural Light and Greek Week and football scholarships, but the Golden Gate Bridge, the New York Stock Exchange, the highways, the power grid: it was for them. For them to use or ignore or destroy. For them, and not for me.

"Faggot," one of them muttered, just loud enough for me to hear.

"Yeah," I called over my shoulder, "I love cock. Come over here, and I'll suck you off. You and all your buddies, best head you ever had." And then ran for my life.

My father had been an outcast like me. When I came home crying after grade school one day, my mother had told me that Dad had been picked on too, that his mother had had to pick BB gun pellets out of his ass with a butcher knife. (Jesus, he'd even one-upped me in the bullying he had endured.) But I also knew my father was weak. If everyone you encountered was an asshole, wasn't it more likely that you were the asshole?

Long before he'd flaked on us, I'd made up my mind to live in defiance of my father's circumscribed life, fleeing persecution at home for persecution at work like a dog clipped to a clothesline, running frantically back and forth, wearing a rut in the lawn. My last semester at Simon's Rock, a friend who lived across the hall had waded through the filth of my room and, with a "You need to read this," thrown a book at me and walked out: *Women* by Charles Bukowski. I was in pain, and Bukowski's wounded, macho bluster made instant sense to me. Bukowski mapped the path to freedom: freedom from the horrors of working a corporate job, from kowtowing to people, from turning out like my father. Reading Bukowski, it seemed radically simple. A bellyful of bourbon was the answer. The trick was just not to run out.

I drank whiskey from a plastic bottle by myself at night in that cold basement, teaching myself Elvis and Johnny Cash songs on my father's guitar, my shoulders, back, and feet aching from work. I drank sloe gin from a flask with the leathery old Native Americans on the bus to Boulder. I drank warm Budweiser before class, then berated my classmates for trying to bluff their way through a conversation on *Lolita* when they clearly hadn't done the reading.

Sorely hungover on the bus back from class one day, my mind flashed to the jug of whiskey I had been nursing for a couple of weeks. Poisoned as I felt on that lurching bus, the thought of that bottom-shelf whiskey actually made my mouth water. I was an explorer; I had ventured deep into the caverns of a new world. But I had been careless, and I had brought something back with me—a malign parasite. I felt the skin on my neck pucker up. I can control it, I told myself, and tried to push the ugly thought away. But I was scared.

I had awkward, drunken sex with one of the carhops from Sonic, a girl I didn't even like. I told Riley about it. It had meant nothing to me. Besides, we were broken up!

That night, she slept with Ben Bertocci. The next night, she slept with Ben White. I drank, I wept, I berated her. I told her never to talk to me ever again. I tracked her every move through my friends. She found a new boyfriend, incredibly also named Ben. Parents, please name your sons Arthur.

My mother ground her teeth in her sleep. My back gave out at work, and I was in excruciating pain for three days, unable to get out of bed. We both started losing our hair. I recalled a cautionary tale from a D.A.R.E drug-education lecture in sixth grade: If you dump a frog into a pot of boiling water, he'll thrash and kick and do anything he can to get out. But if you put the frog in cool water and incrementally raise the temperature, degree by careful degree, the frog won't move a muscle, floating idly in water that gets hotter and hotter until he's finally cooked. But what about frogs like my mother and me, frogs who have adapted to truly frightful conditions and are somehow able to continue living in the boiling water, their flesh scalding, skin peeling off their backs in sheets?

My mother never gave up. Late on Christmas Eve, she stole a Christmas tree for Tashina and me, just backed her car up to the lot and tossed it in.

"You stole that?" Tashina said, incredulous that our pillar of morality was capable of such a clear trespass.

"Well, it's not like they're going to need it now, are they?" my mom said, smiling. "Look, it's even got lights on it!"

≡

I dropped out of CU-Boulder at the end of the semester to move back to Great Barrington. I hadn't spoken to Riley, and I didn't intend to, but I felt powerlessly drawn to her. I had forgiven Bertocci—he had written, begging my forgiveness; he had been wasted, and she had waylaid him!—but Ben White would have to be dealt with. My old roommate James had reenrolled at Simon's Rock to try to get his two-year degree, so I'd meet him in DC, and we'd travel up together. What was my plan, moving to Massachusetts in the dead of winter? Did I intend to settle the score? To win her back? I probably did it because it was the worst idea possible.

Before leaving Colorado, I worked and drank and taken trucker speed and studied for finals until I was worn to a nub. As soon as I got back East, I came down with laryngitis and bronchitis. I spent a week in bed at James's parents' house, worrying I would die, then praying I would. His mother brought me to her doctor and paid for the visit and the antibiotics—$80, a princely sum I had not budgeted for.

After I recovered, I had found an apartment close to my fellow hangers-on from Simon's Rock, a two-bedroom over a doctor's office. The doctor's neighbors had taken him to court to force him to paint the dilapidated old building and won. He had painted it eleven different bright, clashing colors. He specialized in pain management, as did I. It was perfect.

I found a roommate, a girl a year behind me, a girl I had never liked, a girl I had openly mocked. We flipped a coin for the bigger room. She won. I encountered Riley and did nothing. I encountered Ben White and did nothing.

I got a job at a pizza place two miles away (a long, cold walk in Massachusetts in January), and I worked at every opportunity. Even at $4.25 an hour, I quickly saved up the $80 I owed and sent it back to James's parents. They returned my check with a note, thanking me for paying them back but saying it wouldn't be necessary—I could consider the antibiotics a gift for my approaching eighteenth birthday.

I bought six four-liter jugs of Carlo Rossi at eight bucks a bottle and spent the rest of the money on beer. I kept the jugs at the foot of my mattress as I diligently worked my way through them. My puppies, I called them. It was comforting to hear them clink musically when I rolled over in my bed. When I awoke with night terrors, I had only to reach my feet down and touch the cool, glassy surfaces of the bottles to feel better.

An ex-classmate picked me up while I was walking to work later that winter. She chattered about the latest gossip among our friends and then turned her attention on me.

"You seem to be doing better this year," she said encouragingly.

I lived in a room the size of a bathroom, a poster of a mushroom cloud rising over Bikini Atoll after the testing of the atomic bomb hanging over my bed. I existed on rice and beans. I washed my body, my hair, and my dishes with tiny bars of soap I stole from the restaurant where I worked. I cut my hair with a razor blade. I obsessed about Riley, and though we didn't speak, I tracked all the developments in her life—her library job, her new tortoiseshell cat's eye glasses, her life with her boyfriend, the decline of her tiny green hatchback. She had shown up at the end of my eighteenth birthday party, driven me home, fucked me, then left to go home to her boyfriend. I lost it, crying uncontrollably for a long time. When I finally pulled myself together, I heard my roommate sniffling in her room—I had cried so hard that it made her cry. If I was doing better, I was pretty sure "better" for me was still pretty far below normal for anyone else.

"A bunch of us were worried you were going to kill yourself last year," she said. "You were just so nihilistic. The only reason we decided you wouldn't was that you had said suicide was pointless and stupid."

I laughed out loud, surprising both of us. But it struck me as funny: my nihilism was the only thing that had saved me from myself.

I got a better job at a deli, working sixty hours a week or more. I got hammered every night and drank all day long on my day off. One Sunday, we ran dry, and I made screwdrivers with rubbing alcohol. I was on time or early to work each morning, but the first few hours were brutal.

"You es crazy," Ernesto, one of the Latino cooks, said to me one morning as I lugged a huge plastic container of raw chicken wings onto the countertop to be prepped before cooking.

Ernesto mimed drinking from a bottle and pointed at me. "Ery night. Ery day."

I smiled weakly at him, my stomach doing flip-flops at the mere thought of alcohol. I lifted the lid and dumped the chicken wings onto my cutting board. They were starting to go bad, and as the smell wafted up to me, my eyes zeroed in on the clumps of feathers and hair still clinging to them. I dashed for the bathroom, vomit already boiling up my throat and into my mouth, Ernesto's laughter bouncing off the hard tile floor.

Despite my rough mornings, I was well loved in the kitchen. Dave, my boss, paid me well—I made more than my mother—and my savings piled up. I became obsessed with self-sufficiency, dead set on paying my own way. When my father stopped paying child support for Tashina, I even sent money home to my mom, determined—at eighteen—to be the man he had failed to be.

As I was finding my way, my nemesis, Ben White, had been losing his. He was abusive in class and menaced the kids in his dorm.

It was an open secret that he hit women. Still, he hadn't provided the school with the single overt transgression that would merit expulsion. When he shoved his way through a crowd of women staging a political protest on his way to the dining hall, the school didn't waste any time. He was escorted from campus that very day. He built a nest in the crawl space at his girlfriend's house in town and nourished his decline, constantly high on cough syrup he'd shoplifted, barely coherent, hardly eating, vomiting blood, increasingly erratic, increasingly violent.

We were drinking at my house one night. My roommate asked if it was cool if she invited Ben's girlfriend over. She was a genial Florida party girl who could be counted on to knock over every single drink within reach but was still impossible not to like.

"Ah . . . yeah, that's fine, just tell her not to bring Ben with her."

A moment after my roommate made the call, the phone rang again. That would be Ben.

"Hello?"

"Hi, Mishka."

"Hi, Ben."

"Can I come over?"

"No."

"Why not?"

"Because we're not friends."

"I'm coming over."

"Don't come over."

"I'm coming over."

The line went dead.

When the bell rang, my friend Kevin followed me down the stairs. I saw Ben's girlfriend outside by herself: bullet dodged. I opened the door to let her in.

Ben stood up from behind a hedge and tried to skirt past me into the house. Shit. I grabbed him from behind and got him in a full nelson. What now? Ben wouldn't punch me or tackle me if I released him. He'd gouge out an eye, stab me, choke me to death.

He had gotten so thin that he slipped my hold. I shoved him away and scrambled for the open door. As Kevin kicked the door shut, Ben lunged after me. The glass pane in the door shattered.

I turned the lock and slid the bolt into place. Kevin and I braced the bottom of the door with our feet, holding ourselves clear of the broken window.

Ben slowly pushed through the broken glass till his head and shoulders were inside with us. He stared at me, his eyes flat and dead.

"I'm going to kill you," he said.

Without breaking my gaze, he rolled his torso around inside the jagged window frame. Blood instantly darkened his T-shirt, and wet folds of it slid down his arms.

"Kevin," I said, "go upstairs and call the police."

The cops showed up shortly after Ben left, and they grudgingly took my report. After they had gone, my gathered friends laid into me. What the hell did I think I was doing? We hated cops. Cops weren't going to do anything. This would only anger Ben enough for him to actually kill me. I didn't disagree, but I couldn't sit back and do nothing.

Days later, Ben was gone, having fled back to Florida. Had calling the cops worked? No, he had been too easy to get rid of. I recalled a line from Circus Lupus's "I Always Thought You Were an Asshole": "Florida is not so far away / In fact, it's just another grave." That story Ben always told about his friend who had set a girl on fire and buried her in a swamp . . . could he have been the one who did it? I wouldn't feel safe till he was in jail or a mental institution, and I worried that I hadn't seen the last of him.

⸻

One day that summer, my boss called me into his office.

"Sit down, Mishka," he said.

That was a bad sign. I sat down. He closed the office door behind me. That was another bad sign.

"Listen, Mishka, I don't want to tell you how to live your life but . . . it's impossible to work with you and not notice a few things."

Thank God. Dave was just going to ride me about drinking.

"You are speaking of my good looks? Or is it my joie de vivre?"

"The drinking, Mishka. How much do you drink?"

"Jesus, Dave, you scared me. I thought you were going to fire me."

"No, no, you're doing great, my number one guy, I just—"

"I know, Dave, I know, I'm going to kill myself, and I have soooo much to offer and so much potential and blah blah blah, right?"

"No," he said. "I'm not worried that you're going to die. You can drink hard for a long time without dying. But there are things worse than death. I'm more worried that you'll end up behind a desk, like me. Mishka, if I could turn my desk over and fuck it— just for spite—I would."

I laughed it off in the moment, but slowly Dave's dread wormed its way into me. My two-bedroom apartment had become a flop for ex–Simon's Rockers, sleeping seven or eight people at a time, with one in the kitchen and two in the closet. The charm of working to drink/drinking to sleep/sleeping to work had worn off. I could labor eighty hours a week in a hot, wet, filthy kitchen for the rest of my life and have nothing to show for it but varicose veins and fallen arches. How was this lonely drudgery revenge? What would it say on my tombstone, "He Made Great Potato Salad"?

I called my mother, and she helped me reenroll at the University of Colorado. School was the only thing I did well, and I knew college was essential if I hoped to rescue my mother from working poverty. A degree would get me a job, a job would get me money, money would get me revenge. I would slave through the spring and summer, then cross the country once more not to take a stab at college but to annihilate it.

My mom found a house in Boulder, closer to CU, with a finished basement I could live in. The catch was that I had to find a roommate. Fuck, Mom, how would I find a Colorado roommate in Massachusetts?

I asked James, I asked Bertocci, I asked all my buddies. No takers. It came to me at work one day: Scott, a cook in his forties I worked with. He loved Ray Charles, as I did; he had played drums for Lou Reed, and he liked to drink. He would be the perfect roommate.

"Man, I would love to. But I got my kid here. And, you know, this job that I love so much."

"Hey man, no problem," I said, feigning hurt. "It's cool. I didn't even really want you to live with me, anyway. I'm just asking every person I bump into. Hey, Speck, you want to move to Colorado with me to be my roommate?"

Speck was a dishwasher a couple of years older than me, cute with a black bob and penetrating blue eyes. She had been head of the Judicial Committee at Simon's Rock. She had compelled me to write a letter to Pay-Rite apologizing for the shoplifting thing, and she had presided over the session in which I'd had to grovel to graduate. She went by Speck instead of her real name, which struck me as self-indulgent. Why she was working as a dishwasher now, I couldn't figure out, but I knew that I didn't like her, that I would never like her.

"Sure," she said.

⸻

I had been saving up for a car, but I knew nothing of cars. I only knew that I didn't want to get ripped off. My father knew everything about cars. He knew everything about everything. He could gaze upon anything—a bicycle, a vacuum cleaner, a particle accelerator—and see an exploded drawing: all the parts and pieces, their names and functions, how they all fit together. In my world, a car had four tires, four doors, and a hood, under which was a Bunch of Stuff. But my dad understood all the mysteries of its inner workings: when the carburetor spins, it creates a magnetic field, which

separates the gas-o-trons, which are funneled into the catalytic con-
verter by the spark plugs with a cyclic motion that sets the engine
block spinning and—voilà—horsepowers!

Bertocci's dad helped me find a car, a rust-orange 1986 Ford
Bronco II. Paying for the car, the registration, the title, and the insurance took up almost all the money I had saved. But I had a car!
One of the other cooks congratulated me. She had owned the same
model and loved it. It had burst into flames in her driveway one
day. Dave asked me if I had seen that news story about how Ford
Broncos were prone to rolling at even very low speeds. The baker
just laughed in my face.

On a rare day off two weeks before Speck and I were to leave
for Colorado, I walked over to my friend's house on Castle Street to
see if he wanted to go swimming. The door was open, so I walked
in. I was halfway to the stairs before I realized someone was sleeping on the couch. I quieted my stride so as not to wake him or her,
then glanced down as I passed, curious. It was Ben White.

I slipped up the stairs to my friend's room, but he wasn't there.
My heart flopped in my chest like a fish on the dock. The police station was only blocks away. Should I climb out a window? No, I'd
just sneak silently past that jumble of gaunt limbs on the couch and
trot down the hill to the cop shop. They'd bag him, and he would
be none the wiser.

As kids, we had practiced moving silently in order to spy on
our parents fighting. It never worked. A stair would creak, a knee
would pop. I drew a deep breath and crept past Ben White in absolute silence. I marveled once I reached the door. I had done it. Then
I glanced over my shoulder and looked right into his open eyes.

Ben White was out of jail before the end of the day. Zack and
another of my friends paid his bail. Apparently, Ben had just shown
up in the middle of the night with a couple of fifteen-year-old run-
aways in an old gray sedan. Another news item filtered back to
me later that night: the old gray sedan had a couple of guns in the
trunk.

At work, I began setting up my cutting board next to the fire exit in order to make a quick escape if Ben White came in blazing. I slept in a different location each night so he wouldn't know where I was—a night at my art teacher's house, a night in Bertocci's barn, a night on a friend's couch. A minor hood I knew offered to get me a 9mm. No, I would rather die than kill.

Two nights before I was to leave, I got shitfaced at Speck's going-away party, perhaps because I knew there would be no party for me. She was catching a bus the next morning for Philly in order to pack her stuff for Colorado.

I flopped down on a couch and burrowed in for the night. I was exhausted and could not wait to flee Massachusetts. It would be a great relief to hunker down at my mother's house away from all this drama. I'd work less, no more twelve-hour shifts, and focus exclusively on school. "Mishka, you can't sleep here," Speck said, smiling down at me.

"I'm already halfway there."

"Just come sleep at my apartment. You can sleep in a bed."

"The magic of alcohol is that it makes the entire world soft and squishy. I'm fine."

Speck pried me up and walked me, stumbling, back to her apartment. She laid me down in her bed and left the room. I wiggled out of my pants and T-shirt. She had been right. The bed was nice. Soft, clean sheets.

I was just dozing off when she crawled into bed with me and climbed on top.

CHAPTER 4

The Potato Peelings in the Sink Did Not Turn into Vodka as I Had Hoped

H ad I grown? My mom seemed smaller in the narrow, cracked driveway of her Boulder rental, her shoulders a little rounder, the skin on her face softer. She cooed over me, rubbing my stubbly chin and gently mocking my facial hair: "Ooh, I almost didn't recognize you with the mustache! So handsome, like a young Freddie Mercury." She helped Speck and me unload our bags and boxes into the basement, beds already made up for us, dinner waiting on the stove.

After sleeping for a couple of days, Speck and I crawled out of the basement and got jobs at the closest restaurant, the International House of Pancakes. Speck would hostess and was assigned a scratchy blue dress. I was handed a ridiculous floppy chef's hat and a matching navy neck scarf. My clothes now stank not of pickles, as they had when I had been working at Sonic Burger, but of pancakes and bacon.

My mom referred to Speck as my girlfriend once, and I corrected her: Speck was my roommate. We were not involved. We would never get involved. I had warned Speck not to fall in love with me, and she had laughed it off. It would be impossible, she had said; she was even harder than I was. True, we slept in the same bed. True, we hung out all the time, shared all the details of our lives with each other. True, we fucked constantly, in all manner of acrobatic positions. Speck was infertile, so we fucked joyfully, gleefully, like we were getting away with something. I had her hold her arm tight to her side one night, and I fucked her armpit because we had exhausted every other perversion we could think of. It worked, and when I came on her back, we collapsed into giggles. Best roommate ever!

While I had been spasming back and forth across the country, Mom had patiently worked her way up at her customer service job, from phone rep in the trenches to a marginally less degrading supervisory role. Since her collapse in the driveway in New Hampshire, she had never faltered again. She took everything in stride, applying her lipstick in the hallway mirror, then putt-putting off to work in her tired little Nissan Sentra. She had taught me how to drive in that little car, snugly buckled into the passenger seat, her hands folded neatly in her lap: "I know how to do it, but I don't really know how to explain it to you . . . You're smart so I'm just going to sit here and love you, and I know you'll figure it out."

You could plan a day at the beach, wake up to a monsoon, and she'd throw open the curtains and say, "Well, look at that! A perfect day to clean the house! Why don't I put some cookies in the oven, and we can listen to that Beach Boys record, and then there will be fresh cookies when we're done cleaning?" It was maddening—*nothing* got to her. But I was so happy to see her and so relieved to be home—in a rented house I'd never been to that belonged to people I'd never met—that even her high spirits couldn't bring me down.

She'd found a boyfriend, Paul, an ex-plumber from New York who looked like a Neanderthal but was as intelligent as he was insecure, generous and coarse and easily pissed off. But he treated me like an equal, turned me on to Dave Van Ronk and Lightnin' Hopkins, and was good to my mom. I knew it was good for her to have someone.

Still, her attitude baffled me. My father treated us kids like an unpleasant, expensive chore, like buying new tires for an old car or getting a tooth drilled. But my mom had gotten royally fucked; she had built her life around a lie, devoted more than twenty years to a man who'd bailed on her for the most banal trope—a younger secretary and a red sports car. I was poisoned with resentment, not for myself or my sisters but for her, and somehow she could joke about it. It was grossly unfair for this woman, who had always put everyone else first and herself last, to be treated poorly. It made me so angry to hear how rude people were to her at work that I couldn't even be there for her to kvetch about it. I would have taken it all on for her if I could. What I really wanted was to punish those fuckers, but I was powerless.

I loathed my job. My blue-blooded New England buddies at Simon's Rock had ruthlessly romanticized the working class, pontificated at length about the merits of honest, hand-and-back work. My coworkers—weed dealers and racists and convicted sex offenders on work release—these were the salt of the earth? Working full-time, I still couldn't afford to insure the Bronco I'd blown all my hard-earned wages on. It sat silently in the garage like the fossil of some great beast made obsolete by evolution.

I loathed the other college kids. Alone in my basement at night, I imagined their fantastic lives: their Range Rovers and Land Cruisers, their ski weekends at Vail, the coeds in the hot tub, brand-name vodka, cocaine, orgies—tanned, svelte bodies writhing and grinding on each other, pure Sodom-and-Gomorrah luxurious carnality. Their privilege, their excess, their entitlement disgusted me. And I would have done anything for a taste of it.

I was exhausted all the time, dozing off on the bus, at dinner, on the toilet. But, aching and sleep-deprived, I did every reading for every class, every lick of homework. Great Barrington had taught me that fun was pointless, the low road to a life of servitude. A degree was the only way out. I stopped drinking after a humiliating meltdown on the night of Speck's birthday party and ground tirelessly toward my bachelor's.

The English department head raised an eyebrow when I turned in my application for the honors program.

"Your reputation precedes you. People are talking."

"People talk. What are they saying?"

"That you're a good writer with a grating personality."

"I agree with the second part."

A letter arrived a week later: "Welcome to the University of Colorado at Boulder English Honors Program." I mailed my dad a couple of the stories I had written but didn't hear back. I printed them up and mailed them again. Still nothing.

One night after sex, Speck rolled off me, then took my head in both her hands, pulled me close, and spoke into my ear.

"Mishka?"

"You're pregnant?" This was my running joke, more hilarious each time I said it.

I could hear Speck smile.

"No. I love you."

I drew a deep breath. That I had feared this was coming didn't mean I was prepared to deal with it.

"When I said I wasn't going to fall in love with you, I wasn't lying," she said. "I was already in love with you, and had been for a long time. I took that job washing dishes just to be close to you."

"Speck," I said, "I love dogs. I love my mother. And I love rock 'n' roll."

In the silence that followed, I could hear us breathing in time there in the darkness. She would leave. She had to now. It would be the best for both of us.

A month later, I bought some 'shrooms from a waiter who dealt out of IHOP. Walking home with the plastic sandwich baggie in my pocket, I realized I didn't want Speck to eat them with me. Falling in love with me, then scheming, lying to me, and trying to fuck me into loving her . . . it made me angry. It was like she had gotten herself addicted to crack: I worried for her welfare, and I knew I could no longer trust her. And I was mad at her because—crack cocaine!—what the hell had she been thinking?

Tashina would trip with me. Only days after news of the divorce broke, I'd understood how it would work. Tatyana would be the good daughter. I'd be the bad son. Tashina would slip through the cracks. I'd done a couple of cool things with her since I'd been back, like bring her to see the radical feminist riot grrrl band Bikini Kill, but mushrooms would let us reconnect on a deeper level. She was fourteen. That was old enough.

We choked them down, chasing each disgusting mouthful with tons of water, then bundled up and snuck out into the winter night. We were walking up Table Mesa Drive toward the National Center for Atmospheric Research, when the mushrooms hit us so hard we could barely walk. We shuffled off the road to avoid the terrifying headlights of the occasional passing car. The snow was deep, and we made slow progress up the hill, giggling and falling.

I struggled upright at one point. The bright moon shining down made the boulders on the hillside cast dark shadows against the white snow.

"Tashina, look at the black spots on the snow! It looks like a cow."

"You mean, like . . . moo?"

We toppled back into the snow, cackling. I loved Tashina. She loved me. We would never stop loving each other. She was the best sister for not being Tatyana. I was the best brother for feeding her mushrooms and edifying her on the grand, sweeping issues in life, like midnight mountain climbing and David Bowie and the use-lessness of America's police force.

We were half-frozen by the time we got back, post-euphoric but still cognitively disabled. I tried singing the alphabet song to myself, but I couldn't remember what order the numbers went in. Down in the basement, Speck was sitting in a chair, reading. She closed the book when I stumbled in.

"Can we talk?" she said.

"You're pregnant?" I said, grinning.

"Yes," she said.

Turned out Speck had never actually been diagnosed as infertile by a doctor; she had just never gotten pregnant before. I picked up a twelve-hour shift at the International House of Pancakes, from five p.m. Friday night to five a.m. Saturday morning, to pay for the abortion. The graveyard shift was quiet, so I was charged with deep-cleaning all the grills and cooking fifty pounds of bacon for the morning rush. Standing over that hot grill, sweat cutting rivers down my greasy face, the tendons in my back popping and strain-ing, I felt like I was coming apart.

My whole life, I had yearned for an older brother. Maybe that's why I had worshipped Chuong so. Where the hell was he now? In Albuquerque? In jail? Back in Vietnam? Dead? When my mother told me in high school that she'd had an abortion before she and Dad had gotten married, it made perfect sense. That had been the older brother I was missing. What would he have looked like? He would have had some good advice, which would come in very handy right now. Or at least some money.

Speck went back to Philadelphia. I started drinking again. I de-cided I loved her and pleaded with her to come back. Finally, she relented and came back in the spring. I met her at the airport with a dozen roses. It was okay, for a while.

I clashed with my mom's boyfriend, Paul. He had squandered his life on a career beneath his intelligence, and it had left him angry. While I was constantly busting my ass, his sole ambition was to catch a buzz and do as little as possible. He liked me, as he saw his past self in me. I hated him, as I saw my future self in him. We got into screaming matches, nearly coming to blows one night.

I clashed with my boss. Meal breaks were a scam to have you clock out when it was slow so you'd be stuck there a half hour longer. I never took meal breaks, just snatched bites of a sandwich between orders. My manager told me I had to take a meal break, then took my time card and punched me out. I left my hat, scarf, and cook's shirt in a pile on the floor and walked out. I got a job at a moving company run by an ex-member of an Aryan gang. He'd been shot in the head by a cop and become a Christian in prison. He worked us brutally hard. Stumbling in after my third fourteen-hour day in a row, I noticed my hair was frosted gray with dried sweat.

Speck adored me, and I could never forgive her for that. We were fucking in the basement one day, and she was saying all kinds of crazy stuff—how she would die for me, how she could touch my skin in the dark and instantly know it was me. She whispered my name in my ear, my full, loathsome name: "I love you, Mikhail Valerian Shubaly."

I threw her off me. She drew a ragged breath, and before she could begin crying, I heard the sounds of Paul fucking my mother upstairs. I told Speck I never wanted her to touch me again. She left, and this time she didn't come back.

At the end of the summer, my mother got downsized. Such a despicable practice, both the bloodless elimination of jobs for corporate profits and the act of concealing it in a meaningless word like "downsizing," blunting the blade so it looks less dangerous. And hurts more. Was America bent on destroying us?

My mom and Paul made plans to abandon the United States for a caretaking gig in the Virgin Islands with Tashina in tow. My mom finally seemed to be coming around to a hard truth Tashina and I had accepted long ago: Fuck the world. In the eye. Straight to hell. Forever.

Tatyana had cruised efficiently through college, gotten her degree in electrical engineering, and moved to California, where she was pulling down big bucks doing some Internet thing I didn't understand. My father was barely a voice on the other end of the phone. Would I be okay left to my own devices with no adult supervision? Sure, Mom, what could go wrong?

I moved into a college slum blocks away from our old house with Sam Sacks, a movie geek from Boston who had befriended me—the helpless leading the hopeless. I quit my job moving furniture and quickly blew through the money I'd saved as my drinking ratcheted up, a reliable solace in the dark. I had to plead for my old job at IHOP. I made less money at the grill, but it was impossible to move furniture with a hangover.

I studied hard every day and slung pancakes all weekend: the good son. But I was isolated in a relentless circuit: rising, throwing up, going to class, drinking and studying till I passed out. More than once, I awoke in the night, crying hard enough to wake Sam in the other room. Part of me knew I was making progress toward my degree and my plan for revenge. The rest of me just wanted to set the entire thing on fire.

≡

Riley called me drunk in the middle of the night. She had tracked me as I had tracked her in Great Barrington. She was unhappy, she missed me, she loved me. I sold my Bronco at a heartrending loss, then convinced Sam we had to drive halfway to Washington to meet Riley and her roommate in Idaho.

Riley was more erratic than ever. Drunk, she was abusive and even dangerous. It didn't matter: we were in love. I finally had something of my own, our nation of two. Nothing else mattered.

At my mother's urging, I went to the Virgin Islands for the summer. Paul assured me there was work. There was no work. But the drinking age was eighteen, so I drank the local $2.19-a-bottle rum and obsessed over Riley, who was attending a dance program in Maryland. I wrote her letters daily, called her nightly with the calling card my father gave me to call him until he caught on and canceled it. One day, I drank a liter of rum, woke up in my own urine, and suffered some kind of weird nervous collapse, unable to make even the most trivial of decisions for several days. Finally, a menial construction gig came through, removing the internal plywood forms and cleaning newly poured concrete cisterns for a housing development. Brutal work, but I was no stranger to that.

Three weeks before we were to move to Denver so we could start our lives together, Riley erased herself from my life: letters returned, phone ringing and ringing. I attacked the labor at my job passionately, crawling out of cisterns drenched in sweat, coated head to toe in gray concrete dust, my hands torn and bloody, coughing up chunks of clay on my lunch break. After work, I helped Paul break rocks and dig fence-post holes on the property, anything to keep myself from thinking about what had happened, what lay ahead.

I landed in Denver in September, $1,000 in my pocket, unemployed, heartbroken, no place to stay.

Sam took me in. He met me at the airport and drove me back to his apartment, a beery second-story crash pad with a rotating cast of ne'er-do-wells, including Conor, a bartender who was more than happy to serve me despite my being six months shy of twenty-one, and Judah, the only guy I'd met outside Simon's Rock who drank more than I did. The landlord on the first floor despised us. For a heartbroken twenty-year-old, it was a heaven, of sorts. I set about diligently drinking my way through the money I had saved.

⸺

I awoke one night, fully clothed, one shoe off, lying on my back in Judah's bed. The moon was shining through the window, and it was pleasantly cool. I was incredibly thirsty. It took me a minute to get my other shoe off and stand up. I was surprised when I stumbled on my way to the kitchen for a glass of water, because I felt totally sober. I drank two glasses of water and washed my face. I walked around the apartment, calling Sam's name a couple of times. No answer.

Sam's room was dark when I opened the door, so I turned the light on. His bed was empty, a yellow mattress with roses printed on it, a fuzzy blue blanket, a pillow waxy from his pomade, no sheets. I needed desperately to talk to Sam, or someone, anyone. I mixed myself a mug of rum on ice and went back into Judah's room to look at my pictures of Riley.

Riley had sent me two pictures of herself at Yellowstone before I left for St. John. In my favorite she was standing in front of Old Faithful as it was shooting off. One cloud in the brochure-blue sky, assorted tourists in the background. They struck me as unnaturally candid and corny, as if they weren't actual tourists but extras hired for a photo shoot. Some fluorescent letters were silk-screened onto the back of someone's T-shirt, and I could almost make out what they said. Maybe "I Blew My Top at Old Faithful, Yellowstone National Monument." Or maybe "The Seven Stages of Tequila." Or maybe "Mishka, You Are About to Make a Terrible Mistake."

Riley was standing in front, missing all the action by facing the camera. Hands on her waist, elbows out. One hip was thrust to the side, as if those hard hip bones had just sprung up under her skin overnight and she hadn't quite figured out how to wear them yet. There was a slit up one side of her cutoffs where the seam had come unraveled and the white threads trickled down onto her pale, froggy legs. She was wearing a red-and-white-striped T-shirt. The material had been carefully stitched at the arms so that the stripes lined up with the rest of the shirt, encircling her forever, a perfect circuit, like Old Faithful erupting every seventy-some minutes, tourists returning year after year like sunburnt pilgrims. Riley's hair glowed red in the sun like heated metal. Was it hot on her head? Did red hair somehow react to the sun, as certain species of fish only breed under a full moon?

Her eyes were circumspect, one eyebrow slightly crooked from a childhood tumble off her bike. I squinted at the picture and turned it in the light, looking for a clue. Riley was smiling tentatively—great popsicle-red lips, but they were closed, no teeth. She looked tired. Had she been posing like that all day, all summer, all the time I had been gone, the real natural wonder at the national park? Maybe at the end of the season, the Yellowstone rangers took her cutoffs and T-shirt and put them in a pressurized chamber to prevent dry rot, then made her crawl into a tiny, Riley-shaped pit of murky sulfur water under the boardwalk. She would hibernate the entire winter, the volcanic chemicals keeping her fresh, keeping her hair incandescent for the next season's amateur photographers.

The second picture was darker. Riley wore a light-gray jacket, leaning on a weathered wood railing overlooking the silty, bubbling pool. Her stubbornly red hair seemed gray, limp, and defeated. The light in the picture was evening light—no, more mournful than just the end of a day; something bigger was coming to an end. Her lips were waning red, pressed into another tight, painful smile. What's the matter, Riley? If I were there, I'd kiss that close-lipped smile right off your face. Please, Riley, throw your head back, laugh, open mouth, teeth.

I felt something break loose inside me. I was coming unwound. I dug in my cardboard box of clothes for another bottle of rum. When I raked from the bottom up, I unearthed a gallon Ziploc bag of seashells. I lifted the plastic bag out of the box and emptied it on the carpet in the moonlight.

The seashells were beautiful, of course, but also sinister. Loosely piled there, ridges gleaming between folds of shadow like wet human ears. I'd spent a whole afternoon walking around on the beach after a storm on St. John picking them up for Riley—tiny coiled snail shells, perfect miniature scallops, the pink, oval skeletons of black sea urchins. It all seemed so fucking useless now. I grabbed handfuls of them and threw them out Judah's open window.

I needed Sam now. I called information and got the number for the Taj Mahal, Conor's bar. Conor answered after about ten rings. He was slurring, and I could tell by his voice that he was surprised to hear from me. No, he said, Sam wasn't there; he had shown up to get me but left when Conor told him he'd already dumped me in a cab. Conor asked me if I got home okay, but I hung up.

I called my mom in the Virgin Islands even though I knew it was long distance, even though I knew she was on vacation with Paul somewhere. I figured I would get Tashina, and she could give me the number where they were. I let it ring and then hung up just before the answering machine could pick up. I tried again, hung up again.

The third time I called, somebody picked up. I said, "Hello? *Hello?*"

When I called back, it was busy. Tashina must have just knocked the phone off the hook. I realized it was two hours later there and a school night.

I cried for a little while. Then I decided to call Riley's mother. I knew Riley wasn't going to be there, but I just wanted to talk to somebody who knew her. I dialed the number by heart. Her mom picked up the phone. She sounded sleepy. She always did when I called her in the middle of the night.

I said, "Hello? Is this Sandy?"

She sighed. "Hi, Mishka."

"I'm sorry for calling, Sandy. Did I wake you up?"

"No, no, no, I was just falling asleep."

That's what people always say when you wake them up.

"I'm sorry, Sandy. I swear I won't call again. I just wanted to make sure Riley was alright."

Of course she was alright. I knew because I'd had a panic attack one morning after a night of Riley dreams, and I'd called her house and grilled her little sister's babysitter.

"Oh, she's fine. She got accepted to the Washington, DC, ballet, and so she's out there. Do you want her number?"

"I know she doesn't want to talk to me." My voice started to crack a little bit. "I just wanted to make sure that she was okay."

"How long has it been since you talked to her?"

"About two months."

"Oh, Mishka, I'm sorry. I can't make any excuses for her. When Riley doesn't know what to do, she doesn't do anything. She was trying to get in touch with you, I know, but she didn't know where you were."

That was so much bullshit. She'd tracked me down before when she was drunk and lonely and tired of calling her other ex-boyfriend. She knew the number for information. She knew I was in Denver.

"Let me get your address," Sandy said.

I gave her Sam's address, my voice warbling the whole time: 1065 Gaylord Street—is this world *completely* void of dignity? Sandy wrote it all down. Or at least she acted like she was writing it down.

"She'll get in touch with you, I'm sure."

Then there was a little pause. We didn't know what to say. Sandy was Riley's mother; I was Riley's crazy ex-boyfriend calling her house in the middle of the night again. I had seen Sandy about six months before, and we hadn't had anything to talk about. We both loved Riley. Sandy had always been nice to me, or at least polite.

"I love her so much, Sandy."

I was completely gone, bawling.

"I know, I know, Mishka. I'm sorry. I'm sure she'll get in touch with you."

"I'm sorry, Sandy. I won't call you again. I just wanted to make sure she was okay. Good-bye."

"Good-bye, Mishka."

I fell on the floor. I didn't know where my mom was, Tashina wasn't answering the phone, I couldn't call Tatyana, I definitely couldn't call my dad, Sam was gone, Riley was dancing for the Washington ballet . . . there was no one. I was crying pretty hard, I guess. My landlord banged on his ceiling, my floor. It was quiet hours after nine.

I won my own room only when someone else moved out, so I stacked my boxes in ungainly towers and made a nest of old blankets in the corner as I had no bed. My back hurt, but my back always hurt. Sam found me a job in a call center very much like the one that had downsized my mother. The guys talked about sports; the girls gossiped; everyone parroted jokes they'd heard on TV. I'd clawed my way through college to discover that the world was a high school.

Still, after my cooking and construction gigs, a cushy office job was a miracle. They paid you to sit around hungover all day! For the first time in my life, I had more money than I knew what to do with. We drank gloriously: Fat Tire, Blue Moon, Guinness, Mississippi Mud, gallons of Jameson, oceans of shitty red wine. Our landlord refused to turn on the heat, so as the temperature dropped, we found ourselves dressing up for sleep: coat, two pairs of socks, winter hat. I still didn't buy a bed.

My life felt hunched around the space where Riley had been. My second year at Simon's Rock, I got a palmar wart on the callus just below my index finger on my right palm. I picked at it. It grew. I picked at it. It grew. Finally, one night, I got a good hold on it with a pair of needle-nose pliers, took a deep breath, and ripped it out. A jagged sear of pain flashed through my hand and was gone. I looked down. Clamped in the pliers was what looked like a well-chewed piece of cinnamon gum. I glanced fearfully at my hand. There was a ragged hole in my palm, big enough that I could have stuck my pinkie finger in it. I stared at it, unable to look away. Nothing happened. Nothing happened. Then, in an instant, the hole filled with blood, then overflowed. That was my October in Denver: the gaping hole, the horrifying absence, the moment before the blood comes.

Stumbling drunkenly out of the shower one morning, at an utter loss as to how I would make it through work in my condition, I came upon Conor, just home from his bartending shift, cutting lines of blow on the cover of the record player. Who, in good conscience, could turn that down? It would get me through the day anyway. The coke energized me enough to brave the chill and walk to work.

The first half of my shift was fine. God, I was helpful; I had never been so incredibly helpful in my life. Oh, no no no, thank *you!*

Lunch was a pratfall. I walked to the Subway where I ate each day. The counterperson made my sandwich without comment: a foot long roast beef on whole wheat with everything, extra banana peppers, extra jalapenos. I was coming down, a rougher reentry than I'd anticipated. My stomach twisted ominously.

Outside, the cold air in my face calmed my nausea. Just take a bite, choke a bite down, begin the grim process of forcing your body to run on food again. I opened the bag and the smell hit me before I could even get a piece of the sandwich out.

Some people fall to their knees before they vomit. This is poor technique. It's easier to start out in a low crouch, like the position recommended for a plane crash. This angle maximizes the amount of product for your effort. Plus it's easy to sink to your knees afterward if you're feeling melodramatic. I held my tie over my shoulder like a pro as I bent over and wretched on the corner, just bile and water.

People crossed the street to avoid me. I wiped my mouth with the Subway napkins, looked around to make sure no one from work had seen me, then walked a block and sat down, leaving my mess for someone else to deal with. I learned it from watching you, Dad.

Around the corner, a skinny old dude was playing harmonica and singing about "my baby left me." Riley was everywhere now that she was gone. I began to cry.

The guy cut off in the middle of his song, got up, and sat next to me. I tried to stop crying, but I couldn't. He patted me on the back.

"There, there, little brother. It'll pass, it'll pass."

When I was cried out, I stood up and handed my sandwich off to the homeless guy. I knew I should empty my pockets for him, but I also knew I would need to drink later. Then I walked back to work. It just wouldn't do to come back late from my lunch break.

—

When the landlord on Gaylord Street finally became too openly hostile for us to continue living there, we gave notice and agreed to band together to find another place to live. Then no one did anything. Mere days from our impending homelessness, a huge, unseasonal blizzard shut down the city so none of us could get to work. I worked the phone all day, schlepped around in the thigh-deep snow for hours, then spun an intricate web of lies: Conor was my current landlord; Judah's girlfriend was my boss; his friend Mateo's girlfriend, whom I had only met once, was a family friend of ten years, my character reference. By the end of the day, I had snatched our fat from the fire by finding a house bigger, nicer, and cheaper than our current atrocity. I was toasted articulately and then inarticulately by my roommates . . . and still I got stuck with the worst room, a lightless unheated concrete box in the basement, the Well of Misery. Fortunately, Mateo's girlfriend kicked him out, and he took the other basement room. It's nice to have company, even in hell.

Our request for our Gaylord Street security deposit elicited a vitriolic eight-page diatribe from our old landlord, threatening legal action if he ever heard from us again. We performed dramatic readings of it in the living room of our new house, quasi-musicals even, leaping off the furniture, cracking ourselves up. We swore drunkenly to preserve the letter forever. I lost it almost immediately.

I had been driving down to Boulder each week for my final class, a geography lecture, in the battered 1986 Nissan my mother had left for me. After a particularly rough night, I threw up blood on the university quad to the horror of some passing coeds. Fuck it; my father had bailed on paying tuition for my last semester, so at least it was my own money I was wasting. I was so weak on the drive home that several times I drifted dangerously close to the median before jerking the wheel. The next day, I canceled the insurance on my mother's car and parked it in our garage. A banal car accident was not the death I wanted. I began taking the bus to Boulder for class. I slept through the Denver stop on the ride home once and was halfway back to Boulder when I woke up.

Winter came and, with it, darkness. I threw up constantly and lost weight. My eyes yellowed. Each night, the edge was clearly visible. One warm beer in the cardboard twelve-pack felt italicized: if I drink this beer, I will feel like death tomorrow. One swallow in the gallon jug of Carlo Rossi separated itself like a clot of oil: if I drink this swallow, I will throw up tomorrow. A shot of liquor in the bottom of a chipped glass glowed like it was radioactive: if I take this shot, I will puke tonight. I drank them all.

<hr>

I graduated summa cum laude from the University of Colorado that December. I didn't bother picking up my diploma; I had to work. We celebrated with a keg, some coke, and a gift from Paul's son Jesse, an oversmart stoner.

"You're twenty years old. You just graduated college. I figure we're at the moment of grace in your cerebral development where your brain has the optimal ratio of raw computing power to useful intellectual content. Perfect time for the brain-destroying power of protoxide of nitrogen," he said, then handed me two boxes of cartridges of nitrous oxide and a handful of balloons.

The next morning, empty nitrous containers littered the house like shell casings. We labored to kill the keg while listening to the Oblivians and Hank Williams. Everyone in the house had gotten lucky except for the man of the hour, unconscious before midnight. But then I had been a reliable disaster with the ladies for a while. Apparently women weren't attracted to morbid, weepy drunks? They were worse than fair-weather friends; women were just . . . *emotional gold-diggers*, the whole lot of them, I bitched to Sam. He shook his head, then put his face in his hands.

I wound up having three days off due to a scheduling change. No school, no work, money in the bank . . . I went on a bender, Absolut and Jameson and Cutty Sark and Bailey's, vomiting repeatedly, barely eating for three days.

I awoke, gasping, in my bed. The frigid oblong of my room felt submerged, claustrophobic, and futile: a fish tank at the bottom of the ocean. What time was it? There was one small window in my room, four tiny panes tucked down a little well at the base of the foundation. Blocking that window—shutting out even the weak, timid pulse of sunlight that snuck in for a couple of hours each day—would make the darkness of my room complete. I kept meaning to tinfoil the glass and write on the foil in black permanent marker, one syllable on each pane, "FUCK | ING | HOPE | LESS." But even getting a Sharpie and tinfoil together took more effort than I could supply.

The window was dark. Night. I listened carefully. There was no sound. Everyone was asleep.

When I made it to Colorado, I had devised The All-Encompassing Plan:

1. Graduate from College and Make Mama Proud. Do her justice so that, at least in that regard, all her sacrifices haven't been for nothing. I had completed this phase, no small feat considering the cubic footage of alcohol I'd consumed my final semester. Hold your applause, please, hold your applause.

2. Do Something Incredible. This would be slightly more difficult. I had no idea what The Incredible Thing would be. Right now, getting some food down would be incredible, particularly if it stayed there. But The Incredible Thing had to be bigger, of course: something dramatic, explosive, brilliant. I had ruled out acts of violence and terrorism, major and minor—that was maybe the only thing I had learned at Simon's Rock. Self-immolation was still on the table.

3. Become Successful. This most likely involved monetizing The Incredible Thing. Shit, I guess this step ruled out self-immolation, which was unfortunate. I knew of only three ways to get a large amount of money. One was armed robbery, but I couldn't bring myself to do guns. Another was craftiness: cracking safes, counting cards, hacking computers, financial wizardry. With my shaking hands, physical dexterity of a three-legged camel with vertigo going downstairs on a pogo stick and roller skates, and track record of never having gotten away with anything ever? Nope. Lastly, big money could be generated by being outrageously lucky. Let's not even kid about that one.

4. Get Revenge. I'd heard about the process of "making amends," a part of the Twelve Steps wherein some sorrow-soaked sober souse would write sniveling apologies to everyone he had ever wronged in his life: mother, father, sisters, brothers, friends, bartenders, doormen, motel maintenance staff, every single woman who had ever had the misfortune of having any part of his body inside any part of her body, and so forth. The fourth and final phase of my great plan was an inversion of this process. I would come for everyone who had ever laughed at us: the kids who had mocked Tashina for her hearing aids or her glasses, the men who walked over her feelings and took her for granted; the flirtier, more confident girlfriends who had used or betrayed Tatyana, preying on her selflessness; every sneering neighbor, every haughty landowner who had ever condescended to my mother because she was working in the supermarket or cleaning his house. I would come for every bully, any bully, every man who had raped or traumatized or abused any of the numerous women I'd known who now lived in pain and fear; the torturers, anyone who had ever taken pleasure in creating pain in another. I would come for every single rich person in the world; every happy, unworried person in every coffee shop; everyone who had had it easy where we had had it hard. I would come for everyone, everywhere. It would take some planning. A pad of legal paper and one of those mechanical pencils would be a good first step. You know, make a list.

What day is it? Do I work tomorrow? I think I work tomorrow. Am I going to be sick if I sit up? I tried to feel down into my tummy without moving. Wow, I was wearing a T-shirt and socks and nothing else. My stomach felt hard and tight. Not good, but I wouldn't be sick, at least not now. Nothing to throw up.

I sat up slowly and reached for the phone. My head felt like someone had broken a bottle inside it. I dialed time and temperature: "At the tone, the time will be 1:39 a.m., December 15, 1997."

I had slept through the fifth anniversary of the shooting.

A couple of friends would have called, possibly my dad, probably Tatyana, definitely my mom. I checked voice mail.

Nothing. Nothing from my friends. Nothing from my family. Nothing, nothing, nothing.

During the day, I was generally okay. There were people around, and there were limits to how far off the rails you could go in the daylight. Sad, but okay. But at night, and especially alone at night . . .

I had described it to Judah as the Snuffleupagus of Despair. The Snuffleupagus of Despair was like Big Bird's friend who only visited when there was no one else around, except totally different: terrible, horrible, terrifying, horrifying, isolation made flesh, hot breath that stank of cat urine, long shaggy hair that smelled like a dead wet dog washed up on the beach. To gaze upon the Snuffleupagus of Despair was to lose your mind; to touch it was to fold up inside yourself, asphyxiate in the cold molasses of your own loneliness, and disappear completely. Judah had laughed—we had both laughed there in the kitchen—but even then, laughing together in the sunlight, he understood, and it put fear into his eyes.

I had hidden some bottles around the house, you know, just in case. The pint in my sock drawer was gone. The pint in my desk drawer was gone. I pulled on some boxers and went upstairs and out into the screened-in porch, shivering violently. There, under one of the couch cushions was a pint of Captain Morgan. It was freezing cold. I took a huge, chilly pull off it even before I walked back inside. It tasted like Christmas and pancake syrup and poison.

I went back into my room and wrapped myself up in my blankets, sitting up. I drank. When my dad bailed on us, my mother, my sisters, and I swore that we would stay a family, fuck him. After the shooting at Simon's Rock, my friends and I had sworn that, drunk or sober, high times or hard times, we would always stick together.

I hadn't spoken to anyone from Simon's Rock in how long? Six months? A year? I couldn't remember. I dodged my mother's phone calls—kindness now would only make me crumple. Tatyana and I had barely spoken since the divorce. I never called Tashina, too ashamed of how I'd let her down. We had gone head-to-head with darkness and lost.

I took a knife out of a little cardboard box of crap that sat next to my single futon. I had been cutting myself since I was a child, small, secret slashes on the inside of my arm with razor blades pilfered from my dad's wood shop. At sixteen, in a fit of loneliness after a fight with my father, I had carved my torso up with a serrated steak knife. A year later, I put a gash in my leg that should have gotten stitches.

I pulled off my shirt. I unfolded the largest blade and drew it down my left breast as hard as I could, then, before I could stop myself, down my right breast. I gasped with the shock of it, then threw the knife away from me. What was next, my face? My wrists?

The wounds yawned open, the flesh obscenely pink and white underneath, but no blood. Shit, I hadn't meant to do that much. Then the blood came, pouring down my chest, gushing through my fingers and into my bed. I grabbed the bottle and drew from it until I ran out of air.

When my alarm went off in the morning, I was stuck to my sheets. I gingerly worked myself free. The twist of tangled, bloody blankets looked like a murdered hooker. I put on a black T-shirt and made my way up to the shower. When I came downstairs, I packed the gaping wounds with Neosporin and did my best to duct tape them shut. Then I got dressed. I had to go to work.

The winter deepened. Mateo and I continued to atrophy in the Well of Misery, though I had the sense to remove every sharp object from my room. A girl in Mateo's drunk-driving class had totaled her car, decapitating her best friend in the front seat. Only a thin sheet of fake wood paneling separated our rooms, so when they got drunk after class and got it on, I could hear every nuance in minute, biological detail. After a few months of listening to them, I felt like I knew Mateo's sperm count.

I had to endure the sounds of them together, but Mateo had to endure the sounds of me alone. When I started crying one night, he knocked gently on the door, then came in with a jar of wine and sat and talked to me for a while. Another night, he knocked gently on the door, came in and put a jar of wine next to my bed, then left.

Another night, he knocked on the door and asked me if I was okay. I said that I was. He said, "Alright. Then shut up," and walked out, pulling the door shut behind him.

Damon, a gay friend of Judah's girlfriend and our token "normal" roommate, was a grown-up with a real, professional job, but he spent every free hour cruising for ass at Cheesman Park. A steady stream of random dudes wandered through the house, back and forth from his room. It was maddening—sex all around me and just out of reach.

Judah was again unemployed, owed us all money, and only survived by sponging off his mom and his girlfriend. I encountered him in the kitchen several times while I was getting ready for work, wobbling around in his boxers, still up and drinking from the night before though it was eleven in the morning. Slurring his speech, incomprehensible, his sunken chest so white it was almost green. Judah got into a scrap with Sam one night. It's good I had already blacked out, or I might have taken a swing at each of them.

My sadness ebbed, replaced by fearlessness and anger. I accompanied Damon to cavernous gay clubs to take advantage of the hour of free drinks, railed meth off the back of a toilet in the women's room, then made out with dudes for more free drinks. Was I gay? I theorized aloud to Damon how much that would simply my life. He raised one eyebrow, then roughly set me straight: "Yeah, Thanksgiving with my family is a fucking blast. As was high school. You stupid redneck faggot *tourist*."

Too drunk to walk to the bar one night, I drove. When I returned home later, someone had taken my parking spot, so I rammed his car, then parked down the street. The police woke me up early the next morning. I was high on nutmeg when my court date rolled around but still managed to plead my penalty down to just a fine.

When I was escorted out of the building at my customer service job by security, I dumped my cardboard box of stuff in the trash— purloined Post-it notes, pens, a stapler—and hit the closest liquor store for some vodka. I woke up several days later with knifing chest pains, feeling not hungover but mortally wounded by alcohol.

I was plagued by a persistent hallucination, more vivid than any I'd had on mushrooms or acid, more disturbing than coming down from meth. When I closed my eyes, I saw a lush, marine garden, pulsing magically in an underwater cavern: swathes of fluorescent anemones glowing like multicolored lava; phosphorescent seahorses that seemed to be made solely of blown glass and light; fish friendly as dogs, bright as parrots, nimble as serpents; enormous alabaster and ebony octopi with not eight but thousands of elegant arms cascading off them, waving, beckoning.

The moment my eyes closed, water rushed against my face. I was sucked into the mouth of the cave and drawn deeper, deeper. When I opened my eyes to keep from drowning, there was an unpleasant shock of returning to my body. The hallucination was too compelling, too inviting, far realer than my flat life of grays and browns.

As my heart stuttered and skidded painfully in my chest, my skin prickled, and my body filled with fear. If I yielded to the beauty of that underwater garden, if I allowed myself to be lured all the way into the cave, my lungs would fill with saltwater, and I would die.

It was tempting. My wounded heart would finally be allowed to rest. The nausea, the headache that never went away, the constant throb from my back injury at Sonic Burger, the phantom pains, the panic attacks . . . It would all be over. Every day, I said it: *I wish I was dead. I should just die. I hope I die in my sleep.* Here was my chance. All I had to do was surrender.

It scared the fucking shit out of me. I didn't drink for an entire week. When I started back up, it was just wine, a bottle or two a night. No more liquor, certainly no meth, no more lost weekends. I fought to keep Riley out of my head.

Things improved marginally as the weather warmed. I took a job as a door-to-door salesman for a sketchy construction company.

I found a couple of girlfriends I alternated between, a girl from the human resources department at my old job and a black stripper. The dismayed looks she got from her family were almost as enjoyable as the dismayed looks I got from my friends. My girls had three kids between the two of them, children they were careful I never met.

I wrote a letter to my father. Our relationship had been solely financial for some time. We rarely spoke, and I hadn't seen him since I was eighteen. He had bailed on the tuition for my final semester, and a two-year-old chiropractic bill I'd sent him four times still hadn't been paid: $51. I informed him that, with him welshing on his most basic commitments, our relationship was over. I would see him at his funeral. I got no response.

I felt different than I had when I'd landed in Denver in the fall, as if something broken inside me had finally knit together and calcified, if at an unnatural angle. I did push-ups every morning and curls every night, drinking alone in my room. I still threw up sometimes, but it was all business, shoving my toothbrush down my throat in the bathroom or puking out the open car door in a Safeway parking lot before a sales call. And then I wiped my mouth, and I closed the fucking deal.

CHAPTER 5

The Graveyard of Dreams

I moved to New York City in October 1998 with $300. If I hadn't exactly triumphed in Denver, I had survived there long enough to know it was time to get the hell out. New York City had towered in my mind, a noir Shangri-la, slashes of black ink bleeding out of white paper on a page of *RAW* magazine. It was a city built of all the darkness I loved, Burroughs and R. Crumb and Cop Shoot Cop, cockroaches and prostitution and squalor. "I want to be filthy and anonymous," East Village poet John Giorno had written. You could not do that in San Luis Obispo. You could only do that in New York. When I dreamed of New York, I pinioned wildly between arrogance and insecurity. I would thrive in the City, I would blossom, I would shine. Or I would flame out and disappear, bleed out in a gutter with some eloquent execration dying in my throat.

Paul's son Jesse lived in a musty one-room apartment in a glorified dormitory near Columbia on the Upper West Side. He carved out enough floor space for my dingy single futon, pushed his shirts to one side of the closet, and I moved in.

I had never paid more than $200 in rent. In Denver, we'd had a front yard, a backyard, a garage, a screened-in porch, two fridges, two bathrooms, and an extra room in the basement we did nothing with. In Manhattan, I paid $300 to share one room with Jesse. No living room, no privacy, communal bathrooms, and a kitchen that stank of fish oil and kimchee.

New York City was glamorous on TV: lights and celebrities and coke and sex in limousines. My New York was broken, dirty, expensive, desperate. The grit in the subway tunnels—it wasn't stylish cross-hatching like in a Frank Miller comic; it was greasy, organic filth, crystallized human urine, rat hair, flakes of dead skin, sebum.

I knew no one and nothing, so I puppy-dogged my old Simon's Rock cronies James and Zack around the East Village and Brooklyn: Rubulad, Life, Spa, Motor City, Mars Bar. I couldn't afford to buy drinks, so I got loaded before leaving the house, then snuck a plastic flask into bars with me. When I had exhausted the flask, I sponged off Jesse, James, Zack, and any other friend within complaining distance until I had exhausted them all. Finally, I downed any unattended half-empty glass I encountered, more than once winding up with a mouthful of cigarette butts for my troubles.

I hinted, I joked, and finally I begged James to let me join his band, COME ON, named after Chuck Berry's first single. I got nowhere. With growing desperation, I loaned the band my amp, a 1960s Fender Super Reverb, and then my guitar, a 1967 Fender Mustang, in attempts to convince my oldest friend of my indispensability as a band member. James remained unswayed.

I had assumed that my college degree would qualify me for some kind of low-level reporting job at a newspaper, but I had no idea how such a job was procured. I was too crippled by insecurity to apply to a single newspaper. Editorial assistant at *Beverage World Magazine*? I couldn't even fake my way through a cover letter. I wasn't qualified for a job; I wasn't qualified to be alive.

I had to do *something*, even if it was just a postponement of the inevitable—winding up in a rehab and then living the rest of my life on my knees. School had held the real world at bay before. Writing papers was less taxing than flipping pancakes, less demoralizing than answering phones. I asked Jesse what the best writing school in the country was, and he pointed to Columbia, just up the block. If Columbia wouldn't take me, I decided, I'd concede defeat and check in to rehab.

I picked up an application for the writing master's and threw myself into it with abandon. When I wasn't too drunk or hungover to think, I was writing and unwriting and rewriting until the application grew huge in my mind. I scrounged the $75 application fee by doing odd jobs for Jesse's mom in Westchester. Days before I was to send it in, I got a ticket for drinking a forty-ounce on the subway with an accompanying fine of exactly $75. Fuck it, then—I borrowed the money from my girlfriend Shannon's parents. Shortly before midnight on the day of the deadline, I printed the application up, stuffed it in an envelope, ran down to the corner, and dumped it into the mailbox. When the inevitable form-letter rejection came, I'd surrender myself to some grim, state-run facility for a thorough brainwashing.

Finally, James came around. One night at Brownies on Avenue A, he sat me down, bought me a lukewarm Rolling Rock, and asked me to join COME ON. I couldn't even manage to play coy. James had been my best friend since I was fifteen and had often been my only friend, my sole defender. He was simply *more* than me in every way—more confident, older, sharper, more worldly, more talented, ten times the musician I was. It was the ultimate compliment for him to deign to include me in his band. Here was my opportunity to repay him for staying my friend when I had alienated everyone else. I swore to devote myself wholeheartedly to his project, to be as loyal as a dog. Sitting there in our booth at Brownies, I was sure we were on the edge of something enormous.

COME ON didn't just remedy my failures, it inverted them. To be young, naive, hungover, and lonely in New York City is a rotten thing. To be young, naive, hungover, lonely, and playing bass in a rock band in New York City is magnificent. We practiced three or four nights a week at a crappy rehearsal space in South

Williamsburg, five or six hours each night or until we were too drunk to play. Our tour bus would be covered in beaver fur with wheels made of solid cocaine. Our elite security team (to fend off the throngs of screaming fans) would be composed exclusively of pregnant nuns. Our home would be an abandoned Brooklyn firehouse with a polished brass pole that terminated in a hot tub in the basement, with a Taco Bell instead of a kitchen. As I couldn't succeed, James couldn't fail. Together, we were breaking new ground; we were beating a dead horse back to life; we were juvenile gods just beginning to mature into our powers. Someone would notice—how could they not notice? Something would happen. Nothing happened.

I got a call while working at my temp job at Bergdorf Goodman one spring day. I hadn't just been accepted to Columbia. They had awarded me the school's largest scholarship, the Dean's Fellowship. My heart pounding, I got off the call as quickly as I could so I wouldn't get into trouble at work. Even with the scholarship, tuition was still a shitload of money, money I didn't have. I had almost $400 in the bank, the largest bankroll I'd had during my time in the city. My mom made minimum wage, less than I did. Though I never saw a penny from him, my father's income was substantial enough to disqualify me for any kind of economic scholarship. I would probably qualify for student loans . . . but then I would come out of grad school in an even deeper hole than I was currently in. Even before I called my mom, I called James.

"Good job."

He sounded like he was congratulating me for finding a dollar on the sidewalk.

"Do you think you're going to go? I mean, how would you pay for it?"

That made it easy—I didn't even have to ask him what he thought I should do. Zack was less prickly but openly startled. James was the musician, Zack was the writer, I was the drunken brute. This Dean's Fellowship bullshit fucked with the hierarchy of our universe. Of the three of us, I was the most unnerved by it.

When I called my mom, she crowed her delight into the receiver. I had to go, she said, and don't even think about the money; opportunities like this come once in a lifetime. I gnawed at myself about it for days. I had to go. I couldn't go. But there is no more devoted gambler than a man who has been serially unlucky. Finally, I called Columbia back. Yes, I was in.

I lasted at Bergdorf's till May, when a dude who looked like poor, murdered Phil Hartman put his head under the bathroom stall door and offered to suck me off. I boldly returned to the scene of the crime the next day, only to encounter a monstrous rope of semen spanning the eighteen inches from the toilet seat to the polished and gleaming marble floor below. Manhattan's crown jewel of retail was more depraved than any truck stop. Despite my boss's protestations that "You have a future here!" I quit the next day and quickly found a marginally less demeaning customer service gig. Progress!

―

COME ON took every gig we were offered, playing out at least two or three times a month. James's father found us a manager. He did nothing. James's father bankrolled an EP we recorded in Nashville. It did nothing. James's father paid an entertainment lawyer thousands of dollars to walk our demo into the offices of A&R reps. That did nothing.

COME ON went "on tour"—two shows in Massachusetts. We loaded up our girlfriends' cars with our beat-up gear, CDs, T-shirts, and stickers. (We were out to make fans, not money, but it would be inconsiderate to leave our new fans' craving for merch unfulfilled.) Each night, we found our excitement matched with equal or greater ambivalence. We sold one T-shirt. I shared a bottle of whiskey and a foldout couch with the guitar player and woke up soaked in his urine.

Sourly hungover after our Boston show, I convinced Shannon to drive us an hour up to New Hampshire so we could see my old house. As we headed north on I-93, I felt my dread tick slowly up and up and up.

I directed Shannon off the main highway, taking the back way so we could see a little bit of my old gulag. We drove past a small church with a cheap marquis with moveable plastic letters like you see in front of roadhouses but with a more pointed message: THE WAGES OF SIN IS DEATH. REPENT BEFORE PAYDAY.

The roads got smaller and smaller until we were following a barely paved path hardly wide enough for two cars around the shoreline of Powwow Pond. Homemade plastic docks ringed with seaweed floated off the shore like bloated bodies. A woodstove smoldered alone in the middle of a dirt yard in the rain as if its surrounding house had been mysteriously whisked away. Each property line was clearly demarcated, like the tiny lots held national treasures instead of sinking bungalows and rusting trailers: KEEP OUT. NO TRESPASSING. PRIVATE PROPERTY. As we wound our way deeper into the lakeside hamlet, past towering woodpiles and rusting pickups and campers parked among knots of grass, I had the sensation of going underground, into the canted, winding burrows of a rabbit warren. What was my plan? I had no idea.

When we pulled onto 107A, the highway that ran past our old home, I felt like I was going to vomit. Too late to turn back now. Shannon drove slowly toward the bridge by the rope swing. I felt a little chill, but I didn't mention the bridge's significance. What would I say? "I intended to kill myself here once. But I decided suicide would be a mistake. I have since wondered if deciding suicide was a mistake was actually the mistake." No. We rolled over the bridge and on toward my old house.

Nothing had changed in ten years. No new construction, no new signs, no new grass off the shoulder. No one had even painted their houses.

Our house had been rundown, always too cold or too hot. The basement leaked and stank of mildew and cat piss. But right out our back door, there were miles and miles of woods. John Bakie, the old farmer who lived across the way from us, had sworn to me that he'd never sell the land behind our place as long as he lived. I had fled into the woods nearly every single day. One day I taught my black Lab, Katie, how to eat blackberries off the bushes. She got the low ones, and I got the high ones. We must have stayed out there for hours.

When we rounded the last corner before my old house, I saw that all the woods had been clear-cut and the soil tilled. Nothing grew there at all. Only one tall, lonely tree had been left standing behind our house. It made the barren landscape look more ruined than if there had been no trees at all.

"This is it," I said. "Pull over. Here."

Shannon pulled the car over so abruptly it skidded in the dirt. She gave me a scared look.

"Wait here. I'll be right back," I said and hopped out.

I walked out into the dirt where the woods used to be, toward the lone tree. There was nothing else to walk to. A board was still tacked to its base. Jesus, I remembered this tree. I had made a half-assed attempt to build a tree fort off it. That someone had chosen to spare this specific tree . . . it made me so fucking angry. Was someone taunting me?

Our old house was the only one on the road that had been painted. Not just painted but transformed, from its gloomy, coffee-grounds brown to a sunny daffodil yellow, a perfect contrast to how it made me feel.

I leaned on the tree and stared at the house, my eyes burning. They say you can't go home again, and that's not true. You can, but you will find strangers living there, and they will have changed everything you loved, everything that made the place home to you.

It's not unusual for a young man to revisit his childhood home and want to buy it back from the new owner. I had no such desire. We had hated it here, but that hadn't lessened the humiliation of being exiled. I had no desire to return in triumph, to parade through the streets. I wanted to carpet bomb the entire town. No, too quick. I would finance a meth lab or two and watch the place rot slowly from the inside out. Corpses riddled with sores, soil sown with arsenic, dead livestock poisoning the wells . . . I wanted this backwater as ravaged and ruined in the physical world as it was in my heart.

The bankers had tricked us. They had told my mother she had to miss a payment before she'd be considered for refinancing, and then they had foreclosed. Which person had made the decision to throw us out of our home? I imagined a small, detail-obsessed man, his life constricted around money, dedicated to stockpiling it as a useless barricade against loneliness. A man whose sole responsibility was to push glaciers of money around with a keystroke or a ballpoint pen. A man with no thought for whom the movement of these glaciers might isolate or starve or trap or mangle or kill. Had he used the money he made from ruining our lives to buy a hot tub? A motorcycle? Were we ejected by something as trivial as a line through a field in a spreadsheet, a checkmark in a tiny box, a zero instead of a one, a clerical error, a typo?

The paperwork must still exist, filed away in a damp basement somewhere, gnawed by mice, peppered with their droppings. Kingston was a small town. The man probably still lived in the area. I could find his address, track him down. I would illustrate for him how a life could be ruined with a ballpoint pen, a death of a thousand punctures. I would kill him the way he'd killed me, so that he felt the dying in tiny increments. Let the pain mount so he genuinely feared his death until that perfect moment when he was so overwhelmed that he finally prayed for that which he feared most just to be released from pain.

I was shaking. I forced myself to take a breath. Was this all that was available to me, my response in any situation—rage? We had been happy here, sometimes. Between icy feuds, Tatyana and I had played epic games of badminton as the sun went down, giggling and tumbling into the soft grass until it was so dark we couldn't see. We'd gone sledding down the steep hill behind the garage, all three of us in a pile on a flimsy plastic saucer, Tashina screaming from the minute we pushed off until the very moment we hit the jump at the bottom, our three bodies separating for a brief, terrifying moment before hammering down on each other and the hard snow. It hurt—it always hurt—but we did it again and again. Nothing felt better than your own blood touching you, even violently. How long had it been since I'd spoken to either of my sisters? A year? Years?

Before he ran away, Chuong and I had spent hours and hours in the Kingston House of Pizza in town. It came back to me, blissfully unchanged, the warm air smelling of rising dough and melting cheese. Chuong and I must have pumped hundreds of dollars' worth of quarters into the Tetris arcade game. The song played in my head, and I could see Chuong dancing, imitating the little Russian dancer on the screen. Sweet, funny, crazy Chuong, the older brother I'd always wished for, ten years gone. I'd made halfhearted attempts to locate him several times over the years but finally had to strangle that hope. Chuong had been lost forever. He was in prison; he had been deported; he was dead. He had come into this world with so much working against him. Not everybody makes it.

Behind the old house was a crooked apple tree. At its base, my mother had dug a hole and buried our old dog Princess. As a boy, I found dogs as magical as some girls find horses. I had a poster of all the major breeds; I could name their characteristics and identify them by sight. In Canada, I had whined and pled with my mother for a dog till finally she agreed to take me to the animal shelter—not to get a dog, just to play with the dogs there. As soon as we pulled up, I began wheedling anew for one of the puppies barking at our car through the chain-link fence.

"We already have the cats. Your dad said we can't get a dog," she said. "But if we do, we're getting that one." She pointed at a narrow dog the size and color of a small deer with huge, emotive amber eyes: Princess. My father was not amused when we brought her home that day.

God, we had adored her. I thought about Princess's body—her tufted fur that made her hind legs look like the legs of a faun, the line of longer, thicker hair that ran down her spine, the fine, soft fur on her head that we delighted in standing up in a Mohawk, whiskers like an overgrown mouse's, her sleek, glossy, dainty ears, her crooked stub of tail, most of it hacked off with an axe or a knife by her previous owner, her thoughtful, pained amber eyes . . . Now just a pile of years-old bones rotting in someone else's backyard. Her head had been so refined, her forehead sloping gently into her long graceful nose, like the head of some small aquatic horse.

It was too unfair that a stranger had custody of her remains. But what would I do if I had access to the property and no one else was around, dig her up? I followed that morbid, impossible thought. They could line her skull up against those of twenty other dogs, and I would be able to pick her out, even now, because she was one of a kind, and I had loved her that hard. She was so close. It was all so close. And still irretrievably lost.

I had wanted nothing more than to leave this place forever, but somehow being exiled had trapped part of me here forever. I stumbled through the wet, useless dirt back to the car, its headlights just a bright smear through my tears.

⸻

In the fall, I started at Columbia. My teachers were brilliant, not just insightful but so full of books that they spoke almost exclusively in quotes. My classmates were roundly disappointing. I had hoped to stumble upon another Simon's Rock, a school of brilliant lunatics with oversized lives. The Columbia kids were uniformly white, wealthy, and restrained, their dreams as safe as milk—landing a professorship or maybe moving to Connecticut to grow tomatoes, raise children, and write. I had loved writers invested in life, Harry Crews and Flannery O'Connor and Jack Henry Abbott, not language theorists like Thomas Pynchon and William Gaddis. They had read more than I had, and maybe they were smarter, but God, they were as dull as dirt.

Shannon left me in a rage. She was angry enough when she moved out that she paid a couple of my classmates to move the furniture she was abandoning out to the street so I couldn't use it. A wino helped me move it back in. When I offered him a handful of change, he said, "Nah, that's all right, big man. You looked like you could use the help."

I went to class. I went to practice. I wrote. I blacked out after shows, waking up on the couch at James and Zack's apartment, waking up in the practice space, waking up on my floor just inches from my mattress. I did sound engineering for NPR at the Radio Foundation, producing sessions with Ed Bradley, Kofi Annan, Stephen Sondheim, Anthony Bourdain, and Judy Blume. I got mistaken for homeless while barely conscious on the sidewalk outside Motor City bar. I did catering gigs; I worked security; I did marketing focus groups; I got paid to take a series of MRIs. I attended every department mixer and collegiate function in order to get blitzed on shitty wine and fill my pockets with hardening cheese cubes and softening grapes.

I interned reading the slush pile at the *New Yorker*. I got hustled for gay porn. I built myself a tent in the living room and rented out the bedroom to bring my rent down to $200 a month and still had to borrow $1,000 from James's parents in order to stay solvent (a loan they were too kind to let me repay). I chewed ice cubes to curb my hunger, and I recall wondering if I could eat my own hair. At semester's end, I retrieved dry goods that departing undergrads had thrown in the trash.

With great shame, I accepted money from my mother, who had gotten a job working at one of the resorts on St. John. She was happy to give it, she said. Great things were just around the corner for me, she knew it.

Mom was right. Almost weekly, I got tantalizing encouragement. An editor at *Harper's* magazine said my short story was promising despite its flaws. An editor at the *New Yorker* said another story contained "masterful lines," but it went without saying that they wouldn't publish it. And Mom was wrong. My drinking brought on bizarre afflictions; heat rash, a mouth full of boils, lips so swollen I couldn't leave the house, aching and blotchy hands and feet. I smashed a whiskey bottle with my right hand, and when I woke up, my apartment looked like a scene out of a slasher movie. It cost my school insurance $5,000 to get my hand stitched back together by a plastic surgeon. Everywhere I went—trying hard not to ralph in the Condé Nast building, reading Virginia Woolf on the way to band practice, locking myself in the bathroom with the DTs before my literature seminar with Pulitzer Prize–winning MacArthur Fellow Richard Howard—I felt crushed between my good self and my bad self, as they collided and strained against each other.

＝

At my summer job licking envelopes for mailers for a DVD production house, I developed a crush on the receptionist, Allison. I talked to her whenever I could screw up the courage. We had nothing in common. She had perfect posture, perfect carriage, perfect hair. As she walked to the photocopier with unassuming grace, she smelled of shampoo and hope. I slumped, I slouched, I shuffled, I stank. She had gotten her master's in opera and was a gifted pianist, singer, and songwriter. I could barely play guitar, and my voice was an amusical groan, a bull walrus in mourning. Her father was an English professor; her mother was a mom; her parents still lived together in the house where she had grown up; her best friend was the girl next door. I didn't just want Allison, I wanted her entire life.

The vibe during band practice that summer oscillated between resignation and desperation as we failed to make any headway. I had begun to chafe under James's leadership. As my ideas for the band were rejected with increasing frequency, I invested more in the songs I was writing on my own. I four-tracked an EP of boozy rants in my room, *Thanks for Letting Me Crash*, and used student loan money to press a thousand CDs. I was still grimly obsessed with Riley, and I fantasized about taking a bus to DC and leaving CDs everywhere in hopes that one would find her and she would hear the songs I'd written for her. Would she take me back? Would she reach out to me so I could spurn her? I didn't know. The fantasy ended with her hearing the songs and knowing how deeply she had hurt me.

I booked a CD release party at a tiny bar in Brooklyn in January and ran copies of the CD to the *Village Voice* and *New York Press* with no hope of them writing about or even listening to it. The show was a mess. The band I'd put together was drunk and ill rehearsed, and we were plagued with sound problems, but I sang every song to Allison, standing quietly in the back. After we had broken our gear down, she came and found me.

"I have to go, but I just wanted to say that I really enjoyed your show."

"You're leaving? You can't leave."

People were packed in tightly at the tables around us, and they immediately started rooting for me.

"Stay! He wants you to stay!"

"I want to stay, but I have to go all the way back up to the Upper West Side, and I have to get up early tomorrow to go to Rochester."

"He likes you! You know he likes you!"

"Just stay for one more drink. C'mon, I'll buy you a drink."

"A free drink! That's true love!"

"I can't, I've already stayed too late. I'm sorry."

Fuck it, then. I grabbed her and dipped her back and kissed her hard. The bar roared.

After Allison left, a reporter showed up from the *New York Press*. She had heard my CD, really wanted to write about it, and was heartbroken that she had missed the show. I went home with her, but I was too drunk to get it up. In the morning, I couldn't come. The reporter apologized as she was showing me out—she couldn't write about the CD now as it would compromise her journalistic integrity—but she wanted me to know that she really had loved it. Yes, I had potential—potential to ruin anything.

Allison and I started hanging out, then sleeping together, then dating. Sex with her, even filthy sex, felt fresh and clean, health giving, like eating a nectarine. There was no obstacle between her and her pleasure, nothing blocking her tenderness for me. The term "making love" angered me because it was such a deceitful euphemism for the seedy, manipulative grinding I'd experienced. But with Allison, that genteel phrase almost made sense. When we finished, I felt only gratitude and a strange good feeling radiating outward: happiness? I couldn't get used to it.

Nearly all the girls I'd ever slept with had something broken inside. They'd been raped or molested or beaten up or, at the very least, betrayed, taught to hate their bodies, their desires. Shannon had been belittled by a boyfriend as "dirty" because she wasn't a virgin. A girl at Simon's Rock had had long, thick scars across her breasts where a boyfriend had slashed her. I'd had a crush on a girl with scoliosis in a poetry class in Colorado, a crush she'd shared, but her father had raped her for years. We could only get shitfaced and stare at each other.

I couldn't understand Allison and her uncomplicated relationship with her history, her life, her self. We had all been the victims of some evil—hadn't she? After a couple of weeks, I tried to withdraw. She laughed it off. A month later, I tried again.

Allison was singing as she washed the dishes. I loved it when she did that. I felt terrible for what I was about to do. I waited till she finished her song, savoring our last moment together.

"So . . . I think we should probably stop doing what we've been doing."

Allison dried her hands on a dishtowel, then draped it over one shoulder. She turned around, leaned up against the tiny wedge of counter in her apartment, folded her arms, and looked at me.

"You like me. I like you. Why do you keep trying to do this?"

"I just . . . I don't know. I . . . I feel bad."

"Why do you feel bad?"

"You're so nice and so good. And I'm . . . well, not nice or good."

"You're nice to me. I don't want to be good all the time. You're fun. Face it, dude. We get along. Quit trying to fight it."

"I just . . . I don't want to ruin your life."

She smiled.

"What makes you so sure I'm not going to ruin yours?"

She shook her head, then turned back to the dishes.

<hr />

In early 2001, I ran into Jacob, one of the few friends I had made in the writing program, in the university library.

"Hey, man, how's it going? How was your break?" I said.

"Well . . . the social mores of casual New York City interactions dictate that it is gauche to answer that question with any dour or depressing or even specific personal information. So I am fine, and my break was also fine."

Jacob always spoke that way. He could not have made it any clearer that he had a secret he desperately needed to tell. With little prompting, he confessed. He had gotten hooked on speedballs, a combination of intravenous heroin and cocaine. He'd spent his winter break in rehab in Minnesota.

Jacob had shared his secret with me because he needed help, and he knew he could trust me. Though I was barely keeping my own head above water, I tried to repay his faith in me by helping him stay clean. We grabbed lunch twice a week and got together some weekends. When he fucked up, I'd drag him into an empty classroom to yell at him and spell out exactly what he was headed for. If you fuck up when you're quitting drinking, you lose the progress you've made and have to start over. If you fuck up when you're quitting heroin, you die. He made it a week clean, then two weeks, then a month. We were going to be okay.

When our classes ended at the beginning of May, I celebrated to the point of oblivion nearly every night at Don Hill's, a rock club where I worked as a barback. For two weeks, Jacob and I played phone tag. Without my continual harping, Jacob backslid one night and got high. The day after he died, my pager beeped and delivered a message from the other side: "Hey, what's up man, this is Jake. Just calling . . . so we should definitely get together soon."

For someone who was maniacally well-spoken, his last words were maddeningly banal. I replayed his message over and over, sitting at the kitchen table, drinking straight from the bottle, straining to hear some clue, a hidden message, any bit of overlooked information that might explain how he could have so quickly and irrevocably disappeared. His was a near-constant presence in my unconscious and semiconscious hours. Allison found me in my basement apartment one morning, one shoe on and one shoe off, clutching the jean jacket Jacob's mother had given me that still smelled like him.

I stopped writing. I quit COME ON. I drank. A sailboat I was crewing on shipwrecked, and I narrowly escaped with my life. You may recall that something occurred in New York on the eleventh day of September in 2001. When the wind blew a certain way, you could smell the ruins in the air outside Don Hill's: burnt concrete and steel, like you were grinding the form nails down inside a concrete cistern and had let the coarse wheel of the disc sander hit the concrete wall. Under that was another smell, a note of something organic decaying—the sickly sweet scent of rotting meat. Was that how it had smelled outside Auschwitz?

I had tried to keep Allison at arm's length, even as our lives grew entwined. To protect her, I told myself. But that dark winter, she needed me as I much as I needed her. She had been laid off shortly before 9/11, and finding a job after that cataclysm was impossible. Every year, she had treated herself to a Christmas wreath to hang on her wall, but as Christmas approached, she said aloud, mournfully, that she couldn't justify it. I picked a wreath up the next day, the biggest, fluffiest one I could find. When she saw it hanging on the wall, she said, "Baby! It's a Christmas miracle," then burst into tears and fell into my arms.

Allison and I labored through the winter to record an album with my old friend James, an album I was sure would bring my breakthrough. When we finished it . . . what, press up a thousand copies? No way, I probably still had nine hundred copies of the EP I'd made. I shelved it.

I worked at the bar. I drank my wages. I had no plan, not even a fantasy. I had banked everything on graduate school transforming me. Nothing had changed. I was as broke, starving, and helpless as I had been when I'd entered school, but now crushed with $70,000 in debt. It was like that line from *Jurassic Park*: I was so preoccupied with whether I could go to Columbia that I never considered whether I should. Yes, the most insightful line about the hole I was in was from a fucking dinosaur movie.

Writing? I hadn't written a word since Jacob's death. What for? Writing was just another hopeless bulwark against the darkness slavering to claim us. Your precious fancy words, your Salman Rushdie, your David Foster Wallace, your Edmund Wilson . . . when the world narrowed to a pinhole, the smartest thing you could say was just "Badeep badeep badeep, that's all folks."

CHAPTER 6

Are We Going to Be Judged on These Lonely Deeds?

Jacob had completed his coursework days before he died. He had gotten through enough of a novel to satisfy the writing requirement for the fiction MFA. I petitioned the university to allow Jacob to graduate posthumously. It wasn't a small ask, the dean made clear. I told him I would edit Jacob's thesis as if it were my own. After a couple of days' deliberation, I got word back. If I delivered his thesis in satisfactory condition, Jacob would receive his MFA posthumously, the first time the school had made such an arrangement. It was sad, to be there with him on the page, but I dug in. Something was at stake.

I lost four days in February celebrating my twenty-fifth birthday. I cried in Allison's bed when I realized I had missed a crucial meeting regarding Jacob's thesis. I was so fucked up, I couldn't come through for my dead friend.

I would take a year off drinking. Alcoholics couldn't quit drinking for a year, right? My sister Tatyana's first baby arrived three days after my decision to start anew. When she told me his name over the phone, I jumped and threw a fist in the air, denting the low tin ceiling in my kitchen in Brooklyn: Mika.

When I was one, Tatyana, two years older, had dragged me around, calling me "my Mika." When she decided to name her child after me a quarter century later, her gesture touched me and unsettled me. In a way, I would have the child I had wondered about, the child I had yearned for and feared, the child I had taken grim measures not to have. Later, I wondered cynically if she intended him as a do-over for the first Mika, whom she had been unable to retain control over. No, I couldn't let this go dark. Mika was a being the same age as my sobriety. Mika was a fresh start.

As my year of sobriety progressed, I worked to distance myself from the man I had been. I landed a job booking the bands at Luxx, a hip club in Williamsburg. The owner, Eben, was sober and decided to give me a shot when he heard I'd recently stopped drinking. I built a reputation for being tough, fair, and endlessly supportive of the bands. I opened a checking account, then a savings account. I made Mika the prime beneficiary, should something happen to me. I forced myself not to obsess about Riley. Once, I capitulated and googled her name in the middle of the night. It kicked up a picture of her smiling wanly next to a midget dressed as a leprechaun. That could only be interpreted as a warning.

I finally began to relax into being Allison's man. She'd seemed sweet but bland when I'd first met her, with her long denim skirts, her conservative haircut, her passive silence. But she was sharp and funny and fun, and as she grew more comfortable with me, her wit came out more often, usually when I least expected it. As I hesitated in front of the chips rack at the bodega one day, she called me out.

"Everything okay over here? You look like you're puzzling over a Scrabble word. Too many consonants?"

"No. I just . . . I can't decide if I want Cool Ranch Doritos or the regular kind. Look, it's says they're now Nacho Cheesier."

"A real *Sophie's Choice*, isn't it?" She patted my hand and walked away.

Allison was so gifted musically—how was it that people thought of *me* as the musician? It was miraculous to watch the transformation that came over her when she sat at the piano, the unassuming girl become instrument, music gushing forth from her. I tried to encourage her to come out of her shell, to be more invested in her artistic life, to pursue the music that was clearly so important to her. I bought her an acoustic guitar and encouraged her songwriting efforts, even recording and producing an EP of her songs. It felt good.

As the spring wore on, Allison and I rubbed up against each other, in desire and frustration. In the great constriction that followed 9/11, Allison had been unable to find a new job. Unemployment checks had gotten her through the winter, but she was running out of options, out of money, and out of hope. She lost it one night, weeping helplessly as I tried to console her. The next day, I forced her to accept a loan of $500. I called my boss at Luxx, and he made some calls. The next day, she had a job. I had come through again, like I had with Jacob's thesis. It felt great.

But the job— waiting tables at a new soul food restaurant in Williamsburg—didn't provide a lot of hours. Allison wanted to make music together; she wanted to go to the beach together; she wanted to just hang out and do nothing together. I couldn't—we couldn't—because I had to work.

Was the job that demanding, or did it provide me a distraction from a life I didn't know how to live? Sobriety had alienated me from the songs I'd written without quelling the urge to make music. I felt like a reporter with nothing to report. Staring at my schoolbooks, my neglected notebooks, I felt fear and shame. I was trapped in the space between, not quite one thing and not quite the other, anxious and irritable and easily angered.

God, if I was this bad when I was sober, I must have been a nightmare for Allison to be around when I was drinking. How lucky was I that she had stuck it out, propping me up nights, nursing me in the mornings. Riding the bus together one day, I apologized to her again for how I had treated her when I was drinking.

"Mishka, stop," she said.

"You're too forgiving. I just . . . I feel really horrible for how I was for so long. But I swear, I will find a way to make it up to you."

"Mishka, I'm not letting you off the hook. There's nothing for me to forgive."

"But, I mean, all those times I was so shitfaced . . . "

Allison shrugged.

"It was fine. You were never mean. When you were drunk, you were sweet. You would say the most romantic things to me. You tipped the girl at Burger King one day. And then, the next morning . . . you needed me. I wouldn't change a minute of it."

"Wait. Are you saying I treated you better when I was drinking than I do now?"

Again, she shrugged.

"Maybe."

That stuck in my head. I didn't drink, but we smoked weed one night. Then we did ecstasy. Then I started taking pills on my own.

<hr />

The first time I held Mika, my miracle son, my ghost made flesh, I was high on cough syrup and Adderall, and I'd been up for two days. I'd made no travel plans for the winter holidays. Christmas had been irredeemably ruined for me by that rotten twenty-four hours of the shooting and the divorce. I intended to spend it alone, as I had many before. But under increasing pressure from my family, I bought a last-second ticket to California, departing on Christmas Day.

My buddy Ethan invited me over for Christmas Eve dinner with his family. Leery as I was of holidays, strangers, grown-ups, and socializing without alcohol, I forced myself to be gracious and accept.

Dinner was fine, good even. Ethan and his family were welcoming, and the food was delicious. Dessert was a thick, sugary trifle, and I felt a tiny squirm of pleasure in the back of my head. I didn't notice what I was enjoying so much until my second piece. The layers of cake were soaked in brandy. Carefully not thinking, I ate a third piece.

While driving my roommate's truck home, I could almost hear a buzzing at the base of my skull, something alive in there, alive and hungry. It had been a mistake to eat the trifle. It had been a mistake to accept the invitation to dinner. It had been a mistake to even leave the house at this time of year.

My phone rang. Armand, my connection. I picked up. Whoops.

"Yo, Merry Christmas, man."

"Watup, son, Happy Hanukah and all that jizz. What you doing?"

"Just ate with Ethan and rolling home."

"I got some of that shit you like in."

Adderall.

"Armand, it's Christmas Eve."

" . . . "

I had money.

"Ahmn. Fuck, I'll be over in a minute."

Back at my Bushwick apartment, I cut pill after deep blue pill of Adderall into fine lines and snorted them off a CD case while brutally chafing my cock to hardcore porn on my computer. Not great, I knew, but at least I wasn't drinking.

Tremors of pleasure ran through my body, like a woman was lightly raking her nails over my skin. More exciting, though, was the feeling of pleasure to come. Some amazing thing was about to take place. An epiphany. It got closer and closer and closer . . . until finally the feeling began to dwindle without The Amazing Thing ever happening.

The room began to gray. Was something happening to my vision? I glanced over at my windows, covered with thick black curtains Allison had sewn. I stood up from my chair and almost fell over. I had been sitting so long my legs had fallen asleep. I stumbled over to the window in my boxers and pulled the corner of a curtain back: morning. Fuck. I went back to my desk and snorted another bright blue line. I'd sleep on the plane.

After I packed, I crept out to the Duane Reade and bought a four-ounce bottle of generic maximum-strength cough syrup. I felt good, rebellious, subhuman. Everyone was desperate for the shitty drugs that dealers deigned to sell you for too much money if you were lucky enough to know somebody. Nothing like the pushers forcing it on you I'd seen in the movies. You had to scramble, you had to plead, you had to crawl. Fuck them all—the thuggy, condescending dealers, the skittish indie-rock kids lecturing me to "be chill," my idiotic friends who thought coke was cool, my idiotic friends who thought it wasn't. Fuck them all. I was scoring from the *drugstore*.

I hadn't done cough syrup in a while, but, hey, it was Christmas. This would be my present to myself. It's not like I was drinking. I would be down by the time I got to California. Or down-ish. Or I'd figure it out when I got there.

I pounded the bottle of cough syrup in the back of the car service on the way to JFK. Clouds cinematically darkened the sky. By the time I'd made it through security, the cough syrup was coming on strong. I glanced at a floor-to-ceiling window and noticed I was walking sideways like a crab. If I could make it onto my plane, I would be okay.

When I got to my gate, I ducked into a bathroom. I shuffled into a stall, locked the door, and sat down on the toilet. Could I really be this fucked up?

Between my feet, a huge drill bit at least four inches in diameter chewed its way up through the floor, giving off sparks and tattered wafts of green vapor. That can't be right, I thought. The bit reversed itself and ground its way back into the floor, leaving no trace. Get on the plane, just get on the plane.

When I emerged from the sanctuary of the bathroom, I had to close one eye in order to read the flashing red display over the gate. My flight had been delayed indefinitely.

I tried to discreetly look around for a place to sit down. I felt like I was tossing my head wildly back and forth like a drowning horse, my eyes bulging.

There. Seated on a bench ten feet away was Francesca, a bartender from Mars Bar, the open sore of a bar where Zack worked as a barback. Francesca had taken care of us more than once after a night had devolved into chaos.

"*Francesca*," I whispered urgently and fell into the seat next to her.

"Oh my God, Mishka," she said and hugged me.

"I am so fucking glad to see you. I've been up all night, and I'm so fucked up."

"*Me too*," she hissed in my ear.

We hugged each other tightly, then couldn't bring ourselves to let go, as if we were the only thing anchoring each other to the earth. We sat there together for a long time.

Hours later, I made it onto my plane, peaking on cough syrup, barely able to parse language or stand upright. Sleep was impossible. Every time I closed my eyes, my vision exploded into painfully vivid colors. I put my headphones on with no music, just so no one would talk to me, and stared at the gray nubbin on the back of the plane seat holding the dinner tray in place. Tatyana was going to freak out if I was this fucked up when we landed.

Jesus, could two children be more different than Tatyana and I? I must have been a nightmare for her, ending her reign as only child, then suddenly bigger and louder than she, the Second Who Would Be First. I skipped a grade, so she was pushed to do two years in one. The year she was graduating high school for college, I stole her thunder by leaving high school early for Simon's Rock. By the time of the shooting and the divorce, we had already been strangers to each other for years. What had happened, and when?

Trapped on the airplane, staring at the back of the seat in front of me, I saw her without even closing my eyes, maybe five years old, a pretty little girl in the back yard in a long dress of white fabric printed with hibiscus blossoms, smiling shyly, a real hibiscus flower from my mom's garden tucked into her hair. Was there already nervousness behind her smile then, or had the years just inserted it into my memory?

Tatyana had been able to do something I could not. She could play quietly. She could behave. Tatyana could *be good*. That was beyond me. I wanted to—I would have done anything to be good—but it was impossible. I could not control myself. To see her doing it so effortlessly, well, I think that just drove me insane.

But it hadn't been effortless. She put herself under incredible pressure to be good, to not disappoint anyone, and because of that, she was ready to snap at you for the slightest thing. That summer in the Virgin Islands when I was twenty, I remember bitching about her to Mom. What Tatyana and I were fighting about, I can't even remember.

"Mom, she's impossible! You know that! Don't ask me to be a well of patience."

"Mishka, don't you understand? That is *exactly* what I'm asking of you. She's your *sister*, for God's sake."

Well, shit, Mom, don't you ever get sick of being right all the time?

The divide between Tatyana and I had only deepened over the years. Tatyana got excellent grades, excellent comments, excellent test scores. I killed the standardized tests, as I understood that they were important, but my greatest concern in school was exerting the least amount of effort possible. When I did get good grades, I did it only as a raised middle finger to my classmates, either thick or spineless, and my teachers. They could give me study hall, detention, inside suspension, outside suspension, talk shit on my report card—call me "juvenile," "immature," "disruptive," "hyperactive"—but I would force them to give me that A.

Now here I was, with a master's degree from a fancy-schmancy Ivy League school . . . running a rock club. So not necessarily kicking ass, but at least I was *trying*. Tatyana lived on a military base, married and popping out kids with a marine who had proposed to her in a Denny's. She was a *normal*. Jesus, Tatyana, the world has more to offer you than Toby Keith, and you have more to offer it than scrapbooking!

What was worse, she had been better than me. Whenever we had gone head-to-head, she'd won. I finished the test first, but she got every single question right. I got to the bottom of the ski hill first, but the instructor complimented her on her "perfect form" in front of our ski class. She'd fulfilled Dad's wishes by becoming an electrical engineer like him, pulling down a fat salary. I had changed my major from theater to film to creative writing and finally wound up flipping burgers or answering phones for beer money. An overpriced master's I could never pay for had only upgraded me to grubbing in bars. I disdained the life Tatyana had chosen, but, once again, she had won. She had made Mom and Dad proud. She had found a partner, and she'd found her place. Tatyana had even named her child after me, for Christ's sake, and I had no fucking idea who I was.

I looked down at my hands. My fingers were short and stubby, then they were incredibly long, then my fingertips were grossly oversized, like a clown's. The skin on my palms rippled and fluttered, patches of red and white skin organizing into intricate patterns, then shuffling themselves. I had done too much. My teeth were definitely rotting. I had given myself brain damage. If I was still this high tomorrow, I'd shoot myself in the head and be done with it. That thought gave me some comfort, and I closed my eyes.

⸺

I had explicitly asked my mom to come pick me up by herself to ensure that there was no big scene at the airport. Of course, there was the full welcoming party: my mother, Tashina, my brother-in-law,

Bill—a fucking marine, for God's sake, the squarest of the square in his "high and tight"—and Tatyana, who hugged me and immediately deposited my ten-month-old namesake in my arms.

I held Tatyana's baby away from me for a minute, just taking him in. He was the size and weight of a thawed turkey, his useless little flippers hanging limply by his sides, staring at me with the same blank wonder with which I stared at him.

I had nearly become a father twice, at eighteen and twenty-two. My children would have been three and seven. Four years apart, just like me and Tashina. Or like Chuong and me.

I drew Mika to me. He pressed his head against my chest. I put my head down next to his face and took a breath, smelling his fine hair, his soft skull, the nascent promise of his new flesh.

I closed my eyes and had a vision of a nursery full of sleeping babies, each more unique and more perfect than the last, the air over them swirling thickly with boundless potential, the infinite possibilities of their lives. A beautiful nurse in a starched white hat walked among the rows of cribs, bending over each infant to caress the fine eddies of silk on their heads, brush their cheeks with her eyelashes, and whisper a blessing into their tiny, sleeping ears: *Nothing bad will ever happen to you.*

Nothing bad will ever happen to you: it's just the most heinous lie, the worst bullshit imaginable. Millions of bad things will happen to you, a thesaurus, a full set of *encyclopedias* of bad things, a vast, shimmering spectrum of bad things, from stubbing your toe to passing a jagged kidney stone to the day you finally die, The Biggest Bad Thing, which, by then, may not seem so awful after all, because death, in its completeness, at least ensures that no more bad things will happen to you.

But before you achieve that, man . . . you will piss your pants, and you will shit your pants, as a child and as an adult. And not a little bit, where you can almost get away with it; you will shit your pants with such vehemence that you will have to change your *socks*. In fact, your final act on this earth will probably be to piss *and* shit your pants at the same time. Death and taxes are not the only inevitabilities; there will *always* be feces.

You will fall in love. Your lover will cheat on you with your best friend or your worst enemy or both in one action-packed weekend, and you will only find out when you wake up with crabs or herpes or Hep C or HIV.

You will get beat up. A lot. You will get beat up by your brother/sister/mother/father/friends/lovers/strangers. You will get raped. You will get raped twice, once by a stranger and once by someone you know, someone you trust, someone in your fucking family, God damn the world to hell. Your hamster will die. Your cat will die. Your grandfather will die. Your mother will die. Your child will die in your arms. You will pay for an abortion, you will have an abortion—several abortions—and those dreamed lives, those pre-children, will follow you around like starving stray dogs for the rest of your life.

You will be abandoned. She will leave you. He will leave you. They will leave you. Everyone you love who doesn't leave you or turn against you or die will leave you *and then* turn against you *and then* die.

Something will happen to you that is so bad that you will not be able to parse it; you will have no language with which to comprehend what has happened to you, so you will just carry it around in your abdomen like a dead fetus, which will calcify in your gut, a stone baby that grows so large and so heavy that you will lay awake at night and feel it, cold and unyielding inside you, and understand that you have been transformed into just a vessel to transport this profane weight.

You will do bad things to people you hate, and to people you love because you are angry, because you are confused, because you are hurt, because you have become cruel, and because you can't help yourself. You will do truly *rotten* shit, small, mean-spirited shit, petty shit, shit so base, so abominable it will keep you awake years later, wondering if it could really have been *you* who had done it at all, because it seems so foreign in essence from the polite, responsible, even caring person you understand to be your true self. It will disturb you, it will hurt you, you will bleed, it will destroy you, it will murder you, it will kill you to fucking death, over and over, again and again. And you will go on living.

Still, glassy-eyed and sleep deprived and half-crazed in the San Diego airport, I held my sister's baby boy to my chest. It'll be different for you, Mika, my little man. *Nothing bad will ever happen to you.*

When I awoke late in the day, my sister's house was empty. I showered and dressed, then followed the sound of voices out to the back patio.

"There he is," my dad said, as if I'd been gone for hours, not years.

Seven years since I'd seen my father. Like something out of a fable or maybe *The Princess Bride*. I looked at his face. He had aged far more than seven years. He had aged immeasurably, irretrievably, incomprehensibly. His hair gray, his skin not just lined but crinkled, broken veins splashed across his nose. He had crossed the line; he had become *old*.

His girlfriend was way younger than Mom. Maybe closer to Tatyana's age? Long legs, long blonde hair, generic toothy smile. Dad, you swine, did you order her from the factory that way?

I took my place: equidistant from Tashina and Mom, our outsider and our core. On a tiny blanket in the center of our mangled family circle lay Mika, face down, staring at the dirt. We all turned our gazes to him.

"Better than TV, huh?" I said to Tashina.

She smiled.

No one said anything. I stared at the baby.

Mika had pulled our parody of a family together for the first time in ten years—my father from his hideout in northern

138

California, my mother from the Virgin Islands, Tashina from Colorado, where she was finishing high school, me from New York, the very ends of the earth. This battered circle—how could it hold so much power over us? Was it enchanted, a faerie ring?

Bullshit. It had no meaning, held no power. This whole bogus ritual of celebrating the bloodline . . . genealogy meant nothing. It had been a mistake to come here. I'd allowed myself to be duped. Not drinking was making me soft.

Mika picked up a tiny rock, turned it over in his infinitely detailed little fingers, inspecting each and every surface. Another rock caught his eye. He discarded the old rock for a new one, then a new one, one after another. It reminded me of a picture from my childhood of another baby performing a similar inspection. What was that from? Cheap white quilt speckled with checks of bright primary colors, but the baby looking at a clover, not a rock. That baby even looked like Mika. Ah, shit. That baby was me.

I glanced over at my dad. We had probably spent less than a month together since I was fifteen. He was watching Mika intently, his hands on his hips, fingers pointing backward, his thumbs pointing down the sides of his legs. I looked down at my body, my hands on my hips, fingers pointing backward, my thumbs pointing down the sides of my legs. So maybe there was something to it after all.

—

I had no intention of extending an olive branch to my father on this trip, something I think he understood. His girlfriend, Theresa, hadn't gotten the memo. She brought me a glass of lemonade without asking if I wanted one, so I didn't have a chance to decline. I waited patiently while she made herself a couple of sandwiches in the kitchen so I could make my own, but the two sandwiches went onto two plates, not one, and she handed one of those plates to me. It would have been rude not to sit and eat with her.

Didn't this stranger know that I hated her simply because she was inside the same sphere around my father that I had been excluded from? Was she not picking up on any of the signs I was throwing out that I wanted nothing to do with her? Or was she deliberately fucking with me?

She asked me about New York. She asked me about my music. She asked me about Allison. After a few minutes, I realized I had stopped trying to assess if she was an evil genius or a dolt. We were just talking. It was easy. She said something, then I said something, then she said something. Could I make her laugh?

"Are you Catholic?" she said.

"No, but I am religious. Evangelical Defeatist."

She laughed.

By the time she excused herself to tidy up in the kitchen, she had confounded every shitty off-the-cuff judgment I had made about her. Theresa was nice. Not in a wishy-washy way, but in a thoughtful, open, engaged way. I hated being wrong, but I felt relief, gratitude even. Dad's girlfriend wasn't just okay, she was good. Worst-case scenario, she might turn out to be great. What was she doing hanging around my dad?

Over the next couple of days, my dad made a few small overtures to me, asking how I'd slept, if I was hungry. I gave back as few syllables as possible, even going so far as to address him by his first name, Murray, instead of calling him Dad. Still, he was trying, in his stilted way.

The last day, I suggested we talk. Not that I wanted to talk, but no way were we going to just slip back into some half peace. Maybe my family was content to let him skate, but not me. I'd learned one thing since I'd backed down from clocking him with a roll of quarters in the Denver airport: fighting sucked; it was scary and it was painful, but pain was temporary. Taking some lumps or even getting your teeth kicked in was far preferable to rotting slowly from the inside out from the knowledge that you were a coward. Fuck it, I would take the old man on.

If we had to yell, we would yell. If we had to scream, we would scream. If it came to blows, well, I hadn't had a drink in six months and had even made it to the gym a couple of times. Even over the hill, my dad was still a physical specimen. He might win. But if I went down, I would bring him with me. If it went to the ground, I wouldn't just hurt him. I would *damage* him.

I opened the door for my dad, and we walked outside. I could feel a bustle in the air in the house, the sound of my sisters and my mother and Theresa whispering to each other, or maybe just looking at one another. As I closed the door behind me, the tension in the house oddly calmed me. Was this the sensation of completeness a murderer felt the moment before the act?

We pulled up white plastic chairs and sat down opposite one another across the dusty white table. The sun was setting before us, flamboyant sorbet oranges and pinks. It just made the cheap Home Depot deck furniture and the plain concrete patio seem that much cheaper and plainer.

"I'm glad you want to talk," my dad said. "I think it's good for us to talk."

He crossed his arms, not really something people do when they want to talk.

"I don't *want* to talk, Dad. It's necessary. I'm not willing to just let things go back to how they were, like everything's hunky-dory, you know?"

"I understand that. Where would you like to start?"

That was a good question.

"Under the terms of the divorce, you were to be financially responsible for us kids, right?"

"Until you were eighteen, yes."

"And you were supposed to pay for our college, right?"

"Your undergrad, yes. You knew that you were on your own for grad school."

I could already hear him tightening up.

"That's fine. So . . . you bailed on any and all emotional aspects of being a parent. When you dumped Mom, you tried to bury all of us kids with her. All that was left at that point was the financial thing. And you couldn't even do that. I worked full-time the summer I was sixteen and started paying all my own expenses the day I left Simon's Rock, a couple of months after I turned seventeen. From seventeen to eighteen, I got—what—five hundred dollars out of you? If that.

"The last time I wrote to you, it was about a $51 chiropractor bill for the thing with my back that happened when I was seventeen. I had already paid for my final semester at school out of my own pocket. You couldn't pay that bill for $51?"

"It . . . At that time . . . Well, I don't really know exactly what was going on at that time. It was so long ago. It just fell through the cracks."

"I sent it to you four times."

"Okay. Yes. I should have paid it. Is that what you want to hear?"

"It doesn't matter now. I don't need the money. I needed the money then, but I don't need it now. I guess that's the thing. When I was eighteen and needed help figuring out my taxes and my financial aid for college, you weren't around. When I was seventeen, learning how to drive, and when I needed help buying a car so I wouldn't get ripped off, you weren't around. When I was fifteen, with the shooting . . . Hell, way before that! You were gone for a long time before you finally left. I had to figure it all out on my own. And I did. I don't need you anymore."

"You seem to have done well for yourself. You certainly look good. All you kids have done well for yourselves."

"Thanks, I guess. Anything we accomplished, we did it without you."

"It's a good life skill to learn how to do things on your own."

Like he had disappeared for our benefit, so we would grow up right. And not because he was a pussy. What was he thinking, sitting there with his arms crossed? I had known this man longer than I'd known any other man in my life, was supposed to have a deeper connection with him than any other man in the world. I had no fucking idea what was going on in his head. He was probably just thinking what a hassle this was. Anxious for it to be over. Just like me.

"Here's the thing, Dad. If I had a friend who treated me the way you have, well, I would no longer have that friend. Hell, if I had a friend who treated his kids the way you've treated us, I would tell him he was a piece of shit, and *then* I would no longer have that friend."

He didn't say a word, just cinched up tighter and stared at me.

"But I've gotten a lot of second chances. And I'm grateful for that. If you're going to be more responsive, then we can try again."

"It doesn't make me happy, not seeing you or hearing from you for years at a time."

That was the closest I would get to him telling me he had missed me. Hearing those three words—I miss you—would have been better. But that was one lesson he'd taught me: Life is not about getting what you want. It's about living with what you get.

"Okay, Mishka. If you're willing to try again, I'm willing to try again."

"Great. Then you've gotta stop bullshitting us."

He sputtered a little, then drew himself up.

"And how have I bullshitted you?"

You really have no idea how easy I'm going on you, do you, Dad? You have bullshitted me in many ways, great and small; you have bullshitted me in every way. Our entire relationship, from the day I was born, was a lie. When you built me that little wooden box for the set of toy tools you'd bought for me, that was a lie. When you taught me how to tie a hook on my fishing line so it couldn't be pulled loose, that was a lie. Every single thing you ever did to make me feel like I could count on you was a lie.

But those years and years of lies, a lifetime of lies, they were such a towering, inseparable clot that they threatened to overwhelm us both. Just cop to one lie, Dad. Give up one lie, and we can move forward.

I presented him with one lie I knew he would never cop to.

I'd never forgotten the unsigned letter, in his handwriting, that Mom had found in the back of one of his books while dividing up their stuff before the divorce. Though not addressed, it was clearly written to another woman before he and Mom had separated. Over the years, that letter had grown huge in my mind. It was not a letter but The Letter: concrete proof that Dad had betrayed us. After she had let me read The Letter, Mom had sworn me to secrecy. I wouldn't violate that pact. Not exactly.

Dad was incapable of admitting he was wrong. He would swear he had never cheated on Mom, I would stand up and walk away, and we would be done with this. It would be a relief to go back to not talking. And this chat would keep Tatyana and Mom off my back because I had tried; they had seen me walk out here to try.

"Dad . . . you said you never cheated on Mom. Again and again, you come back to that, that your marriage was over before you started fooling around with your secretary or receptionist or whatever the hell she was. I know you did. I'm not going to tell you how I know. But I know."

He took a quick breath, then puffed it out through his mustache. He looked away. He looked back at me.

"This conversation is between you and me."

Only once, when I was maybe eleven years old, had my father brought me in on a secret. After a big fight with my mom, he had taken me for a drive and sworn me to silence in our Ford Aerostar minivan. Then he told me, "Mishka, sometimes the worst thing you can do is win an argument with a woman." His intensity that night had chilled me. I had never forgotten it, would never forget it. He had not just never loved Mom; he had hated her.

"Fine. I won't say a word to anyone about this."

This was a strange turn. What was he going to say? I had prepared for cruelty, violence even. But I wasn't prepared for this, for information, for secret knowledge.

"Okay. This is the truth, so help me God. Lis and I had . . . become friendly before I was able to have the conversation with your mother—"

"Conversation? Dad, you just *informed* her that you were filing for divorce!"

She had cried so hard over the next ten days that she lost ten pounds. I told her she should market the Surprise Divorce Diet Plan—lose ten pounds in ten days! All it'll cost you is three easy payments of $19.95, your marriage of nineteen years, your house, and your happiness.

"Are you going to let me finish? Okay. My therapist told me that my marriage to your mother was over. I fought her on it. I almost walked out, quit therapy then and there. But once I realized she was right, I knew I couldn't go back. Once I'd seen it, I couldn't unsee it. As soon as I could, I booked a trip back to New Hampshire to tell your mother. I had dinner with Lis several times. She stayed over once before you kids were told. I regretted it then. And I regret it now."

He let out a deep breath.

"You had better not tell her that. Your mom *or* your sisters. I am trusting you here."

He was. It wasn't the gutting confession I had hoped for, but it was something.

"I won't tell anybody."

We sat there in silence for a moment. The sun was nearly gone. It had roiled through its beautiful end while we hadn't been paying attention.

"What else?" he said, frowning like he had just been told he needed a root canal and was bracing for more bad news.

"I mean . . . there's more. There's a lot more. I didn't prepare a list. Honestly, I didn't think we'd get past that first one."

"That's good. I mean . . . that's good?"

He looked at me.

"It's a start."

I stood up. He stood up. We shook hands. Then we went inside. What the fuck happens now?

———

My father asked Theresa to marry him, and she said yes. I wanted to be a prick about it, but Theresa was too kind. Besides, we were trying to play nice now. Before they could marry in a Catholic church, Dad had to have his marriage to my mom annulled.

It wasn't bad enough that he had divorced my mom and tried to divorce us kids. Now he was trying to rewrite history, to purge us from the official record, to deny that any of us had ever existed. It infuriated us all. But the most infuriating thing was that my mother was going along with it. She knew it was an insult. She knew it was bullshit. She knew it was incredibly painful for all us kids. But she refused to stand in his way.

"Fuck it, Mishka," she said. "I'm out of tears. I am bone dry. If he wants it gone, fuck it, good riddance."

In order to get the annulment, my dad had to sit for interviews with a priest, then write something up establishing that the marriage had been flawed in its inception. Like a fucking essay on "What I Did over My Summer Vacation." They'd been married nineteen years, bought three houses together, and raised a family—how could he argue it wasn't a legitimate marriage?

I pestered him to read what he'd written. He sent me a couple of paragraphs. They were more tantalizing than satisfying. There was nothing about me or Tatyana or Tashina. I could almost see where he had nipped out the juicy bits, the parts that might explain why he had shut us out, how he had been able to shut us out. I knew he'd written about us, about me, and it burned me to know I would never read it.

When the heat went off in my Bushwick apartment that winter, the landlord declined to turn it back on. Tired of seeing her own breath each morning, my roommate, a girl I'd worked with in Colorado, found a new space, an open loft in a warehouse. Reluctantly,

I agreed to move in with her and her friend, my fifth move in as many years in New York.

My dad was between jobs, so my roommates and I chipped in on a plane ticket, and he came east to help me build out the loft. I took some time off from Luxx, and for four days we worked every waking hour. I wasn't a total failure at carpentry, but my dad, man, he'd line a nail up and drive it flush with the stud with one strike of the hammer.

Allison brought us takeout food and leftovers from her job at the soul food restaurant. Each evening, she marveled at the progress we'd made. Each night, I slept like the dead. Each morning, it took me several minutes to get out of bed because my bones hurt, my teeth hurt, my fingernails hurt. It was the happiest I'd been since I was a kid.

After framing, sheetrocking, taping, and spackling four separate rooms, the last thing left to do was to hang my door. My dad set the frame in place, then looked at me.

"How do you want it hung?" he said.

He was covered in drywall dust—not just his hair and his face; there was also a light dusting on the lenses of his glasses, though he'd been cleaning them all day. Dust in his eyelashes, even.

"Well hung?" I said.

He grinned and rolled his eyes.

"Hoo boy. Gets it from his old man, I guess. I'm doing it so it will certainly be hung well. But do you want the door to swing open when you twist the knob, or do you want it to swing shut when it's open?"

It would be most convenient for the door to swing shut. But what would be the most difficult for him to do?

"Can you make it so the door just stays however I leave it?"

Three minutes later, he called me over. I wobbled when I got off the ladder. I was so fucking tired. *We* were so fucking tired.

Dad gently pushed the door. It swung shut and clicked quietly into place. He opened it three inches and took his hand away. The door didn't move. He pulled the door five inches open and took his hand away. The door didn't move.

I started laughing. He started laughing. You had to give it to the old man sometimes.

＝

The anniversary of my year off drinking came and went. I kept going: working long hours at Luxx, boxing at Gleason's gym, tinkering with guitars, practicing guitar and squeezing out a few songs about my old life, reading but carefully not writing. My dad and I talked, not a lot, but a little. Tatyana was doing okay; she had her nest and her baby and her husband. My mom was doing okay without any help from me, still down in the Virgin Islands with Paul, selling advertising for the local newspaper. She didn't make much money, but they didn't pay rent or car insurance, and she had lots of practice living close to the bone. Even Tashina seemed to have found her happiness, going to college in Toronto for radio production. What made me happy? I mean, *besides* alcohol.

I loved Allison. She loved me. We never fought. She was never mean to me. She was patient when I got squirrelly, which was often since I'd quit drinking. Allison was beautiful, and I loved every Allison she was: I loved her at my side while I worked the door at Luxx; I loved her singing my songs with me, on stage or at home; I loved her in Rochester, opening her Christmas presents like a little girl while her parents looked on. I loved her sober (to support me in my year off), as I loved her after one drink, the taste of wine or vodka-cranberry in her open mouth, as I had loved her wasted—Alcoholison. When I woke her in the middle of the night to show her how the plastic wrapper on the Tylenol PM made blue sparks in the dark, she didn't get angry. I loved her in public, and I loved her in private, gasping underneath me. I loved her asleep, her eyelids fluttering in a dream, loved her so much that I missed her even while I was beside her, while I was inside her. But . . . was this it? Were we just to go on loving each other forever?

I got an email from Riley. I had kept my name off the utility bills in every apartment I'd lived in and paid to keep my number unlisted. But finally she had found me.

I read her email. Then I read it again. Then I deleted it. Then I rescued it out of the trash can, created a folder called "Work," secreted it there, and turned my laptop off. I closed the lid, zipped it into its carrying case, and stuck it under my bed. As if that would keep me safe.

I was finishing a guitar I had been working on for months, an old Hagstrom neck and body I'd found in a pawn shop, which I'd wired with Jazzmaster pickups—The Hagmaster. I had finally gotten all the electronics up and running, and I was ready to take it for a test drive. Before I strung it up, I opened a can of lighter fluid to clean the fretboard. I put some on a paper towel and rubbed all the old gunk off the fingerboard. The lighter fluid smelt oddly comforting, familiar. I sniffed the paper towel, greasy from the lighter fluid, gray from the dirt. Then I took a deeper breath. Then I opened the container, emptied my lungs of air, put my nose right over the opening, and drew its scent as far inside me as I could. God, it smelled so fucking good. I started shaking.

I knew it would be a mistake to write back to Riley, but I couldn't help myself. I let fly, all bile, just raging at her. She wrote back. I wrote back. Then we were writing to each other.

She was in Washington, DC, as she had been for all six years since she'd broken off contact. She had been trying to track me down. She knew I had gone to Columbia and had even screwed up the courage to call my old apartment less than a month after I left there. I had slipped up and put my name on the Con Ed bill, I recalled. Riley had never stopped missing me. Riley wanted me back.

Tatyana and Bill were down in Virginia for some military training. They had invited me down to see Mika. I booked a hotel room outside DC and caught a bus down a day before I was to meet

Tatyana. I would not sleep with Riley. I could not sleep with Riley. But I had to see her. I had to know.

When I got off the bus, she was nowhere to be found. I sat down in the bus station to wait. Ten years now with Riley, ten years with her absence, ten years of a rusty fishhook in my heart for her to twist whenever she got bored.

I waited for more than an hour. Of course she wasn't going to show. To lure me down here and then not show up, well, that would be the perfect punch line to this long, humiliating shitshow. The explanation I'd come so far for? The explanation was that life did not owe you an explanation for your suffering and that you were an idiot to expect it. It was what I deserved. Then there she was: a woman in her mid-twenties, reddish-brown hair or maybe now brownish-red. Heavier not just in the hips but everywhere, especially her face. She looked worried and anxious, late and stressed, more fearful than excited.

I had been remembering Riley as I'd first seen her at Simon's Rock in the fall of 1993. But had I even been remembering the actual experience of her on the lawn like a delicate rainforest sugar glider, fearful of being trampled? Or was I remembering the *memory* of that experience from being heartbroken over her for the first time, when I was seventeen? If you taped a song off a CD, and then taped that tape, and then taped *that* tape, well, with each new copy, the song got duller, weaker, diminished, until the music was finally swallowed by noise. Remembering Riley—compulsively, desperately, insanely—hadn't diminished her. It had perfected her. Memory hadn't preserved her but transformed her. The Riley in my head had become better, brighter, more alluring as the years had passed. For the real Riley, time had had the opposite effect.

Go, I thought to myself. It was stupid and crazy to come here. You have your answer. Stand quietly and slip discreetly out before she sees you. Then run. And don't look back.

She saw me. We both froze. Then she walked directly toward me.

We didn't hug or even shake hands.

"Hi," she said, breathlessly.

For years and years I had been imagining this moment, encountering her again, and all the brilliant, cutting things I would say.

"Hi," I said.

⸺

She drove me to my hotel. I made her wait in the car while I checked in and ran my bag upstairs to my room. This would unfold exclusively in public places.

We got a table at a fake Mexican chain restaurant across the street. We ordered, and a mute food runner put two limp, greasy Southwest Caesar salads before us. We discussed the banalities of our lives. She was finishing her master's. It was okay. She was excited about having been accepted to a PhD program in Montana. I passed her the two CDs of songs I had written about her. And then we both went silent. I looked down at my salad, as appetizing as a dissected, formaldehyde-soaked frog.

"Why, Riley? Why did you just disappear on me?"

I looked at her. She looked down.

"You were cheating on me," I said.

"You've cheated on me."

"Yes."

"Yes," she said. "A boy at the dance program in Maryland. It's terrible, and I'm sorry."

"I . . . I don't even care about that. It's actually a relief to get confirmation. I knew something was going on."

She didn't say anything.

"Where did you go at the end of the summer? I mean, I know you went to DC to dance. I called your house one night when I was shitfaced, and I talked to your mom."

"She told me."

"I guess the question is *why*. Why did you go? How could you? You didn't just get accepted to that program randomly one day and leave the next morning. You knew you weren't coming to Denver; you knew you were going to DC. You knew that for a long time. And you pretended everything was okay."

"Yes."

"Why didn't you tell me? You just disappeared. It was like you died."

"I was afraid you'd react badly. You were just . . . you were kind of unstable then."

I laughed.

"If you thought I was unstable before you disappeared, you should have seen me after. I went insane."

"I'm sorry."

"It's okay. I'm not insane anymore."

She didn't say anything.

"Why didn't you want to be with me? I loved you. You loved me. Or you said you did."

"I know. I don't know. I just . . . I couldn't go to Denver. I didn't know why, but I knew I couldn't go. Something bad was going to happen."

"Something bad did happen to me."

She didn't say anything.

"Fuck it, whatever, I'm not going to be a crybaby. You made the right decision. You should have told me, but you're right. It would have been a mistake for you to come to Denver. I was out of control. It would have ended badly."

"I should have given it a chance. Maybe it would have worked out."

"No. No, you did the right thing. It was crazy. *I* was crazy."

"Maybe it was crazy. You were certainly crazy, but I was crazy too. We were so young. But we're not crazy anymore . . . "

"Riley. Are you kidding me?"

"Mishka, I . . . I've never stopped loving you. The whole time, you were the one. I knew it, but was I was too afraid to see it through. I'm not afraid anymore."

This whole thing, coming down here to meet her, had been a rotten idea. What was I going to do, pull out a yellow legal pad, give her the specific dates and times I'd cried on the bar or wept myself to sleep, and punish her for each one?

Riley was damaged. A loaded, unkind word, but there was no other. Not just her brain or her mind but the very core of who she was. She had been damaged by the men who had raped and abused her, as a child and as a teenager. Then she had damaged herself more, out of rage at them and out of rage at herself for being powerless to stop them. Then she had damaged me, out of pain and out of malice. And then I had damaged her, and myself in her name.

Inflicting more pain on her wasn't going to undo any of that. It wasn't going to make me feel better about the hell she'd put me through. It had been torture, absolute torture. And it was nothing compared to what she'd endured.

"Riley."

She looked up at me, miserable. She was still so beautiful.

"It's okay. I forgive you."

Her face opened up.

"I forgive you. And I wish you every happiness. I hope you have a great life. But I won't be in it in any way. I will never trust you again."

I insisted on paying for the salads we didn't eat, a petty revenge I allowed myself. We said good-bye in the hotel parking lot outside her car. She stepped close for a hug. I shook her hand, then turned to head inside.

Light was flowing through me. It was over. It was done. Riley had been leaving me for nearly ten years. Now she was finally gone. For the first time in my life of weakness and idiocy, I had done the right thing. I was free.

"Mishka."

I looked back.

"Can I use your bathroom? I'm sorry, I should have peed at the restaurant."

I hesitated.

She rolled her eyes.

"Come on. I have a long drive home ahead of me."

"Ah . . . yeah, that's fine. Sure."

She followed me into the hotel. We walked up to the second floor in silence. I opened the door with my key card, walked in, and turned on the light in the bathroom. Riley pushed the door to the hotel room closed and, without a word, knelt at my feet and pulled my belt open.

———

Riley dropped me off the next morning at a little country store at the entrance to some military base where Tatyana was going to come pick me up. I felt completely out of my mind.

We had slept a couple of hours at most. My will had folded instantly with her on her knees in front of me, staring deep into my eyes, my cock in her mouth. Riley wanted to do everything, everything we had ever done, everything she had never let me do, everything either one of us had ever thought of. She had brought a Polaroid and wanted me to document every depravity.

And I wanted it all. I wanted to roughly fuck her mouth till her eyes watered and she gagged; I wanted to come in her mouth, come on her face. It sickened me, and it made me hate myself, but I goaded myself on: here is what you wanted; take it now, take all of it, all you can stomach.

I professed to love my mother above all others and to hate my father for the ill he'd done to her. I'd aced my women's studies course; I loved my Bikini Kill and Liz Phair records; I read women authors and went out of my way to support female musicians at the club. But in my personal life, all that shit went out the window. I'd taken Riley for granted when we'd been together and cheated on her repeatedly. When I'd finally driven her away, that's when I decided I couldn't live without her and dove headlong into hateful obsession. I professed to hate the men who'd abused her, who'd dehumanized her, who'd treated her as a sexual possession . . . and then, in my mind, I'd done the same thing.

I had locked myself away from the rest of the world in Riley's name. Speck had been great—salty, tender, insightful. We could have been happy, had I let her in. Shannon had been jealous and paranoid and insecure . . . but maybe she wouldn't have been had I not been writing songs for Riley during every waking moment, even mumbling her name in my sleep. And Allison . . . God, I had a real woman, a real person, real love waiting for me patiently at home. She deserved better than me at my best. She certainly didn't deserve this.

I went into the bathroom of the country store. The stack of Polaroids felt heavy in my pocket, like a folded flick knife with blood on the blade. I sat on the toilet and took the pictures out.

I hadn't wanted pictures. I didn't want a single one. I wanted Riley as she had been, not as she was now. Too late, I realized I had loved her absence, not her presence. But the Polaroids were repellent to me not because I wanted to continue my worship of Riley's ghost but because they were concrete proof of my weakness. In my infidelity, it had finally become clear: I loved Allison, Allison in my head and Allison in the flesh, her and only her. I was free of Riley forever. And all I had to do to win my freedom was betray the one woman I loved, the woman who truly loved me.

I forced myself to take in each and every picture. Grainy, out of focus, Riley's speckled flesh harsh white in the flash, our genitals red and inflamed, all else in dark shadow like child pornography or a snuff film. Still, I felt sick desire growing in me. I threw the pictures on the floor. I put my head between my legs and cried.

I could never tell Allison about this. I could never tell anyone. I would just have to hold in my heart the knowledge that I had done a horrible, horrible thing. God, to do something like this sober . . . it proved that you had evil in your heart.

I collected the Polaroids from the floor, tore them up, and dumped them in the trash. Then I walked out to wait for my sister.

≡

Walking home after work at Luxx one night, I thought again of my father and the neglected acoustic guitar in its case under his bed: the strings slowly tarnishing, then rusting, as he didn't learn to play and didn't learn to play and didn't learn to play. One day, the rust would eat all the way through. Those strings would finally break.

When I was a small child, I told my mother I wanted to be "a wandering minstrel," just traveling town to town, playing my songs. Other dreams had moved me temporarily over the years, but that dream had never left. I had moved to New York to naively chase my dreams of being a musician and a writer and putting some kind of mark on the world. I had wanted a big, rambling, rambunctious life, but my life here in New York had been more circumscribed than anywhere else.

I decided to buy a van, put all my shit in storage, abandon my loving girlfriend, and hit the road, touring the country nonstop for a year. I felt sure the road would transform me. My fearlessness and devotion would win me a deal with a small label and a small (okay, medium-sized) advance. Of course I would drink—it would be impossible to do without drinking—but that was incidental. With the advance from the record label, I could buy an RV, and Allison would join me, singing backup, playing Wurlitzer and harmonica. I could almost see her, curled up in a sunlit corner of the tiny breakfast nook, playing one of the harmonicas I'd bought her, working her way through another song.

≡

A year later, I came back to New York, broke, unemployed, and exhausted, with nothing to show for my efforts. I'd gotten discouraged trying to book shows, then fallen behind schedule, then found myself just begging my way onto bills on the night of a show, lucky to sell one CD or cadge a few free drinks for my troubles. Sure, I had padded my press kit, but there was still no one at the shows.

Yes, In Music We Trust, a record label in Portland had expressed interest in hearing a full-length album, but "record label interest" and two bucks will only get you a slice of pizza. I moved in with Allison and only made my first month's rent because my van got hit by a drunk driver, a young princess in a colossal, gleaming white boat of an SUV, who gaily wrote me a big check and asked for a signed copy of my CD.

Eben, my old boss from Luxx, got me a job as a night manager at the legendary music venue The Knitting Factory. I saved every penny I could, borrowed money from my uncle, and diligently set about making the record I was sure would rescue me from obscurity.

But the man I'd become on the road—depressed, resentful, self-obsessed, leering at women, convinced both that he was utterly worthless and that the dimwitted world had ungraciously failed to recognize his genius, eager to do any depraved thing to escape the eternal present of the drunk—well, he was unwilling to retreat back into the darkness from whence he'd come. I thought up a name for this asshole: Narsissyphus, from Narcissus, the legendary hunter so enamored of his own image that he starved to death staring at his reflection in a pool, and Sisyphus, the hubristic king damned to roll a huge boulder to the top of a steep hill in Hades, only to have the stone tumble back just before he reached the summit, forcing him to begin anew, over and over again for all eternity. Narsissyphus incorporated the worst of both characters: he was a man erotically transfixed by his own repeated, myopic failures. Probably not someone you want as a roommate, let alone boyfriend.

≡

I went out on a ten-day tour and drunkenly cheated on Allison. That first night back, I felt physically sick with guilt. Allison knew something was up. I have always been horrible at concealing the truth.

It was late, and I was exhausted, so we just ate and called it a night. We got into bed and turned out the light, trying to ignore the silence hulking between us. We lay there for a moment in the dark. I could almost see my infidelity, writhing obscenely above us in the night. It was okay, though. We were just going to fall asleep. When we woke up, it would be gone. I would never do it again, and we could go on with our life together.

"Did . . . did you cheat on me?" Allison said, her voice trembling out of the darkness.

Allison loved me, and I loved her. I knew that she didn't want to believe that I had betrayed her. I knew that I could lie to her face, that I could tell her, no, I hadn't, and how could she think that? I knew I could manipulate her, that I could partly force her and partly trick her into believing that something she knew to be true was a lie. And I knew that to make her believe a lie would be an evil thing to do to someone you loved.

"Yes," I said, "and I'm so sorry."

I'd never said a word to Allie about Riley, and it had eaten at me. Coming clean about this was the right thing to do, one lonely right thing in the sea of wrong things I'd done. And that small right thing was our undoing.

≡

That spring, the people I loved the most in the world had my dream come true for them without me: the band Allison played in with my best friend James—my ex-band!—signed to a major label. They were at practice; they were in the studio; they were on tour. Allison had little time for our music and less time for me.

The Knitting Factory hadn't totally fired me, but I had been demoted from night manager to security, then found myself having to beg just to get on the schedule. My record—mostly love songs I had written to Allison while on the road—had stalled.

I felt like I had fallen down a well, a well so deep it led to hell. What was worse, I could see a tiny circle of sky and hear the sounds of the living world. I saw Allison for a couple of hours each week—I could smell her delicate blond hair; I was even infrequently allowed to touch her translucent skin—but she wasn't there. We had sworn we were going to live together, die together, forever and ever! And now Allison had disappeared, like Speck had disappeared, like Riley had disappeared.

No, that's not right. Allison was playing shows, going on tour, doing photo shoots with my best friend James, who I never heard from anymore. Allison was right there in front of me, bolder and brighter than she'd ever been. It was me who was disappearing. I could see it in her face: each day I was a little meeker, a little smaller, a little feebler, until one day I would disappear altogether, and she would finally be free to go on with the rest of her life. Chilling as it must be to watch someone die, it must be more chilling to watch yourself die in her eyes.

Allison and I split. And "split" is the right word. I felt like a Siamese twin torn from its other half. In the middle of the night, I packed up my stuff and moved onto a friend's broken futon in Greenpoint.

I struggled to keep it together. Eben got me another job at a new club on Ludlow Street named Pianos. I started playing bass in a band called Beat the Devil. I went deep into credit card debt to finish my solo record.

I slept with the singer in Beat the Devil, and the band careened out of control. I got into a drunken argument with the label dude from In Music We Trust, and he declined to put out the record. I got fired from Pianos. Again, I bottomed out. Again, I got sober.

I found an apartment with a random gay dude from Craig's List named Esteban. I got a temp assignment. I felt lost and afraid, so I worked hard, as I had always done. My temp assignment turned into a lucrative but meaningless desk job, cooking the books for a crooked general contracting firm that did renovations in the Bloomingdale's building. When I had paid off the credit card debt I had accrued, I offered to send some money home to my mother. But while I was frittering away my student loan money and failing as a singer/songwriter, she had been on the upswing. She'd left

Paul and moved to California. Selling time-shares there had made her enough money that she even bought a condo.

I should have been happy for her. But by saving herself when I had failed to, my mother had undone my raison d'être. By apologizing, my father had robbed me of the nemesis I had been striving to best. I couldn't be angry at him now—he called me at least three times a year! Or maybe just twice. Tatyana had made the grand gesture of naming her first child after me, but when I was on my endless tour, she'd kicked me out of her house, and we'd again stopped talking. Every time I thought of Tashina, I reminded myself that I owed her a phone call. But what I needed to say—I know that, though I swore I'd never abandon you, that's exactly what I've done—was too hard, and the phone call stayed unmade. I burrowed back into alcohol.

But in short order, it wasn't just alcohol. Long hours hunched over a tiny makeshift desk at work aggravated the fickle vertebrae I had injured when I was seventeen. A girl got me started on Vicodin, then Percocet, then Oxycontin. The painkillers did little for the pain, but the high got me through my workdays. My on-off relationship with Shilpa, the singer from Beat the Devil, had turned abusive, so Klonopin and Xanax got me through the nights when she ranted and raged, throwing bottles and mics at my head.

The anniversary of the shooting, then Christmas, then New Year's, then my birthday came and went with no card or phone call or my email from my father. I sent him a card with $20 in it for Father's Day, baiting him: #1 DAD! He didn't respond. Fuck him, anyway. It had been a mistake to try again with him; it was always a mistake. Best to just cut it off clean and walk away. Trying to have a relationship with him, best-case scenario, was a sentence of life in prison without parole. Why fuck around? I'd take a good, honest execution, just get on with it and get it over with, thank you very much.

I managed to patch things up with In Music We Trust, and in the fall of 2007 *How to Make a Bad Situation Worse*, the record I had nearly killed myself to make, finally came out. Nothing happened. I did a national tour, only able to book shows as "the bass player from Beat the Devil." Nothing happened. Beat the Devil broke up.

A part-time girlfriend gave me a full scrip's worth of Opana. Those little pink pills—they looked like cherry-flavored Sweet Tarts—were a dream come true, a vastly superior way to escape myself. Opana cut up beautifully, nothing like that gravelly aspirin-and-Clorox cocaine I strained to get up my nose in bar bathrooms, no coating to scrape off like with Oxycontin. The postnasal drip even tasted good: chemical-like (which I didn't mind) but also slightly sweet. Like Sweet'N Low.

Alcohol, by that point, only made me feel normal. It slightly lifted my spirits and cleared my mind enough that I could string a sentence together and sometimes even crack a joke. My problem wasn't that I was drinking too much; it was that I couldn't drink enough. Alcohol no longer made me feel good; it just made me feel not bad. But snorting Opana made me feel like those old, corny oil paintings of Jesus where he is not just bathed in light but illuminated from within. A couple of lines of that shit, and my body was bursting with love. I could perform miracles, heal with the touch of a hand.

Opana wasn't cheap, but who cared? I was paid well, in cash, off the books. And these bills, they weren't wages. You earned wages at a job. At a job, you learned skills, you made something, you exerted yourself, and you moved forward. I falsified documents with Wite-Out and pencils and a scanner, expended the least amount of energy possible in order to rip off our contractors—men with jobs, men who performed work, men who actually built things. My weekly payout was just a kill fee for my wasted life. When my boss put the thick envelope in my hand each Friday, I felt a base thrill mottled with shame, as if it weren't money at all but some particularly carnal pornography, fascinating as it was repellent.

Money could never buy what I wanted: revenge, the hatred and fear of the public, Allison. So I bought what it *could* buy: drugs. How much do I want? Well, how much have you got?

I cut up line after line of pink powder with my work ID for the Bloomingdales building, hoovered them with rolled-up yellow Post-its I'd stolen, pointlessly, from the office, and nodded off in incredibly strange positions. Taking off my clothes and getting into bed became mutually exclusive: I either slept in my bed with my coat and shoes on or naked in the hallway.

I woke up for work in the mornings with bemused surprise: Wow. Made it through another night. More than once, I found myself shuffling to work on Monday morning wearing the same clothes I'd left in on Friday. I was on time, and my work got done, so my boss rolled with it.

I quit Opana and then published a cavalier, remorseless account of my romance with it in the *New York Press*. Friends I hadn't heard from in years wrote to me, wondering if I was okay; total strangers created blank online profiles just so they could write to me to give me the number for Narcotics Anonymous. I wrote back to everyone, assuring them all that I was okay: it wasn't something I did; it was something I had done and was now finished with.

I was invited to meet Dave Blum, the editor in chief at the *New York Press*. I was a good writer with interesting subject matter, he told me over dinner, and he would use me as much as he could. He had an agent he wanted me to meet, as it sounded like I had a book in me. Finally, I was a writer. I might yet do some good thing with my life. I celebrated my progress by filling another Opana scrip at the Union Square Kmart.

My aggressive apathy at work finally paid off. On the first day of spring, a Thursday, my boss let me know that Friday would be my last day. I felt anger and terror. Was I supposed to beg, to wheedle, to plead for an explanation? I laughed and said, "Okay."

I burst through the door to my apartment that night, furiously crushed up a couple of pills of Opana, stuck my rolled-up bill in the chunky pink powder, and snorted as hard as I could. As the drug came on, I sank to the floor, overflowing with righteous fury and chemical bliss.

When I awoke from my nod, I dragged myself to a bar and went home with a girl I'd met at a show. Alone in her bathroom, I got colossally high. The next day, Friday, I showed up to work on the nod. They gave me my last envelope after lunch and sent me home early—"home" in this case being the Midtown apartment of my drug supplier. We did lines off her parents' antique furniture, fucked on their white leather sofa. We ground up Oxy and Opana and Adderall and coke, mixed it into a huge multicolored line, then did "Lady and the Tramp," with her starting at one end and me at the other. When we met in the middle, we collapsed laughing, naked, then high-fived. Junkies rock!

I awoke that night on the street in Brooklyn, bleeding from my forehead. When I made it to my feet, I saw a yellow cab. I raised my hand to flag it down. The taxi slowly became a police car, and as I slowly lowered my arm, it slowly drove past.

CHAPTER 7

The End of the End

When the housing bubble burst in early 2008, my mother's good fortune burst with it. Her sales slowed, then died, then was let go. A year after her peak prosperity, she was on the verge of losing the home she'd only been able to buy by grinding for fifteen years after losing our family home in New Hampshire. I was still so enraged by that public degradation that I was determined to do anything in my power to prevent it happening again. I flew out to California and brought every penny I had—$10,000—to my mother so she wouldn't lose her home. She declined the money. My life's savings, the sum of all the wealth I had accrued in my time on the planet, wasn't enough to save her house. God, I had failed and failed and failed.

Instead, she recruited me to sell her belongings on Craig's List before she got kicked out, a humiliation with which I was by now intimately familiar. The last day of my visit, I was to help my mother move into a room she had rented in her friend's house, like some delinquent teenager.

I sullenly posted ads on Craig's List for the furniture she had bought while she was flush: a set of overstuffed arm chairs for a loving couple to read in; a red velvet love seat for the lovebirds to cuddle on while watching a movie; a bed large as an island, enveloping like a cloud, where the lovers would begin and end each day together. It had never happened for her; it would never happen. My mother and her friends, the first wives, had been conned. Each had borne and raised her man's children on the promise of "till death do us part," then been cast off, discarded like an old stroller, useless now that the last brat could walk and feed himself. My mother, the woman I loved more than any other, more than *every* other, more than any other being on the planet . . . no good man would ever love her. The good men had kept their promises and stayed married. The successful men had bought new women, women half their age. If my mother's loneliness became too much, Mom would take a man like me: A failure. A loser. A critically flawed man-child.

I posted and reposted her ads all day long, fuming in silence. The instant my mother went to sleep, I railed thick, chalky lines of Opana and chugged her box wine, as I had when I was a kid, then stumbled around her house, gawping at her belongings, as enraged as I was impotent.

When my mom accidentally threw away my hoarded Xanax, I pitched such a tantrum that she not only went through the trash looking for it, she then begged some Valium for me the next day off a girl she knew from work. Wow, I thought, I've even got Mom scoring drugs for me now.

We got drunk playing Scrabble one night, and my mother expressed concern that I was going to kill myself.

"Mom, I promised when I was a kid, and I promise again," I said. "As long as you continue to live, so will I."

"And when I'm gone?"

"Well, you won't be around to bust my chops for breaking a promise, will you?"

She smiled at me sadly. "Well, I plan on living to be ninety, so you'll be sixty by then. You may be ready to go."

"We can catch the same bus."

"Two for one. Kids ride free."

We made light of it in the moment, but it depressed the hell out of me. My own mother seemed resigned to the fact that, best-case scenario, she and I would be kicking off at the same time.

═

When I got back to New York, I returned to that living death, the working life. I begged my way into a job at another construction company in Queens as office manager, a position with more responsibility than the gig I'd previously been fired from. My lack of qualification for the job was only outmatched by my lack of desire to actually perform it.

After a straight month of subpar performance, I got bumped back to a tiny, unheated, windowless office flooded with an inch of standing water. In the move, I found a file cabinet drawer of expired cough syrup samples. Anything cherry-flavored makes me gag from drinking too much cough syrup as a teenager, but these were grape flavored. They got me through a couple of idle weeks.

High on morphine one night, I got a call from the iconoclast comedian Doug Stanhope. He'd heard my songs, he said as I listened in stoned disbelief, and he was a fan. He brought me out on the road, opening for his bleak "fetish comedy" with my songs of drunken-hearted despair. I played to the biggest crowds of my life. People started clapping before I'd even finished—clapping for *me*. I churned out a couple more bleak, druggie dispatches for the *New York Press* to accolades from my friends and even a couple of fan emails. I sold hundreds of dollars' worth of T-shirts and CDs; I took photos with fans; I signed autographs. People picked fights with me; one guy even took a swing at me. I'd been waiting for this my entire life.

These occasional debauched weekends on the road made work bearable, and they made it unbearable. I imagined Stanhope as a foulmouthed, mushroom-gobbling Tinker Bell, silently sprinkling some powder of indeterminate origin in my hair as I hunched over a desk, then whisking me off to a depraved, hedonistic Neverland of free drinks, free drugs, applause and adoration and autographing boobs. Too soon, I was neatly deposited back in front of my hated computer monitor, my pen caddy, my monthly desk calendar, always coming down from something.

One of my most cherished moments was getting booed at the end of my set in Seattle, only to have Doug bound up on stage and come to my defense: "Hey, Fatty! Yeah, you, the date rapist in the back, booing my friend. What do you do for a living, *file shit*? Mishka's a fucking *artist*, man." The crowd roared with laughter. My chest burned with pride. Days later, I was back at work, filing shit. It was funny, funny in a way that made me want to jam my fingers in the paper shredder so I could never work again.

Finally, my chaos alienated even Stanhope. He had been a little thrilled when he found out I was every bit the drunken mess my songs promised. Had that thrill diminished when they held back some of his pay to cover a table I couldn't recall breaking? Or when the club had to call the cops in Portland? Or was that Tacoma? Was it when I had to retain a criminal lawyer? Or was it just the same thing that had plagued me my whole life, that I was almost good enough but not quite?

After one particularly chaotic trip, the show offers stopped coming. Then Stanhope stopped calling. Then he stopped picking up my calls. Then he had a new opener. The carnival never stopped, but if you were careless, it left town without you. Doug was going on with his life. I was left to deal with mine.

My roommate Esteban worked as a dispatcher for a gay escort service and did phone sex from the apartment. I felt for him. Poor fucker was surrounded by sex but unable to get any for himself. In the nearly three years we had lived together, he had never had a dude over. The muffled human sounds that occasionally seeped out of his room—were those pornography or him crying? I couldn't decide which I found more repellant: the thought of my morbidly obese roommate masturbating to gay porn or a human being feeling an honest emotion in such close proximity.

Esteban ate terribly—White Castle and TV dinners and heaping plates of fried chicken, plantains, greasy rice and beans—and his weight steadily increased. Esteban blacked out on the toilet, naked, his long black hair hiding his face. Esteban vomited in the bathtub and didn't clean it up. Esteban locked himself out one night, so he smashed a window in order to get back in, badly cutting his arm. Another night, he showered drunk, then opened the wrong door on his way back to his room and fell down two flights of stairs. Our eighty-year-old landlady, Doris, found him at the base of the stairs, naked, bleeding, and barely conscious.

Esteban wasn't all bad. He was friendly to the ragged parade of sad women trooping in and out of my half of the apartment. Like me, he sang in the shower. My sympathy for his situation was not entirely destroyed by having to live with him. We had a kind of grim understanding, like characters in a Beckett play: each of us deserved the mute horrors of the other.

Bleak as my life was, I knew I had to succeed at my job. But work was impossible. I was useless for hours of the workday, sweating and nauseated and lightheaded. My mother had sacrificed so much for me. It was time for me to sacrifice for her. Just be the good son, I told myself, and get it together.

I finally did some research on my magic bullet, Opana. It was a Schedule II synthetic opiate more powerful than Oxycontin, morphine, and pharmaceutical heroin. Indeed, Opana was so treasured by junkies and other opiophiles that it had been pulled off the market in the 1970s after a string of pharmacy robberies. In the 1989 Gus Van Sant movie *Drugstore Cowboy*, Opana was the pharmacy bandits' drug of choice. A commenter on an opiate message board wrote, "I've been shooting heroin for 27 years and I've never had anything like this." What had I gotten myself into? I would kick it, cold turkey.

Removing painkillers from your life means inserting pain. My back knotted, then seized. I writhed my sheets into wet vines at night, gulping handfuls of Advil and Aleve, unable to sleep. Each night that passed, I grew more and more exhausted but somehow never got so tired that my body could take the sleep it needed. I felt possessed, like my skeleton was writhing under my flesh. I was visited so often by phantoms—a hanged man; an impossibly tall faceless man in a dark robe; the skeleton of a child; a dancing, empty dress; a drowned twelve-year-old boy, naked except for a dripping hooded sweatshirt—that I half convinced myself that my room was haunted.

The pressure I put on myself to succeed at my job failed to motivate me to work hard. It only made me hate myself when I couldn't force myself to try. My boss threw money at me, but I couldn't be paid to care. The nihilist in me rose up, and I decided to see how long I could go without doing any actual work, trying to make my situation completely unbearable in hopes that something would happen, anything. Finally, I made it through an entire day without doing a single work-related thing. Nothing happened. I quit in disgust.

≡

The day before a December show with Rumanian Buck, a band I'd started with Aaron and Chen, my two most constant friends, I swung by the Christmas party at Pianos for "just one beer." I progressed rapidly, from beer to shots of Jameson, to bumps of coke, to drinking late into the morning with the metal security gate pulled down, to a near-fistfight with a cab driver who refused to take me over the bridge into Brooklyn. I glanced at the clock in my room when I finally shuffled in. My "just one beer" had concluded at 11:55 the following morning, fourteen hours and over $120 later.

I woke up in the early afternoon, still drunk, unable to get back to sleep. I kept drinking. It was the only way I was going to make it through the show that night at Santo's Party House.

I took one of those big twenty-milligram Adderalls once I got to the club. Just before we went on, I snorted the blow still in my jeans pocket from the night before. Remaining upright was a challenge if I stood in one place, but as long as I kept moving, I was okay.

The show was fine. It's not like it was my first time playing fueled by chemicals alone. Chen's guitar was too loud, but it covered up any changes I may have muffed.

Afterward, Chen threw me the keys to his van. He was wasted and going home with some girl. Fine, I was okay to drive. Or at least more okay than usual.

When I went outside to bum a cigarette, a girl with pale skin and pale blue-green eyes was leaning on a rail, drawing angrily on a Parliament. Her hair was bleached so white it was nearly gray, trailing down to the middle of her back like mist. She'd been at one of our other shows, chasing Aaron around, shitfaced. I'd stared at her tight jeans and thought, *I* deserve that girl.

She turned her eyes up at me when I walked outside.

"You're hot," she rasped.

"You're hot," I dumbly returned.

She blew out a lungful of smoke.

"You wanna go?" she said.

"Sure."

She turned to a friend of mine, who was standing next to her.

"Is he a rapist?"

"He's never raped *me*," my buddy grinned.

That satisfied her. She threw down her cigarette, stamped it out, and looked at me expectantly.

"One sec," I said. I walked back in the club, grabbed my jacket, and threw the keys to the van at Aaron. They hit him in the chest and fell to the floor.

"Tag. You're it."

He looked at me, then down at the keys on the floor.

"Aw, fuck, man, come on, I can't—"

A moment later this girl and I were in a cab, headed back to my place. When I asked her name, she lifted her head from my crotch to answer, "Oksana."

Oksana peeled her clothes off the minute we got into my apartment. She climbed up into my loft bed and laid there, full, firm breasts and a taut, muscular body. I felt like I was staring at a pile of amphetamines: I knew that it would ruin my life, and I could not wait to get started.

When I couldn't manage anything even remotely resembling an erection, she mocked me. "What am I supposed to do with *this*?" she said, flicking my useless cock, shriveled like some frightful war relic.

Later, she wept raggedly and spilled a sorrowful tale. A week after her father died of cancer, her brother had committed suicide, and she had found his body. Her fiancée had died a year previously from a drug overdose. Now her mother was dying of cancer. It seemed unreal, so much grief in one short life. I wouldn't have believed her story had I not heard stories to rival it.

It had clearly taken a toll on her. It was eerie watching her flip from coquettish to enraged to weeping to laughing hysterically, like a TV changing stations when someone is sitting on the remote. I couldn't make sense of all that loss—no one could—but maybe I could distract her for a minute, make her laugh? God knows I didn't want to be alone.

In the morning, I came to my senses. I could not tangle with her again. She was damaged. I mean, we all were. This world chewed you up. Especially women. But something about Oksana was different. I was like wet matches, but she was like wet dynamite.

She was a sweet girl, I told her, with a lot going for her, but we should go our separate ways. I wouldn't be good for her. She laughed, then pouted, but eventually she left. My self-preservation skills were finally getting better.

Six weeks later, I was still waking up to Oksana. I avoided her, ignored her texts, calls, and emails. I dodged her at my band's shows, hiding behind mailboxes and potted plants like some soused private inspector. But Oksana was everywhere I went, not just shows my bands played but every show I went to, brash and flirty in one of those dresses where it's obvious the girl is naked underneath, eye-fucking me while carefully writhing a nipple free from the top of her dress.

When I quizzed her as to why, in a city of nearly 9 million people, she had glommed on to a penniless problem drinker with no interest in her, she couldn't explain her fascination with me. When I politely rejected her, she sniffled into her wine. Then one of those three ghosts she'd summoned that first night—brother, father, lover—would rematerialize. Tonight was her brother's birthday; it was the anniversary of her father's death; it was the anniversary of the wedding she'd never had, she'd had a horrible vision of her fiancée's dead body in a dream. The cancer had finally killed her mother, and, no, she didn't want to talk about it, but she couldn't stand to be alone, not tonight.

To resist her now was to court disaster. She would flip out, screaming. She'd throw glasses, throw punches. She'd demand to see the club's manager and make insane accusations. Without a doubt, Oksana was crazy. Not kooky or offbeat or eccentric—crazy, like slash-your-tires, stab-you-with-a-broken-bottle, burn-your-fucking-house-down crazy. Of course, the only quality that eclipsed her mental instability was her physical beauty. God, she looked amazing, hair and skin so white it appeared to luminesce in the darkness of my room, illuminated only by the glow of the digital numbers on my hated alarm clock, her body so long and narrow but still curvy and muscular, like a pale serpent. Poisonous, of course.

But those calves, the calves of a high school track star . . . and the first time I stuck my hand up her dress, she was soaking wet. Her eyes, intense and mercurial blue-green, like absinthe, one of them looking right at you: clocking, measuring, thinking, and understanding. And the other one in some fucked-up parallel universe—Cocainia—untouched by reason, logic, reality, or a single word of warning that came out of my mouth.

Each time I encountered her, I coolly assessed that sleeping with her even once had been a mistake. Then I made a mental list of the specific ways in which sleeping with her again would tragically compound that mistake. Then I got shitfaced and took her home.

My loneliness was so intense, it was like a physical affliction. Disappearing into her body was the quick fix that made the condition worse. As neat a trick as it was to feel lonely in a crowd, it was some next-level shit to feel alone while you were *inside* someone else. She had accused me once of wanting to fuck her doggie-style in order to pretend she was someone else. I wanted her facing away so I could pretend I didn't exist.

Every time I woke up next to her, I'd hate myself for my weakness, for my willingness to drag others down with me, and I'd resent her for allowing it. Demeaning as that pattern of attraction and repulsion was for me, it must have been baffling and exquisitely painful for her.

My mother was back in the Virgin Islands, as she had free lodging with the owners of the property she'd managed the first time she'd fled the country and her hard luck. I bought a ticket for a three-week trip with my diminishing savings. Not cheap, but it'd be worth it to see my mother, dry out, make a break from Oksana, and dodge a couple of weeks of the miserable Brooklyn winter.

St. John was gorgeous. The weather was divine. We were broke. God fucking damn it, Mom and I were always broke. My daily chore was to harvest all the green papayas and ripe coconuts I could find on our side of the island. Eggs with fried shredded green papaya for breakfast; a can of tuna and a coconut for lunch; stuffed green papaya or green papaya lasagna for dinner. Jesus, canned tuna and eggs, the protein of poverty, every day of my pathetic life. We even went chicken hunting one day, giggling together, trying to snare one of the birds that had gone feral on the island with the long hooked pole I'd made to reach the mangos on the tops of the trees. All we got for our troubles were some funny looks from the local West Indians.

My mother and I alternated sleeping in the one available bed—a dilapidated old mattress with springs sticking into your back—and on the hardwood floor on a cushion from a deck chair that had been the dog's bed until she died.

Dry out? After years of rampant inflation, the price of local rum had risen to the princely sum of $4 a bottle—cheaper than orange juice. Alcohol wasn't sinful; it was sound financial planning, cheaper and more transporting than food. St. John may have been the worst place in the world to dry out, but at least I had finally made the break from Oksana.

I hadn't been back in New York for an hour before we were back in bed together. Jesus, I wasn't even drunk. We had sex twice. After the second time, she cried. I couldn't bear it anymore. I told her for the umpteenth time that we had to stop this, now and forever. It wasn't good for me. It was very bad for her. She shouldn't prostrate herself before any man, least of all me. Finally, she seemed to understand.

I locked my apartment door behind her, then walked over to the window to make sure she had actually left the building. I didn't know whether to feel sympathy or contempt for her frenzied attempts to pump hope into something so obviously hopeless. Oksana, it's a dusty fiberglass skeleton, like a prop from an Indiana Jones movie; no amount of CPR is going to bring it to life. I pitied Oksana, but pity wasn't love. If anything, pity was the opposite of love.

I crawled back into my bed and curled up in relief. Felt like a cold was coming on. I'd try to sleep in hopes of feeling better before my door shift in a few hours.

"You piece of shit, you're a fucking *doorman*," the drunk chick said, her lip curling with contempt around the last word as she swayed in front of me. "Is this what you wanted to do with your life? Check fucking IDs and be an asshole?"

Point taken. It was pitiable, indeed, to be a thirty-two-year-old doorman on Ludlow Street in February. I'd lorded over Pianos four years earlier, a night manager high on power, drunk on top-shelf liquor. I'd had to beg the guy who fired me for a gig as a lowly doorman, like a dog returning to its vomit. Was I going to be *that guy* and inform her of my scholarly achievements? "Ivy League doorman" was like a garnish of edible orchids and coils of paper-thin-sliced blood oranges placed next to a huge, steaming dog turd.

I reached for the most sarcastic tone I could muster.

"Okay, I was kinda undecided before, but now I'm *definitely* going to let you in."

A stupid line, less than I wanted to say and more than I should have. I stood between the girl and the door, so there was absolutely no confusion. Working in bars for ten years, you learn that monosyllabic grunts and hard stares are the best way to deal with irate partygoers denied entry. If everyone hated me, well, it was my job to be hated, and I was good at it.

The drunk chick—short with flat, dead-looking mousy brown hair, wearing an ill-fitting green party dress with a parka thrown over it to combat the cold weather—mad-dogged me as her boyfriend tugged meekly on her tiny arm. All her color, even the color of her clothes, was washed out, as if she were just a crappy, sunbleached, low-rez printout of herself.

"This is your life? This is what you *do*?" she said. "Stand out in the cold and watch everybody else party and get fucked up and dance and get laid while you stand here? Are you happy? Are you happy with your life? Is this what you came to New York to do, to be a fucking doorman?"

Which finally hit a nerve.

It came out half hiss and half growl, the most cutting thing I could think of to say.

"You have bad skin."

The nearby eavesdroppers recoiled. It was true; her skin was pitted and pallid and uneven. Sometimes cruelty flows through me unchecked.

The chick took an unsteady half step back with a huff of pain, then lunged at me. I swept her to the side with one arm, and she stumbled into her boyfriend.

Themy and Jimmy, the two bouncers, Greeks with chests so thick their girth must have exceeded their height, stepped in and quickly moved the girl and her boyfriend down the block.

The Greeks were old-school mafia strongmen. They liked me because, unlike most of the other doormen, I was comfortable with violence. Getting jumped was the only redeeming part of the job. I was allowed to fight back, spinning some frat boy's head with a hook or just dropping him with a kick to the side of his knee before the Greeks moved in. When a guy with his foot in a cast menaced me with an upraised crutch, I told him that if he hit me with that crutch, I would break his other leg, and he would crawl home. The Greeks laughed about that all night.

My right sinus, the one behind my preferred coke nostril, throbbed like someone was trying to jam a pencil into my brain. "Folks, please have your IDs out!" I called to the line and started shuffling more people into Pianos. My fingers were sticky with snot on their IDs. Weekend nights like this, all the fucking amateurs were out. Gone were the day-trader financial slime and their sublime, disgusting plastic porno angel dates. Even the clubby Israelis and Eurotrash had fled, replaced with fattening sorority girls, short men with adult acne, glasses, and black Amex cards, and foreign tourists, flabbergasted to be expected to both carry ID *and* tip their bartenders. I hoped I got every one of them sick.

I glanced at my cell phone to check the time while a chubby girl in leopard print, stinking of garlic, nicotine, and bubble gum, rooted sloppily in her purse for her ID. A text had come in from Oksana: "im pregnant. its yours. thought it wld be selfish to tell you but fuck that. so tx a fuckin ton. i hate you with all my heart."

I didn't get off until 4 a.m. It wasn't even midnight. Looking like a long night.

—

Shuffling back to Brooklyn, 4:30 in the morning, four miles to my Bukowskian alcoholic flop in Greenpoint. This was a measure of the progress I'd made from walking to my job at the pizza place in Massachusetts in February when I was seventeen: my frigid winter's walk was now two miles longer.

The Williamsburg Bridge alone remains undiminished after ten years in the city. As you climb, all you can see in front of you is the cracked gray asphalt lit orange by the sodium streetlights, the growl of trucks rumbling up from either side. But when you pass the juncture where the bridge splits in two, glance back over your left shoulder: the night city yawns open with promise, glittering orange and black. If your eyes are blurred with tears, the city dissolves into a series of shiny orbs centered on the glow of the streetlights and neon signs, like alien eggs, a tiny, bright speck surrounded by a sphere of shimmering amniotic fluid, glimmering with hope, soon to burst open with new life.

Then the great gulf of swirling black water—the bridge is high enough that the impact of your body hitting the surface is usually enough to kill you—and the sight line narrows again to gray asphalt ringed by chain-link fencing, the path now angled down, down into Brooklyn.

—

Morning came late in the afternoon. My skin felt slick and greasy against the bare mattress. In the shower, I made the water as hot as I could stand it, then gingerly lowered myself into the bathtub.

As I lay there, I realized it was bullshit. No fucking way Oksana was pregnant. How many nights had we been together in total? Five? Seven? She told me she went on the pill like two days after the second time we fucked. Which was both too late and jumping the gun, if you thought about it.

Though I couldn't pinpoint exactly the last time we had got it on before I'd left town, I knew she'd been on the rag. I remember being surprised when Oksana offered up her ass without preamble. Afterward, I was kind of stunned when I rolled off her to go to the bathroom and noticed the white cotton string hanging from her crotch. It was increasingly rare for me to encounter someone more debased than I was, but that moment with her, well, it had saddened me.

I remembered cleaning up her blood in the bathroom the morning after. Jesus, the bulk of my life seemed to involve cleaning up blood in the bathroom the morning after. So she'd been on the rag then and couldn't have gotten pregnant. And that was when? The night before I left for the Virgin Islands.

Lying in the bathtub, the water hammering down, I tried to count the weeks on my fingers like some big dumb monkey. Okay, four weeks. She wouldn't have even missed a period yet. It was impossible for her to be pregnant! An awful accusation to make, faking a pregnancy, but Oksana had lied at every opportunity, lied with passion and conviction and boundless creativity, anything to manipulate a situation to maximize the attention she got.

Oksana had modeled nude for a painter friend of mine but swore she hadn't fucked him. I kept texting her about it until she thought she was busted. I had been kidding around. I had no inkling she'd actually done it until she confessed. The first time she went home with me, she said it was just to get a rise out of Aaron, who had turned her down. After the third time, she declared that she wasn't just in love but that she had loved me from the moment she saw me. Didn't seem fair that love could be retroactive like that.

I had gingerly removed her from Pianos one night when I was working. The next day, her hand was in a splint—she spread the word that she'd had to make a trip to the ER for a sprained wrist. But she hadn't fallen when I carefully carried her out. And the splint disappeared after a day or two. And, shit, that night I'd expressed concern to a friend of Oksana's about Oksana's mother's death, the friend rolled her eyes and said, "She cooked us dinner last week." Lie after lie after lie.

This pregnancy thing had to be bullshit. I hoisted myself out of the shower, dried off, and wandered to the window.

Brooklyn in winter is the only thing that makes both Los Angeles and suicide seem equally appetizing. My building faces the highway, the front windows opening onto the brick balustrades of the majestic Brooklyn-Queens Expressway. We are in the last dying breath of Greenpoint, a jumping-off point, the last way station before you finally give up completely. Immediately to our left is a string of crumbling industrial buildings stinking of rotting lettuce and raw chicken parts, with decrepit RVs permanently parked in front, tiny, stooped men emerging from them late at night to empty white plastic buckets of human waste into the street. Somehow, I still manage to get my car towed every couple of months.

Beyond that, over the bridge to Queens, is a huge graveyard, First Cavalry Cemetery. Driving past it, what you notice first is that the skyscrapers in Manhattan are the same size and shape as the tombstones.

Behind us are yards that process scrap metal—the heavy grilles from abandoned air conditioners, copper wiring from abandoned buildings, junk cars, stolen catalytic converters. The monolithic upright teats of the sewage treatment plant glisten behind the scrap yards. Men covered in grease, stinking of alcohol and other chemicals, their humanity well atrophied, haul shopping carts overflowing with metal viscera in that direction every late afternoon, their daily pilgrimage. There but for the grace of Mom go I.

Escape in front of me, salvage behind me, death to the left, and to my right, The City That Can't Get to Sleep. Sometimes you don't need to reach for a metaphor because you live right in the center of it.

Have you seen me? You may have, driving by my apartment one late night or early morning. My window flashes by too quickly, just a glimpse of a troubling tableau: a naked man with a pale, hollow chest and raccoon eyes, his hand clutching something dark that you can't quite make out: A bottle? A knife? A gun? Did it worry you? Did it register at all?

I did not disappear because I was moving past you with tremendous speed. I disappeared because your world is flowing past me as I stand here—drinking, watching, waiting—absolutely still.

≡

I called Oksana. She'd already made an appointment with Planned Parenthood. So it was real.

I heard myself offering to sell a guitar to pay for the abortion. Such a dick move. Broke as I was, I had enough money left over from my old construction job to just cut her a check.

She sounded surprised that I had offered money, even in a shitty, reluctant way. She said the pregnancy was her fault and her responsibility. If I would just pick her up at the clinic afterward and let her recover at my house, that would be fine.

≡

That snowy first Monday in March, I drove slowly into Manhattan, feeling like a villain. There was no parking by the clinic. I parked illegally around the corner and put my hazard lights on. Then I paced back and forth in the falling snow, from my car to the entrance of the clinic, trying to scoop Oksana up quickly so she wouldn't have to walk far in the snow while I avoided getting a parking ticket.

I had almost given up when I saw her, a block away from the exit, walking toward the clinic, looking vacant and confused. I called to her, wondering how I could have missed her, got her seated in my car, and then drove her to my place. She slept most of the day. I dropped her off that night when I headed into the city to cover another door shift at the bar. I told her I would get her safely to her door, but she insisted I just drop her at the subway. It occurred to me that I'd never been to her apartment, that I had no idea where she lived, not even the neighborhood.

"Will you call me?" she said mournfully after she got out. She looked so pitiable there with the snow coming down.

"No," I said. "I can't. This mistake we've been making . . . we can't make it anymore. We've done something we can't undo." Cruel? Yes. But less cruel than letting her continue to injure herself on me.

She gave me one last mournful look, then hunched up her shoulders and trudged away.

Three days later, I met up with Chen at a show. He didn't have rent money for his rehearsal space. Some money had cleared from eBaying a guitar, so I brought him $250 so he could get current.

I got a text from Oksana, inviting me to her birthday party down at Lit Lounge.

"Jesus, Chen, look at this," I said, showing him her text. It had only been three days since I'd picked her up from the clinic. Were we now supposed to do shots together?

"I know, I know. I just got the same text."

I texted her back and politely but firmly declined. I'd been serious when I said we could no longer see each other, I told her. Yes, I'd hurt her, and that sucked, but it was also inevitable. It happened to everyone who touched me.

But, together, we had crossed a line. We had come too close to a seriously untenable situation: an unstable cokehead and a morose drunk with zero real affection for one another, bound together forever by an unforgivable sin: the thoughtless creation of another unwanted human being.

That's how I had started. And now . . . well, I wasn't a monster. Monsters did things. Bad things, true, but I didn't do *anything*. I was more akin to a catfish—a mundane scavenger, a bottom-feeder, nosing around in the dark, living off anything dead and rotting, primitive and ugly, with no conscience or even consciousness, living just to fruitlessly copulate and consume. The best thing—the only good thing—I was capable of was making sure my father's mistake ended with me.

My phone buzzed angrily in my pocket, a flurry of caustic texts from Oksana. I read them all, one after another, but didn't respond. If I had learned anything from this life, it was how to absorb an attack without reacting.

Chen said that he'd try to calm her down. He was headed in that direction anyway, so he'd stop off for one drink and placate her. He could do that, have just one drink. What a friend he was to sign up for dealing with a drunken, angry Oksana.

I got drunk. I met another girl, Laura. We got drunker in some shitty fake Irish Midtown bar. She stayed over. We made out but didn't sleep together. I was supposed to want it. That was all there was, right? The Wetness and the Darkness, liquor and pussy, animal pleasure and oblivion? This was what I did; I got drunk and slept with women. That night, I just couldn't force myself to do it. There was a gaping chasm inside me. You could throw woman after woman into that pit. Hundreds! Thousands! You'd never even hear them hit bottom.

The next day, Laura and I were heading to my car so I could drive her to the subway. I unlocked her car door and held it open for her. I heard a yell.

"Hey, asshole!"

I looked up and instantly recoiled: Oksana. Rumpled party dress, fishnets in shreds, her mascara dripping onto her cheeks like black fangs. Jesus, had she slept at all?

"Oh boy," I said to Laura. "Um . . . just get in the car and lock your door, okay?"

I slipped around to the other side and managed to get inside and get my door locked before Oksana reached the car. She hammered on my window, howling.

"I can explain, I swear," I said to Laura. We both knew I couldn't.

When it was clear the glass wasn't going to break, Oksana planted herself in front of my car so we couldn't leave. I turned my wheel to the right, and she moved to my right, her hands on the hood. I cranked the wheel to the left, and she moved to my left. Shit. Drunk and in high heels, Oksana was still pretty quick.

I slid my hands on the wheel like I was turning right and again, she moved to the right. But the wheels were still pointed to the left, so I pinned the accelerator and peeled out.

Oksana squawked and flung her hot coffee at my windshield as we were escaping. I blew through a stop sign, then turned the windshield wipers on, which just smeared the coffee across the whole windshield.

"This happen to you often?" Laura asked with a wry smile.

When I dropped Laura off at the Bedford L, I had another text from Oksana: "Just so you know, I fucked Chen last night. U r the biggest asshole I have ever known."

Chen and I had been through all kinds of shit together. He'd played drums for me on my first tour six years earlier. He'd lived with me when his marriage was falling apart. He'd driven ten hours through the middle of the night to pick me up when my van died in Athens, Ohio, on tour.

We were thick as thieves. The winter before, I'd worked some ridiculous security gig for a Hennessy party one night and nicked a $300 bottle of cognac on my way out. Chen and I had worked our way through the bottle together, him on the floor and me in my bed, sipping it out of coffee cups and giggling in the dark.

Jacob had told me, before he died, that he was honest about different things with different people in his life—his mother, his girlfriend, his drug counselor. But there was no one person with whom he was totally honest about everything. If he had just one person with whom he was totally honest, he was sure he could kick heroin. Chen was that person for me. We told each other the stuff we couldn't tell anyone else, not just our triumphant nights or petty struggles but the real shit, the fear, the weakness, the mounting darkness.

Chen had plenty of girls. Ladies loved him. That he would take my loan and then go sleep with a girl with whom I was embroiled in such an acrimonious separation, three days after she'd had an abortion—impossible.

As I was walking into my building, my eighty-year-old landlady peeked her head out of her apartment.

"Um, hi, honey, I'm sorry to bother you . . . "

"Oh, no bother, Doris, what's up?"

She tottered out into the hallway, clinging to the door frame for support. She had been quick and spry when I moved in but lately had been going downhill quickly. I did everything I could not to bother her, even slipping my rent under her door so she wouldn't have to climb the stairs to my apartment.

"Well, your girlfriend rang my bell this morning. She said she had to get into your apartment. I don't have a key so I couldn't let her in."

Good God.

"Uh . . . wow. Um . . . you did the right thing, Doris. I don't have a girlfriend. No one should be going into my apartment other than me and Esteban."

"Okay, hon, that's what I thought."

"Thank you so much, Doris. I'm so sorry that she bothered you."

"Oh, it's okay, sweetheart. Have a good day now."

This was spiraling out of control. What was Oksana doing in Greenpoint before noon anyway? She lived in Manhattan. I called Chen at work.

"Hey, man. Uh . . . you didn't sleep with Oksana, did you?"

"What? No, of course not. Dude, I would *never* do something like that to you."

"I mean, I don't have any claim over her so I couldn't really be mad about it. I would just want to know."

"Dude, *no*. She's yours. I'm with Kara anyway. Why would you even ask a question like that?"

"She texted me this morning saying you guys had got it on."

"Ugh. Man, she's just trying to find other ways to get under your skin. Don't let that bitch get to you."

"Okay, man. I . . . I'm glad I called you about it."

But something about it stuck in my head.

Sunday, I got drunk at Pianos, trying to put it all together. When I was drunk enough, I called Chen and asked him to come pick me up. As we were driving over the Williamsburg Bridge back into Brooklyn, I told him that I knew he'd lied to me, that I knew he'd been with Oksana, and he just needed to tell me.

He told me to fuck off, that this was total bullshit. What kind of an asshole friend was I to accuse him of something like that? I jumped out at the McGuinness exit ramp while the van was still moving and ran off.

One of them was lying to me. Oksana had reason to. She had a history of not just mildly plausible lies like this one but ridiculous confabulations. Why did I believe her and not Chen?

I went to Daddy's, another bar. I drank more, then went outside. It was raining, a warm, light, cloying rain, like hangover sweat. It couldn't be true.

I called Oksana and cussed her out for sowing doubt about my friendship with Chen. She screamed at me for a while. Then she broke down and started crying.

"What the fuck," she said between sobs, "I couldn't believe it either."

I hung up. Was this her greatest performance? Or was she for once telling the truth?

Then I got the craziest idea.

I sent Oksana a carefully worded text: "Just so you know, Chen has herpes. You may want to get checked out."

Seconds later, my phone rang. It was Chen.

"What the fuck, dude, why are you going around spreading lies about me?"

He was livid.

"What are you talking about?" I said.

"You told Oksana I had *herpes*. I don't have fucking herpes!"

"Chen," I said, "you are fucking *busted*. I texted Oksana thirty seconds ago. The only way you would know is if she had called you in a panic after she got the text. She would only be panicked if you guys had fucked. You are totally busted, you fucking asshole."

Chen started talking, but I hung up; then I turned off my phone. I couldn't breathe, like I had been kicked in the throat.

Oksana had wanted to see me on her birthday, and I'd refused. Chen had gone to see her, Chen had gone home with her, and Chen had fucked her *three days* after she'd had an abortion.

I paced in front of Daddy's. I was floating in a cesspool with two humans devoid of humanity, reduced to just their appetites, one for sex and one for love. It was vile, and it was chilling. Of the three of us, who was the most debased?

Tragic as Chen and Oksana were, I was worse. I would eat anything, drink anything, snort anything, do anything just to escape. If Chen wanted sex and Oksana wanted her twisted version of love, well, at least they wanted something. What I wanted was the absence of everything: nada, nihil, zero.

Now there were real casualties. Oksana and I had created and destroyed a life. And what about Oksana? She was someone's daughter. She was crazy, but it was crazy born out of pain, pain I'd only added to. Because I couldn't stand to be alone. *Because I wanted to get laid.*

I thought of my sisters, Tatyana and Tashina, and how many times I'd seen them cry because a man like me had hurt them. I thought about them waiting outside an abortion clinic in a snow-storm, wondering if the drunk they'd been sleeping with was actually going to show up to give them a ride. Christ, Oksana was younger than Tashina, younger than my baby sister.

I thought of Oksana going under the knife and then, only days later, laying under Chen just to get revenge on me, a worthless man who had only magnified her feelings of worthlessness. This certainly hadn't been a walk in the park for me. I'd been shedding friends at an alarming rate these last few years, and now I'd lost my confidant, my confessor, my last unconditional ally. But Oksana seemed to have lost her self entirely.

I stepped back into the bar. I pounded the drink that I had left sitting by the door. I grabbed my coat off my barstool. On my way out, I pounded the drinks of the people smoking outside, then stumbled out into the rain.

My mother, my poor, beleaguered mother. She had sacrificed so much to make sure I got what I needed from the very day I was born: milk and colorful toys and stuffed animals and then Legos and mac 'n' cheese and shin guards and a baseball glove right up to losing the fucking house, just so I could go to school to turn out to be . . . what? A doorman. A drunk. A liar, a weasel, a waste. I began to cry.

At fifteen, in those horrible twenty-four hours of the shooting and the news of my parents' divorce, I had decided in a self-pitying fury that I was brilliant and doomed. At thirty-two, it was more painful to discover that I was neither brilliant nor doomed, just an entitled, self-hating crybaby.

I was no tortured artist. How little I had created between my benders and my hangovers . . . I'd intended to die in some gutter motel, a bottle in one hand and a guitar in the other, long before I made thirty. I hadn't even followed through on that. I had lived into my fourth decade only out of inertia, bored and captive to my own limitations like the normals I hated, except dead broke.

And the *potential* I'd been hounded about since I was a kid? The only potential I had fulfilled was my tremendous capacity for failing. It wasn't just that I had been hustling in NYC for ten years without making it as a musician or a writer. I had never even made it as a bartender.

What was that first, worst hurt, that trauma of key importance that would explain all the shitty behavior that had followed? The hopelessness of my adolescence—the shooting, the divorce, losing the house—it had warped me, like one of those sad sea turtles whose shell has deformed to accommodate the six-pack holder that has ensnared it. But I had been a prick long before that.

I couldn't remember a time when I hadn't been an asshole, all the way back to when I was probably five years old. At the kids' table one night when my parents had friends over for dinner, I punched Tatyana in the face so hard that I knocked her tooth out. I mixed soy sauce and seltzer water, told Tashina it was Coke, and then ridiculed her when she trusted me, drank it, and gagged. I stole, I lied, I pooped in the bathtub. I ducked down in the backseat of our car whenever we drove by the police station, convinced they were going to throw me in jail.

From the first moment I had known myself, I had understood that I was worthless. My mother had tried desperately to sway me over to the other side, but she'd never succeeded, not for any lasting time. Weakness was more repellent to me than anything else . . . and when it came to weakness, Jesus, I hit it out of the fucking park. Not a lick of self-control, a crawling slave to my appetites, tugging at my prick the minute I was left alone like a chimpanzee, a prisoner of my fears and anxieties and doubts, so fucking soft, all resolution crumpling at the slightest momentary desire. How could I fault Chen or Oksana for their weakness? Weakness coursed through me like I was an antenna; I drew weakness out of the air around me.

A small, exquisitely painful truth came to me. Nothing bad had ever happened to me. I had nothing to blame my bad behavior on. I'd had a few bad breaks, but who hadn't? Yet I had reacted by burrowing so deep into my own pain that it became all I could see. Had I ever once been happy in my life? I fanned through my memories like a stack of index cards. Yes. Once.

One evening before we had left Canada, my dad had taken me for a walk after dinner. I must have been very young, maybe four. He was wearing brown polyester slacks and a yellow, short-sleeve, button-down shirt with black shoes. I was wearing brown corduroys and a yellow, short-sleeve, button-down shirt with bare feet. I was just like him, except little. My dad was the coolest guy in the world. I realized that, because I was a little like him, I was a little bit cool as well.

The memory made me emit a stifled half-sob. A woman walking past me took a hopping step away, and her boyfriend gave me a look. Nothing to see here, folks, just another damaged Brooklyn man-child with bad tattoos and a drinking problem and daddy issues. More plentiful than pigeons, much less exciting.

═══

In the wee hours of May 13, 2009, I began to drink. The preceding day had been a stressful one. I'd been recruited a month earlier to join my old pal Zack's band, Freshkills, for a ten-day tour of England starting the next day. After the sun went down, I ate some Adderall so I could stay up to pack and do other last-minute errands. At around 2 a.m., it became clear that I was actually going to finish everything I needed to do, so I cracked open a Coors Light. Far from my first choice, but it had been a long time since I'd allowed myself to keep hard liquor or even wine in the house.

I worked my way through the six-pack and polished off an old vial of cocaine I had in my drug box, a miniature wooden chest that had been a gift to the groomsmen at Chen's wedding. A couple of days after our blowout, he had confessed to sleeping with Oksana and quit our band. A couple of days after that, he met me at the practice space to pay me back.

"Mishka," he said, "I'm sorry."

He held out the money he owed me. I counted it and put it in my pocket.

"Thank you for paying me back," I said. "And now, you're dead to me."

Shortly after 3 a.m., I left the house lugging my effect pedal board and a duffel bag my mom had given me over twenty years earlier, when we moved to the United States. "You're a big boy now," she had said, "and it makes sense for you to have a grown-up bag." I headed toward the rehearsal space to meet up with the rest of the band, stopping off at a bar just before last call to suck down a couple of Jameson doubles. A hired minivan picked us up with all our gear, and we were on our way.

I was pretty loose by the time we got through security at Newark Airport. I wanted to make sure I slept as much as possible on the overseas flight, so I chewed up a couple of Xanax when we were at our gate. My band mates had to carry me onto the plane.

There may be no better country to drink in than England. Why had no one mentioned to me that it was legal to drink on the street there? Though we'd never met him before, the first guy we crashed with had beer, coke, and weed laid in for us. Someone—not me— even sprang for a bottle of whiskey.

England was a welcome interruption from the knot of trouble my life had become. Our shows were uniformly unmemorable (at least I don't remember them), but with 9 percent beer and cider at every corner store and codeine for sale over the counter, I went for it like we were playing sold-out stadiums. I felt light in a country where no one knew me, unencumbered by the cell phone that had lately brought so much bad news, so many direct personal attacks that I'd had to change the number I'd held for ten years.

I starved myself so I could spend the little money I'd brought on intoxicants. While most of my band indulged in steaks and scotch, the drummer and I drank in the park like hobos. I was accustomed to a near-constant stream of chemicals, but coupled with the lack of food, they wreaked strange havoc on me.

In a dream, I encountered Allison in a bombed-out parking lot after a busted gig. She was leaning against an ancient pickup truck. Her honey hair glowed in the imperfect urban dark, her big eyes wise with patience and pain. Most of her weight rested on her right leg, and her right hip jutted out sinisterly, as if her disappointment in me had calcified under her skin. She looked older but defiantly beautiful, like a Dust Bowl–era migrant worker, determined to survive. One child straddled her cocked hip, and another stood next to her, holding her hand and peering out at me from behind her leg. Neither of them looked like me. Allison told me that my father was dead and I had been charged with seeing to his burial.

The funeral home was a disaster. The coffin was propped up on two sawhorses, and the lid didn't fit right. I started screaming at the director—my father at least deserved to be treated with dignity in death—and accidentally knocked the coffin over, spilling my father's gauze-wrapped corpse onto the floor. When I bent over to cradle his body to try to get it back into the coffin, I felt it twist under me. I heard old bones grind, and I felt his teeth, sharp in my shoulder, as his skull tried to bite me through the disintegrating shroud.

On the flight home, I vigorously abused Virgin Airlines' complimentary cocktail policy even after the stewardesses stopped walking the aisles offering them. I'd totter back to where the flight attendants were strapped into their tiny folding seats, trying to sleep, to get them to refill five plastic wineglasses—one for each band member, I told them. Then I'd totter back to my seat and drink them all myself. Still, despite glass after plastic glass of crappy red wine, I was unable to achieve "the click," as Tennessee Williams put it, to reach that drink that "turns the hot light off and the cool one on, and all of a sudden there's peace."

I needed to talk to someone, anyone. Zack. He'd known me through all this. He'd have some insight, or at least he'd be able to make me laugh. Zack was asleep. All my band mates were asleep. The entire plane was asleep except for me. I closed my eyes.

It was never just darkness. Covering my eyes didn't just shut them off; they kept looking, kept searching. On the plane, my vision swam. Afterimages became objects, then morphed into other objects, advancing and retreating at the same time. I pushed deeper into the swirling field in front of me, seeking something, anything: a sign, an omen, any kind of information at all.

I saw an old man—maybe only fifty-nine, so younger than my father, but absolutely an old man—washing glasses behind a bar. Silver hair, gray-yellow face, thin shoulders and arms, fat tummy, hunched back. It was me.

I would get weaker and fatter and grayer and more pathetic, the weird old barback at some old-men's bar in the Village that took pity on me, that guy who had once been in a band you'd heard of but never listened to, a guy who was supposed to do Some Great Thing but then had done nothing.

That vision I'd had of the underwater garden in Denver, Jesus, eleven years before? I had been convinced my life was in danger, that if I went too deeply into the underwater garden, I would die. I had been wrong. This vision was worse. More banal and bleaker, like some *Twilight Zone* deal with the devil.

Alcohol would never kill me. It took singular focus to die from alcohol, focus that I lacked. Instead, alcohol would keep me alive for an eternity, in suspended animation, like a fetal pig in a jar of formaldehyde, except alive, just barely. It would slowly strangle all the good out of my life, until my life was so base that death would be a release.

I would create nothing: no songs, no stories. All I would create was pain. As I had hurt Oksana, as I had hurt Allison, as I had hurt countless others, I would hurt countless more, any person foolish enough to care about me, every person foolish enough to care about me. As I had hurt my family, I would hurt my family. I would go on hurting my family until I finally died, and then the last thing I would do in this world would be to hurt them some more.

I opened my eyes, my heart hammering. I knew what lay ahead, and it terrified me.

CHAPTER 8

Breaking the Beast

By thirty-two, I'd been chasing oblivion for nearly twenty years. Sure, I had taken a couple of breaks, but I'd always known it was temporary. I was like a painter, I'd told myself, and my drinking was like a large, complex painting that had gotten away from me. I needed to take some time away from it, but eventually I would return to finish my masterpiece. That chilly spring of 2009 was different. Before our plane even touched down, I'd sworn to myself that I would I quit drinking. For good.

The first days were misery, but I'd endured misery before. I stuck it out, through the chills, the shakes, the night terrors, weeping in my sleep, the poison sweats, my writhing spine, the clacking-too-fast heartbeat, the phantom pains, the nameless dread, the invisible death in the room. I tossed and turned all night, sweating my sheets into wet piles of slush. I awoke smelling like dry-cleaning fluid. Worst were the waves of shame and humiliation, so powerful that they manifested solely as a physical sensation, like some cold hand was slowly strangling my soul. I felt bad about nothing in particular, and I felt bad about everything. I didn't want to die; I wanted to never have lived.

After a couple of days, I got through the acute physical withdrawal. I walked to the grocery store in slow motion, then had to sit down on a bench to rest before I could make it home. I was reminded of National Geographic clips I'd seen as a kid of listless Ethiopians so malnourished and sick from dysentery they could barely move, then felt horrible for comparing my plight to theirs. I had done this to myself. Still, had a fly landed on me, I'd have been hard-pressed to shoo it away.

After detoxing, I felt less bad without actually feeling better. I avoided Esteban. I ignored my phone. I rarely left the house. I was subject to abrupt, intense depressions. They happened with so little warning and derailed my mood so definitively that I can only compare them to the childhood experience of walking through our house in socks and suddenly stepping in a cold puddle of dog piss pooled on the hardwood floor.

Sleep was the only respite available from the life I didn't want. Fittingly, it constantly eluded me. I sleepwalked through each day. I submitted to jarring, sweaty, unsatisfying naps like a cranky infant. I went to bed shortly after sundown like an old man. The minute my head hit the pillow, my heart raced, my blood itched in my veins, my eyes sprang fully open for the first time that day. I had been anaesthetizing myself for so long, it appeared I had actually forgotten how to fall asleep. I tried to remember how I'd done it in the past and could recall neither the process nor the experience.

When sleep finally came for me, I wished it hadn't. My drinking sleep had been a negation, a thought bubble filled only with Z's. Dreams had been such an infrequent occurrence that even pleasurable ones had been jarring. My sober sleeping life was crowded with deformed creatures, bizarre symbolism, and people from my past, rendering it more vivid, meaningful, and exhausting than my waking life. Everyone I had ever loved gathered on a street corner to throw a party in my honor when a tractor-trailer careened out of control and killed them all. My family turned evil, and I dismembered them in a grisly, methodical manner only to have their limbs stitch themselves together so they could rise up and attack me again and again.

Sobriety was relentless. Sobriety was life without eyelids. Sobriety was a bare white room with painfully bright fluorescent lights, buzzing constantly. I felt like I had braved some Herculean task equal parts agony, anxiety, and boredom—let's say seventy-two hours of cramming for a certified public accountant exam, only to be rewarded with life as a CPA. Like I'd fought my way out of the ninth circle of hell only to be rewarded with the eighth circle of hell. Still, progress is progress.

I forced myself to tidy up, performing maybe two solid hours of work over an entire day. My life had become so small—my buzzing, overheating laptop, a desk I'd found on the street, an end table I'd found on the street, a rolling office chair I'd found on the street. The only piece of furniture I owned that hadn't come from the garbage was my dresser. It was a nice, rugged piece, dovetail drawers, each front a broad, unbroken expanse of handsome blonde wood. Allison had bought it for me five years earlier off Craig's List. She'd wanted me to have something nice. Three of the drawers now failed to close properly because I'd piled stuff on them when they were open—dirty clothes, guitar parts, jugs of wine, books, porno mags, plates of old food. The top was shellacked with gray matter, dust and lint that had stuck to the moisture left by cups and bottles. When I scrubbed that off, I found deep scratches in the wood from cutting lines with a Bowie knife.

When the cleaning was finished, my sunlit living room oppressed me. It felt like a crime scene after the broken bodies had been moved, the tape taken down, and the floor and walls scrubbed with bleach. Though there were no obvious signs of violence, pervasive bad mojo hovered in the air.

I refused to allow myself to hope that this was a new beginning. That always ended in heartbreak. If someone hadn't already opened a dive bar called New Beginnings, then that was just another way in which humanity had disappointed itself. I couldn't even put a name on this time. No wishing, no dreaming, and "Hope" was just an ironic name for a prostitute. Focus on the basics; just keep the body alive. Eat—good food, raw fruits and vegetables. Drink—water, just water, gallons and gallons of it. Get sunshine. Bathe. Sleep.

≡

The best and worst thing about drinking was that it had paired so well with other vices. STD testing would have been pointless when I was drinking; I slept around enough that the results would be obsolete by the time they came back. But after three weeks of sobriety and solitude, I figured I should find out what diseases I was carrying. There wasn't one specific encounter or potential affliction causing me anxiety, but I knew my lifestyle was what one might call a "risk factor." I biked down to the free clinic on Atlantic Avenue and took a number.

While I waited, I was handed an alcohol questionnaire to fill out. I love New York, and I believe in social welfare, but I knew that in Great Recession–era Brooklyn, there was no way anyone was actually going to be reviewing these. Fuck it, why not be completely honest? God forbid you learn something about yourself.

The questions—"Have you blacked out?" "Has your drinking caused tension with your friends?"—applied to the previous thirty days. I hadn't had a drink in three weeks, but if I was honest, I had to check the yes box, question after question. They didn't provide an upside-down answer key like I'd seen at the end of quizzes in magazines, but I realized I didn't need one as I double-checked my work: *A plus!* A gold star! What do I win?

I turned the questionnaire in with the rest of my paperwork and took a seat. Almost right away, my number was called. I got dirty looks from people who had gotten there before me and were still waiting. That's kind of odd, I thought as I was ushered out of the waiting room.

I was led down a hallway and into a side office where a portly balding man sat behind a desk. He was holding my alcohol questionnaire.

Motherfuck.

I sat down.

"My name is Brian. I wanted to go over some of your answers on the questionnaire we had you fill out."

Good heavens, whatever on earth for?

"The input that you've given us here indicates a pattern of alcohol use that could lead to long-term health problems, including alcoholism or addiction to other substances."

I brushed aside his mincing questions about my drinking. He had seen my hand. I wanted to see his.

If I would agree to sign a few papers, he said, he would enroll me in Project Link, an outreach program for drug and alcohol abusers. They would help me get on Medicaid and arrange for me to see an addiction counselor each week. I'd have to provide contact information for a friend so that, if I went AWOL, they could come track me down. After six months, I'd have one follow-up interview. Then I would be free to return to my wicked, wicked ways if I wanted.

My body filled with dread and resentment. Finally, finally, finally, I had been found out. I was hopelessly, irreversibly caught. And also, I faced a great opportunity.

Do or die, motherfucker, I thought, do or die. I signed up.

I was led back to the clinic waiting room to mull over the dark days ahead. When the room had emptied out, the receptionist asked me what my number was. She huffed when I told her.

"Where were you? We called and called, and you didn't respond!" She didn't wait for an answer, just led me back to the examination room.

A harried looking doctor with graying brown curly hair and wire-rimmed glasses came in. She introduced herself but didn't offer her hand. She picked up my folder and briskly began asking me questions about my health, number of sexual partners, and drug and alcohol history. I forced myself to answer every question honestly. It felt terrible. It must have sounded even worse.

I listened to the rationalizations coming out of my mouth. "We looked and looked but we couldn't find a condom." "She didn't seem like the kind of girl to sleep around." "I knew that I was clean." "She said she couldn't get pregnant so . . . " And my recent default response for every difficulty that had risen up in front of me: "Fuck it. At this point, what difference does it make?"

In each instance, in the moment, in the dark, I had let myself off the hook. But as I spoke to the doctor, a diagnosis became clear. I was, simply, an asshole. It was one thing to put myself at risk—my life was mine to throw away if I chose to do so—and another to put other people at risk, people who cared about me and people whom I purported to care about.

The doctor frowned at my paperwork, then looked closely at me.

"Are you feeling okay? You look tired."

"Yeah, I just . . . I've just been here for a long time, and I haven't had much to eat today."

She nodded knowingly.

"I know we've had you answer a lot of questions today, but as long as it's okay with you, I'm going to ask you two more."

Hit me, I thought. There's nothing you can ask me that's going to make me feel worse than I already do.

She didn't wait for a response before continuing.

"You have listed your occupation as 'musician/unemployed/asshole.' You have the rare distinction of achieving a perfect score on our drug and alcohol abuse questionnaire, checking 'yes' to every single question. Oh wait, you don't inject drugs intravenously—yet.

"You engage in all manner of risky sex with multiple partners around the country, which makes you a very effective vector for spreading disease. You have engaged in and continue to engage in selfish, self-destructive behavior that will negatively impact not just your health but the health of those unfortunate enough to be intimate with you.

"At twenty-seven years of age, Janis Joplin, Jimi Hendrix, and even Jim Morrison had each created a body of work that guys like you are still ripping off today. At thirty-two, you seem to have done nothing. Or at least I have no idea who you are.

"So my two questions for you are: What do you intend to do with your life? And what exactly is your fucking problem?"

The revelation several days later that I was clean brought me little comfort. I wanted to be punished for my hideous transgressions, my wasted years. A physical at St. Vincent's, my first in ten years, brought similar results: my blood work was boringly normal. I sought bad news from a reliable source, the dentist. I'd last been to the dentist's office a decade earlier, at my mother's insistence and on her dime. I'd had a cavity but declined to have it filled— I knew better ways to spend $300. I braced myself for the news that the dentist was going to have to tear all my teeth out and start over again clean.

"No cavities," the dentist stated flatly in his Russian accent.

Um . . . did you check the ones on top? The ones on the bottom? What about the ones in the back?

"See you in six months," he said, wiping his hands on the paper bib his assistant had clipped around my neck.

"Guess all those years of drinking mouthwash paid off."

Not even a smile. Maybe the "cavity search" joke I'd made on the way into his office had pissed him off. Well, no offense, dude, but if I went ten years without a cavity, no way I'm going to endure this every six months. Put me down for sometime in eight years.

At home, I stared at my boyish face in the mirror. Big feminine eyes. Long eyelashes. A bump on my nose from the second time I broke it, in the fight with Zack and Ben White. My skin was no longer gray, the whites of my eyes no longer yellow, and I'd lost a roll of bloat under my chin. I was still raccoon-eyed, but I'd been like that since I was a kid. For all my egregious, repeated mistakes, my aggressive self-abuse, I appeared unscathed. No kidney damage, no liver disease, blood pressure and heart rate good, no root canal necessary, no painful, humiliating STD, not even a single cavity. What a sham.

I had only ever wanted to live to be seventeen. Turning twenty-one had been a dark relief—I no longer required a responsible adult's consent to get blitzed. Turning thirty had brought a different kind of satisfaction. "Thirty?" a friend had scoffed at me that day. "We didn't think you'd make eighteen."

Surviving past thirty had been not just an accident but a mistake. I'd reached an age where my friends didn't just die in tragedies—murder, suicide, overdose, drowning—but also from cancer. I had far exceeded my own life expectancy, and, worse, there appeared to be a lot more ahead of me. It seemed bleakly ironic to me that someone who had craved, deserved, and worked so hard to achieve a tragic, early death appeared doomed to live forever.

"You're not indestructible," my mother had warned me, Jesus, millions of times. I had assented throughout the years, but now I had a final, undeniable rebuttal: there was now actually more evidence against her thesis than for it.

All I had wanted was to be erased. I had been such a self-destructive failure that I had even failed to self-destruct. So where do we go now, Sweet Child o' Mine? There is no Google Maps for your life. There is no clearly marked destination—a red dot—with an illuminated blue line showing where you should go and how you should get there and when you have deviated from the correct path. There is no owner's manual for your life, no Idiot's Guide, not even a shitty map scrawled on a cocktail napkin with nearly illegible directions. And that really sucks.

My anxiety, not especially low in the absence of my various beloved medications, went through the roof. It's much easier to ac-
cede to the grim fact of an early death than it is to deal with the
long, fumbling open question of what to do with your life.

Tracy Helsing, a bartender who moonlighted as a personal trainer,
dragged me to the gym where she worked once or twice a week.
She never asked me, just texted me where to meet her and when.
At the end of each session, she didn't ask me if I wanted to work
out again. She didn't ask me when I was available. She didn't ask
me if a specific day or time worked for me.

"Thursday at four."

"I can't do four. I have . . . a thing."

"Thursday at two."

"I . . . Fuck it. Okay."

"You stand me up, I'll kick your fucking ass."

Some days she worked out with me. One day, I looked over
and saw that she was doing shoulder presses with the same weights
I was. My heart jumped. I could lift as much as my trainer! Yes,
Mishka, congratulations, you swarthy, macho man, you. With all
your hard-won progress, you are now as strong as a girl.

The boys in Freshkills were supportive. Perhaps too supportive. While we were setting up for practice one day, Johnny tuned
his guitar, then eyed me.

"Looking real good, Shubaly."

"Right," I said.

"No, seriously. Color in your cheeks. Less like a corpse dragged
up from the bottom of a reservoir."

"You trying to fuck me?"

"Maybe later. No, I mean . . . it's really good, what you're doing." He glanced down at his Pabst Blue Ribbon, then put it down
behind his amp. "Should we not drink around you?"

Suddenly, everyone was listening.

"Naw. You didn't create this problem. I did. It's not fair of me to ask you to change what you do. Just don't, you know, offer me a drink or anything."

Zack shot me a look and grinned.

"Mishka, I haven't offered you a drink in *years*."

⸺

By that summer, my odd jobs and various dead-end gigs had almost totally dried up. I'd pissed away the ten grand I'd saved from my construction gig. I had $70,000 in college debt. I had to do something to make a buck.

I knew nothing of real jobs. I had been fired from all but one of the jobs I'd held in the last six years. I was capable of getting out of bed in the morning now, so, Christ, back to the temp agency? I was proficient in core office skills such as passing the buck, ALT-TABing, and looking busy. No, functional alcoholism was the only way to face a forty-hour workweek. Nine-to-fiving it in some soulless cubicle with a Dilbert cartoon over my desk would undo me. Surely I had one marketable skill. I had a master's in fiction . . . so that qualified me to pump gas or squeegee windshields on the corner or round up the shopping carts at Target.

I was getting desperate when I got a call from Mike Stewart, an old friend and bar owner. They were looking for a manager at Beauty Bar on 14th Street. Was I interested?

I had extensive experience in the internal workings of bars . . . and had even worked at a few. I'd been fired from every bar job in the same way—a meeting with the bosses in which I was informed that there were no bad feelings on their end, and in fact everyone really liked me, but then there was always the same gesture, a shrug with the arms out: What do you want me to do? I understood. My role was to echo the gesture—What do you want *me* to do?—then put the keys on the desk and go out and get truly bombed.

But I was a new man, a guy who didn't drink and didn't sleep around and even did the occasional push-up or walked around the park. I knew, too, that if I were to drink, it would be catastrophic, not just a beer at the end of the shift with the Sunday hardcore matinee veteran doorman. How I longed for one drink. Only one drink, any drink, even something banal and milquetoast, like a vodka cranberry. Sure, just one magical, simple concoction of vodka, juice, ice, and lime to the brim of a cold highball wider than the Pacific Ocean, deeper than the Mariana Trench. Soon I'd be limping through my shifts, having been up till noon the night before, sweating bug spray and trying not to shit my pants, too woozy to stand, obsessively checking the clock until I allowed myself my first drink, and then struggling not to get blitzed until after the money had been counted.

And the temptation while working at a bar . . . wow. Bottle after bottle of top-shelf liquor, the shit I only drank when someone else was buying, Belvedere and Grey Goose, Bombay Sapphire, Glenlivet, Patrón. Working in a bar, alcohol is part of your salary: a gratis nightly sousing is your employee meal. I had rage-drunk my way through more than one $50 bottle on a slow night, then stumbled home, feeling like I'd been paid well. Sure, I had walked out with $19 after tipping out the barback, but I must have drank up at least $150 worth of profits! Even the mid-level scotches, Dewar's and J&B, smelled enchanting. J&B was my mom's drink—old lady scotch. I drank an entire bottle of J&B alone one night, bringing that green glass to my lips and tilting my head back, the scotch careening down my throat like golden fire.

I wouldn't just lose the job if I drank, I would lose Mike as a friend. Having alienated all family, except for my mom, and every girl I'd dated (and a few that I hadn't), my few friends were all I had. Taking the job wasn't just a bad idea. It was the worst idea possible, a Rachael Ray–worthy recipe for disaster, apocalyptic and catastrophic and ready in thirty minutes or less.

I took the job.

The training I received was basically "Wear a blazer and keep an eye on what's going on." I hadn't worked in bars, at odd jobs, and on construction sites for twenty years just so I could go out and buy a blazer *now*, and to work in a bar, no less. I wore plain black T-shirts, which I felt was enough of a concession. I placated stumbling, slurring girls, irate because the doorman had maligned their honor by presupposing they were too drunk to come in, and dudes baffled that their assemblage of flip-flops, khakis, wife beater, backward baseball hat, gold tusk medallion, and liberal dousing of Axe Body Spray didn't meet our dress code. I chased off the creeps, pinballing hopelessly from girl to girl to girl, their desperation growing. I even pitched in behind the bar when it was busy. That was incredibly bizarre, the foam from an overfilled pint of Blue Moon sliding tantalizingly over the back of my hand like the touch of a dead lover, my nose, eyes, hands, and brain full of Corona, red wine, Jameson, vodka, vodka, VODKA, everything I wasn't allowed to have. I held fast.

The only thing I had trouble with, aside from the blazer, was keeping an eye on what was going on. When the bar was busy, sure, I watched for drunks and pervs and Europeans and didn't do a bad job. But when the bar had only a few people in it, well, I talked guitars with the doorman, read the paper, basically did anything except watch the bar.

I kept my appointments with my addiction counselor, but they were a joke, worse than a waste of time. I was nodding out on morphine at my first appointment (I'd quit drinking but not pills, as the thought of quitting everything was too hard to bear). My counselor hadn't noticed. He talked to me like I was a child or a parolee or some kind of savant. I left the mandatory group therapy sessions wanting to drink more than I had when I walked in.

I grimly pissed in a cup, feeling like a criminal. When my counselor didn't bust me for the drugs that must have shown up, I felt like a cash cow. Project Link was supposed to be my lifeline. Now it made me picture a rusty chain yoking my ankle to a cold iron ball.

I had agreed to go to a counselor in good faith, intending to engage fully. The fastest way through darkness was right through the middle of it. I had actually looked forward to talking about some of the shit I never talked about, perhaps even yelling and screaming and crying. At last, catharsis! But this wasn't *Good Will Hunting*. Therapy was like high school: just keep your head down, complete the work with the least effort possible, fulfill their low expectations of you to perfection, then get the hell out of there. It was a colossal disappointment. But everything else in my life had turned out to be a colossal disappointment, so why had I thought therapy would be any different? I lacerated myself for being naive enough to hope for relief of any kind. I walked around that summer like a tightly coiled spring, just waiting for the slightest thing to set me off: Push me. Please, just push me once. Give me one good excuse to destroy you.

And then the fight at Beauty Bar. Javad out cold on the floor. I'd been enraged by the asshole who had sucker punched him, rage that, for once, wasn't misplaced. But I'd let the jerk get away. Going home in a cab without my bike, then waking in a fury and running all the way back into the city to retrieve it. Gasping my way through Brooklyn, through the nauseating memories of my curdled life. And then stumbling upon—somewhere after exhaustion but before heat stroke—peace.

And the sleep! I had suffered from the entire spectrum of sleep issues my entire life: tossing and turning, kicking and punching, insomnia, night terrors, crying in my sleep, sleepwalking, sleep talking, even a light sprinkling of bedwetting as a child. How I had envied Allison, who simply closed her eyes and slept! Sleep was something I stalked, chased, and then choked into submission. As soon as I had left home, I'd gamed it, taking Tylenol PM or NyQuil, muscle relaxants, anything.

But when I lay down the night after my crazed run, I felt myself surrendering the minute I closed my eyes. It was like grabbing the heaviest stone I could handle and diving down into a cold, dark loch. Instead of slowing, as on a normal dive, I descended faster and faster into the velvet fluid. When I realized that I had gone too deep, that I would run out of air before I made it back to the top, I opened my lungs and, impossibly, breathed. I swam deeper and deeper, breathing in huge, luxurious lungfuls of midnight blue water.

For the first time I could remember, I woke up in the same position I had laid down in. This was miraculous! I had dreamed so furiously all night—vivid, beautiful, narrative dreams—that it felt like I had been doing work all night. But I wasn't groggy; I was alert, ready to go. I hadn't been looking forward to anything in the day before me, but for some reason I couldn't wait to get to it. Then I tried to get up.

I hadn't moved the entire night because both my legs were broken. Femurs, tibias, fibulas. Ankles too. My feet, yes, every bone in both feet was broken, including those bones in your toes—metatarsals? Thank God my upper body had been spared. I tried to sit up.

No, my abdomen was trashed too, like someone had run over it with a car. Absolutely ruined. My shoulders and neck too. My goddamn arms were sore—how could you hurt your arms running? If alcohol were as harmful to your health as running, I would have only ever gotten drunk once.

I tottered out of bed, chewed some Advil, and hit the shower. After finishing my breakfast and morning coffee, I didn't feel so bad. Sore as I was everywhere else, my back didn't hurt. One rib in the middle of the right side of my back had been trying to turn sideways since I was seventeen, when some small but vital cog had crumbled while I hunched, sweating, over a cutting board at Sonic Burger. I had tried chiropractors and massage. I'd drank. I'd tried every pain medication, legal and illegal, that I could get my hands on. Nothing worked. The meds got me high yet did nothing for my back. But today, for the first time I could remember, my back was okay.

Sure, everything else hurt. But that was a new pain, a proud pain, opposite in essence from the wincing shame of drinking. For once, I ached from doing something good. Perhaps the best way forward would be to treat running like any other dangerous unknown that had entered my life: if the first fix didn't kill you and only made you hurt for a day, why not see if you could get away with doing a little more?

The next day, I tried it again. Don't think about it, I told myself, just socks and shoes and a T-shirt and those ancient Umbro soccer shorts you stole from Tatyana in high school, then out the door. People do this every day.

Then I was again out on the sidewalk in front of my apartment, gangly and unsteady and blinking in the too bright sun like a newborn giraffe. Don't look around, don't think, just one foot in front of the other.

It was merciless. They say you never forget how to ride a bike, but I had forgotten how to run. How old was I when I had first run, two? One and a half? That instinctual knowledge had abandoned me. The soles of my feet slapped the pavement painfully. Every muscle in my stiff legs wailed. The shock of the impact reverberated up my body, jarring my knees, my hips, my aching shoulders. My head wobbled on top of my backbone like it was going to fall off. I slowed to a walk after a couple of blocks. This wasn't working. What was I doing differently this time?

Aha—I wasn't livid with rage, as I had been when I'd left the house the day after Javad got coldcocked. Here, I thought, was one problem I could solve. I'd spent most of my adult life fighting to keep my temper. To run, I'd have to let it go.

Nothing made me crazier than when someone hit me in the face. My blood started thumping through my veins just thinking about it. I squatted down and glanced around. No one looking. I smacked myself hard in the face, twice. I stood up.

Let go.

I ran.

I lumbered stiffly forward, my ancient Adidas Sambas scraping the pavement. The air felt scratchy whisking in and out of my lungs. I couldn't get my breathing to line up with my footfalls. How did I not know how to do this? Then, suddenly, my feet synced up with the rasping sound of my breathing. I was doing it.

I ran down Driggs, dumpy little two- and three-story buildings lining the street. Past McGolrick Park, across McGuinness Avenue. I felt sick heat growing in my chest. The muscles on the tops of my thighs ached. Then they burned. Then they were boiling under my skin, about to cook their way through at any moment. Something bad might happen—should I stop?

No. That was my weak self, the one who whined and cried and drank in bed. But Christ, that mounting fire in my legs! It was like running through hell. But if you were running through hell, I reasoned, the solution was not to stop but to keep going. Let the weak half suffer; let him bleat until he fled or died completely.

Fuck you, I thought as I ran. Fuck this entire filthy, nepotistic city, this malignant tumor of old money and condescension, cock-teasing me with opportunity just to whip it away, this city that had tempted me and ignored me and exhausted me. It's not that I wasn't smart enough or good enough, just that I wasn't some Upper East Side blue blood or the son of a Connecticut millionaire. It's not fair, and that's exactly how you fuckers want it.

My mouth was dry as straw. Phlegm collected in my throat, but I couldn't swallow, so I coughed and choked on it. My bones screamed with each pounding step. I was doing structural damage, I had to be. People stared at me. I stared hard back.

Fuck you all with your tiny, self-contented little lives, your Urban Outfitters wardrobes, your fancy fucking phones, your designer weed, your coffee tables of repurposed lumber, your vintage eyeglass frames, mocking the Poles or the Puerto Ricans or the black kids at the automotive high school. This isn't your private playground.

And fuck the Poles and the Puerto Ricans and the black kids at the automotive high school for mocking the gentrifiers—being from here doesn't just give you a pass. All of you, what the fuck did you ever do with your lives? You ate and you slept and you peed and you paid too much for a pair of shoes you didn't need.

I felt like I was fighting as I ran, kneeing some invisible enemy in the face with each step, punching another face each time I swung my arms forward, my eyes fixed ahead on the ever-advancing hordes. I thought of all the people who had fucked me over, listed their names in my mind, then destroyed their faces: grade school martinets, cruel gym teachers, high school bullies, bosses, cops, landlords, tyrannical administrators, ex–band mates, ex-friends, ex-lovers . . . Yes, fuck my traitorous father—obviously, so much of this lay at his feet—but also fuck my sisters for being able to live without spontaneously igniting; fuck my mother for coddling me and making me soft and weak like my father . . . Who was left?

Me.

Fuck you, I thought.

You blame this country and this town and these people and some dark, nebulous force like there is some grand, cosmic conspiracy to hold you down. Not only is that not true—the exact opposite is true! EVERYONE has tried to help you since you were just a kid. You wouldn't let them. The darkness and the failure you claimed to battle against, that was your food and drink. You cherished your pain. You held it to your breast and nursed it like a newborn child. You did this to yourself.

"Not fair!" I had been crying since I was a baby. I'd imagined my life to be so goddamn hard, but Christ, my friends in New York, they'd never met their dads, or their dads had been junkies or alcoholics, or they'd died in prison. Or my friends had been raped and beaten by their fathers till they *wished* their fathers were dead. I had been right—life was unfair. But it had been unfair *in my favor.*

I felt cold to the core. Here was the hideous truth: *I* was my problem. I recalled that Latin saying "Every man is the architect of his own fortune." I had been the architect of my own hell. Brick by brick, I had built my own prison. I had written my own nightmare.

I caught a flicker of my reflection in a passing bus—sweaty, red-faced, scowling, fists clenched. I was only barely shuffling forward, but I felt like my heart was going to explode. I stopped, gasping and shaking, barely able to stand. My body needed to stop running.

But where had listening to my body gotten me? My body needed alcohol. Gallons of alcohol, white grain liquor, the cheap shit in the plastic bottle with the twist-off cap, thundering over me like a waterfall in a shampoo commercial, my pores drinking it in. My body needed a woman, many women, a platoon of soulless femme-bots, a legion of barely legal nymphs, cheerleaders, gymnasts, ballerinas and figure skaters and contortionists, oh my! My body needed opiates. Just a handful of pills, espresso grind, thank you, and don't bother wrapping it up. I'm getting that "to stay." Super-size it, make it a pound, make it a kilo, make it a bale, fill the hold of a small airplane, conscript every man, woman, and child in a small war-torn country into an army devoted solely to growing poppies, cooking them down, and sending that shit up my nostril. My body needed to stop running. God fucking damn it, my body doesn't get what it wants. I started running again.

There was no question I was running from something. I'd been running my whole life. Convulsing from one side of the country to the other. Living like a fugitive: keeping strange hours, avoiding the people I loved, waking up feeling hunted and exhausted, and doing it all again the next day. I had been trying to escape a horror that followed me everywhere I went, terrorized by fear itself.

I was running again, now literally running. But something inside me had pivoted, and for the first time I had the bizarre sensation that I was running *to* something. Instead of running away from my fear, I was running straight into it. What lay on the other side? I had no idea. But it couldn't be worse than the life I had led.

I crawled home, feeling like I had lost a fight. Still, for the first time in as long as I could remember, I had fought back. I opened the door to my building with shaking hands, then pulled myself up the stairs to my apartment by the banisters. I almost fell taking my shorts off in the bathroom, but I managed to make it into the shower without major mishap.

Quitting drinking had been simple subtraction. I had removed alcohol from my life. Becoming a runner would involve something entirely different. I would have to start completely from scratch. No, I wasn't even starting from scratch. First I had to dismantle the old structure, pull each rusty nail from each warped plank, break crumbling concrete from rusty rebar. Only then would I be able to start from scratch.

I would have to tear down the asshole I had been and build a human being in his place. How, I had no idea. It would take patience and commitment, two things I had almost wholly purged from my life. My greatest fears were trying and failing. In order to become a runner, I would have to try incredibly hard, and I might still fail. That sober thought was more frightening than any drug-addled hallucination.

When I got out of the shower, I got onto my computer. I looked for a local race longer than five miles so I'd have something to push for. They had seven-mile races, didn't they? Well, no. A 10K race was only six miles, and I knew I could do that. I signed up for the Staten Island Half Marathon to be held on October 11, 2009, less than two months away. Thirteen-point-one miles. It was farther than I had ever run in my life.

CHAPTER 9

Congratulations, You've Rejoined the Human Race

My days were long now that they didn't start at noon and end at sundown. Whenever I was angry or depressed or frustrated or just didn't know what to do with myself, I went running. That added up to a lot of time on my feet. Walking to the bathroom in the morning after my nightly plunge into the depths of sleep became a treacherous ordeal. Sitting down or standing up became a creaky, complicated process. Running stirred parts of my lungs that hadn't seen oxygen in many years, and breathing in the hot steam in the shower, I coughed up all manner of marine life that had shaken loose. Still, I came home from every single run feeling better than when I'd left. My head felt better, anyway. My body was trashed.

I'd taken an anatomy class in high school and thus imagined I had a decent grasp of the human body, its parts, and how they worked together. I understood running to involve coordinated contractions and relaxations of the calf muscle and the gluteus maximus, the two muscles that made up the leg. So why did every cubic inch of my legs hurt? My toes, my arches, my heels, the tops of my feet, the sides of my thighs, the insides of my thighs, odd bumpy muscles in my hips, weird places in my butt . . . from my love handles down to my toenails, the only place I poked that didn't hurt was my kneecap. My lower legs glowed constantly with a warm ache, from the tender surfaces of my shins to deep within my calf muscles to the very bones themselves. I stopped getting high and even quit smoking. Running was tough enough without handicapping myself.

My godmother, Marilyn, my father's only sister, had been diagnosed with abdominal cancer the year before and had already slogged through several rounds of chemo. My mother called one day to tell me Marilyn might not win her battle. I got back in touch with my father, and we made plans to go up to Saskatchewan to visit her in November. As much as I dreaded a long-distance field trip with my dad, I hoped visiting Marilyn with him might help me crack the riddle of my father. The last time I'd seen Marilyn, in 2003, I'd asked about my grandparents. "My family starts with me and my husband," she'd said, looking away from me. "You won't see any pictures from before that."

She was hiding something, from herself and from us. What was it?

=

Rage had been the only thing that could get me out the door and running, but through Marilyn's illness, I discovered something that could keep me going long after my anger had burned itself out. When I walked down the stairs and hit the sidewalk, I had a laundry list of people to be angry at, things to be angry about, a list so long that I felt I could never get through it. But the longest I could stay mad while running was maybe an hour and a half, and that was really milking it. Stewing in my anger that long put power in my legs, but it exhausted me emotionally. By the time the anger had cooked itself down to nothing, my defenses had fallen. Other feelings crept in. Sadness, yes, and regret, but also love, even hope. So, not totally dead inside after all.

While I trained for the Staten Island Half Marathon, I thought about Marilyn. I pictured her face, deeply creased from long hours in the sun, her kind eyes, her smile. I tried to think about the future, *her* future: Marilyn alive and well and happy, driving the combine on their farm, cooking pierogi and venison sausage, playing with her grandkids. As I had forced myself to sit in my anger, I forced myself to sit in my love for Marilyn. Thinking about how much I loved her and the love she had shown me over my life, I finally began to feel better.

Through friends I met a girl named Izgi, a Turkish immigrant with dark hair and eyes and a cute accent. She worked as an auditor for a blue-chip accounting firm and had her own apartment in Soho. Somehow it didn't bother her that I made $300 a week babysitting drunks at a bar till four in the morning. She allowed me an open destiny and made no judgments about my old life.

"The past, you say it's in the past, so? . . ." She cocked an eyebrow at me and shrugged. "Everybody makes mistakes. But not everybody is so brave to say 'I was wrong.' To me, you have only been a gentleman."

Not everyone was so forgiving. While I was running to the park one day to do some pull-ups and push-ups, a male voice called out from an open second-story window, "Fuck you, Mishka!"

Maybe just one of my friends, some good-natured ribbing?

"You suck, asshole!"

I guess not.

—

"Making amends" is an integral part of the Twelve Steps. In my darkest hour, I had never considered going to Alcoholics Anonymous. I didn't do groups, I didn't do programs, I didn't do structure. I was hardheaded, and that had gotten me into trouble, but to pretend I wasn't would bury me. I had gotten sober as I had gotten fucked up: alone, by my own will, on my own terms. I had harnessed my hardheadedness, as I had harnessed my anger, and they served me now. This idea that I had to be humble not just before a God I didn't believe in or people I'd hurt or nonalcoholics but before *everyone* and that my "recovery" would last the rest of my life . . . fuck that, all the way, in every way. I'd been a living apology my entire adult life. I'd had my fill of submission. I quit drinking so I'd no longer have to be humble, so I could take charge of my own life.

AA's concept of amends was bullshit. If you'd punched a guy in the face, there was no way to unpunch him. The harm you had done, you couldn't undo. Nothing would make it right, and it was dumb to dangerous to believe that something as quick as a hand-written letter would balance the scales. You had to live with the knowledge that you had evil in you, that you had done evil, and that you had the potential to do more evil in the future. Let that burden guide your hand down the line.

Still, I wasn't so stubborn that I couldn't see I owed apologies to a lot of people. I'd apologized to my band mates almost daily for my behavior—drinking all the drink tickets, doing all the coke, not doing any of the driving, getting into shit with the other bands, wandering off into the night trashed, costing people money, worrying them, annoying them, pissing them off. But in the second half of 2009, I began anew with apologies that I would finally back up with action in the real world. I wasn't simply going to grovel again for forgiveness for the trespasses of the night or the week or the month before, I was actually *no longer going to continue to do* the things for which I was now asking forgiveness. I intended to apologize one final, definitive time.

I chased down and cornered the friends I'd been in bands with who'd been irradiated by the most fallout from my toxic life. I called them, emailed them, or pulled them aside at band practice. I was careful to make eye contact, apologized specifically for the nights I remembered, then gave a blanket apology for the nights I couldn't remember. Nothing stuck.

Jimmy snorted, waved me away with a hand, and said, "You're fine."

Zack rolled his eyes and said, "Stop. I mean, okay, sure, I hear you. But don't make this any more awkward than absolutely necessary."

Jason stared at me for a second, his eyes quickly lighting up. "Awww! Wouldja listen to this guy? Ya big lug! I love this guy!" He pinched my cheeks, then put me in a headlock. "Folks, ain't he the sweetest?"

Time and again, I set myself upon Mitchell. Mitchell and I had been in Beat the Devil together for a couple of years, an intense, difficult time with lots of grueling nickel-and-dime tours, inebriation, and screaming matches in the practice space, the bar, or the street. Each time I tried to apologize to him, he shrugged me off. I would collect myself, then set upon him with renewed fervor. Finally, he got annoyed.

"Dude, every time I see you, you apologize to me. Knock it off."

"I feel like you're not hearing me."

"I hear you, man. I'm not brushing it aside. It's just . . . you really don't have anything to apologize for, okay? I mean, we were *all* fucked up. If you drank or did more blow or pills or whatever, well, you got us that beer 'cause the clubs loved you, or it was your friends who hooked us up with the pills. And blow . . . Jesus, if there's a team of accountants tracking who's done more than their fair share, well, I don't think *you* are gonna be in the first wave of people they audit.

"You're a hard-ass and that's fucking annoying, but we kinda have to let it go because you're harder on yourself than anyone else. You were never belligerent or mean or spiteful or . . . You never started shit with me or with anybody. In fact, I remember you being pretty patient and talking me down more than once when I wanted to fight *you*. You were only ever a danger to yourself.

"You just . . . once you started drinking, you would sort of wake up from the depressed fog you'd been in. Then you'd get really funny, just awesome to hang out with—I mean seriously, a champion drinker . . . Later in the night, you'd get slurry. Then you'd be asleep or nodding out at the table. At the end of the night, we'd carry you somewhere and have to pull your cowboy boots off and throw a blanket over you. You were never an asshole. It was just kind of . . . sad. This great big excitable puppy dog of a guy who was totally falling apart."

When October 11 rolled around, Izgi and I schlepped down to the Staten Island Ferry at an hour of the early morning I could only recall experiencing from being up all night. She held my hand on the boat, bouncing with excitement in her seat. I felt no excitement, only exhaustion and dread. I focused on the ferry. This vast powerful ship, had it been here the entire eleven years I had? In a city where nothing came cheap, this boat ride—a mundane but completely satisfying pleasure—was absolutely free. What else had I missed?

When we entered the corrals for the race, I felt sorely unready. The other runners were stretching and warming up next to me, some of them already shiny with sweat, alert and well scrubbed under their visors, wearing logo-emblazoned athletic apparel of patented synthetic materials, hydration belts, iPods, and $200 digital watches. It's a run, you fucking clowns; we're not going to the moon. I wore gym shorts and an old black undershirt, capped off with a couple days' beard and a bad case of bedhead. It must have looked like I'd lost a bet.

These runners, they were players. Doers, decision makers, shot callers, winners. They were normals—the people I'd feared and condescended to my whole life, while secretly wishing I could just effortlessly *live* like they seemed to. This half marathon was a farce.

I was not a runner. I was a mangy, flea-bitten coyote among pure-bred greyhounds. When the gun went off, I half expected them to turn on me and tear me apart.

As we began to run, I had one goal, one word in my mind: *finish.* Just get this behind you, another example of you biting off more than you can chew, one more mistake rolling under the tires. Carry Izgi and Marilyn with you, hold their tender, smiling faces in your head like talismans, and get this done. Then get the fuck out of here.

We wound through the gray, chilly streets of Staten Island, the sides of the course lined with people with signs and noisemakers and streamers, cheering on their loved ones. While I ran, I imagined the white blood cells in Marilyn's body regenerating after chemotherapy—one cell with each footstep. If I could make it, she would make it.

As the miles ticked by, I thought I might be able to finish in under two hours. I hammered the last couple of miles so hard I could feel my heart beating in my eyeballs. I made it in at 1:46:50. I would never win any awards, but that was not bad. Not bad at all.

On the ferry back to Manhattan, I thought about the miles I'd run that day in wonder. Not just further than I'd ever run in my life but more than twice as far as I'd run when I was thirteen, before everything had gone to shit. I thought about all the miles I'd run in preparation for the race. These runners, they were not my people . . . but I was a runner. What's more, I hadn't crawled across the finish line, or walked, or even jogged. I had been *sprinting*. As many miles as I had traveled, I had more miles in me.

Later that month, just days before we were to leave to visit her, Marilyn's condition took a downturn. She had concealed the depth of her illness, something that must run in my family. My father paid through the nose to change his ticket and rushed to her side.

His flight was delayed four hours due to an unseasonable snow-storm. He made it to the bedside of his only sibling—his last living link to his past—minutes after she died.

It fucked with me. Marilyn was the first immediate relative I'd lost. My godmother always made it clear that we had a special connection, that she had a special love for me. Losing her in such a tantalizing manner was hard. I'd spent the bulk of my life not just angry at my father but wishing an ironically cruel fate on him. When his little sister died minutes before he could say good-bye, I didn't feel momentarily bad for wishing him ill; I wanted to cradle him in my arms like a child.

My father suggested that I try to trade my ticket to Saskatche-wan in for a trip to California to visit him. I told him I would try, but no guarantees, Dad, airlines being airlines. To my surprise, the airline gave me full credit. I booked a flight out to Sacramento for early December. I couldn't not.

He lived in the tiny town of Sutter Creek in a cute little house surrounded by a garden with his wife, Theresa, and grouchy little Himalayan cat named Rosie. I had named my old van Rosie. They had painted the house the same light, cheery yellow I had painted my bedroom. Jesus, we even had the same model electric tooth-brush. None of that prevented me from walking on eggshells in their too quiet, perfectly ordered house. No pictures of Tashina; the only pictures of Tatyana and me were grade school photos from the 1980s—a happy fiction.

I found *How to Make a Bad Situation Worse* on his shelf of CDs, the album I had killed myself trying to make, the album I had pinned so many hopes on. Angry as I was at him, as chaotic as my life was at that time, I'd somehow managed to mail him a copy. I pulled it off the shelf to inspect it, a relic from my old life. The cellophane wrapper was still on.

One day while Theresa was out of the house, we tried to "have a talk." I cornered my dad about some ancient gripe about the divorce, and he lashed out.

"Every time I see you, you have some bone to pick with me. What are you trying to get out of me? What are you trying to get me to say? That you have been a complete and utter disappointment to me?"

I started welling up.

"Thanks, Dad," I said. "I've been waiting to hear that from you my entire life."

Thirty-two years old, crying in front of my old man like a baby.

———

A couple of days later, he brought out a small shoebox after dinner.

"After Marilyn's funeral, your uncle Dwight and I went through some of her old stuff. He gave me a lot of her pictures. I thought you might want to see some of them."

"Dad, I know I've said this, but I'll say it again. I'm so sorry she died. And I'm terribly sorry for the way she died. That must have been heartbreaking."

He took his glasses off and rubbed his face with both hands, then put his glasses back on. This was a trademark Dad move. He had been doing this exact same thing since I was a little boy. I had forgotten about it, and it made me sad.

"Well, she was pretty out of it for the last couple of days anyway. I don't think we would have been able to have much of a conversation. I've made my peace with it."

Again, trademark Dad. A bloodless, cerebral evaluation of the situation, emotions dealt with briskly, the same way you might hold your breath, pick up an errant cat turd with a paper towel, and quickly dump it in the trash.

Dad opened the box and dumped the pictures on the coffee table. One by one, we turned them over. I was reminded of the first card game I'd played as a small child: Memory.

"The last time I saw Marilyn, I tried to talk to her about your parents, you know, find out a little what they were like. She wouldn't talk about them at all."

"Well, the thing is . . . my parents were alcoholics. Alcoholics and drug addicts, both of them. All kinds of pills. When I was there, they kept it together. Mostly kept it together. But when I went away to university, things really went to shit."

"How do you know? I mean, you weren't there."

"Marilyn told me a little of what was going on. And I could tell, a little. But on one of my trips home, I went out for a walk. Can't remember exactly why, maybe I was going fishing or something. But I stumbled upon this pile of bottles. Bottles and broken bottles. A mountain of them. They weren't just drinking more, they were drinking *a lot* more.

"I avoided going home after that. I really don't know exactly what they put Marilyn through. I didn't want to know. I guess I'll never find out. But I know that she never forgave them."

He thumbed through the pictures on the coffee table. One leapt out at me: my father, maybe nineteen or twenty, shirtless, with a broad, charming grin. Slung effortlessly over one shoulder was a man with gray hair and black-framed glasses: my father's father.

"Holy shit, Dad. I've never seen a picture of your father before. I'm going to go out on a limb and guess that you weren't incredibly close."

He raised an eyebrow at me.

"After I got my PhD, your mother and I drove out to the farm. I showed it to my father. I mean, I was proud. I had worked damn hard for that. You know what he said? 'Don't let that make you think you're any better than us.' That was the last time I saw him alive."

"Sounds like it's a Shubaly family tradition, not talking to your dad for years."

"My father wasn't a particularly easy man to get along with."

I laughed.

"Dad, I think I've said those exact same words."

He looked at me. Was he going to get angry again? He gave me a half smile and shook his head.

"I'm going to let that one slide. I will say this: I'm glad that we are in closer touch now. When I don't hear from you for a long time . . . well, it sucks."

"Sucks for me too, Dad."

We went through more pictures: my dad and his sister as little kids in their Sunday clothes; my father with a string of fish he'd caught; fields and hay bales and tractors and hand tools and barns; adults I didn't know socializing together at the table or on the couch or in the yard, every single one of them with a drink in hand, empties scattered around the frame.

"Jesus, I haven't thought about this stuff in forever," my dad said. "It was not an easy start, you know, growing up on a farm. Even now, approaching seventy, I can still hear my dad's voice in my head like he is in the room."

"I don't know, Dad, I feel like you made it through okay. Nice little house in California. Hot tub. Woodstove. Grumpy old cat. Your wife is amazing. I really think Theresa has done more to get you and me, you know, talking again than either one of us has. And all just by being her normal, generous, patient self. I envy your life, Dad."

"And I envy yours, my son."

I snorted.

"How can you say that, Dad? I mean, yeah, things are decent right now. Or at least better than they've been. Izgi's great. But I have $167 in my bank account right now. I owe $90,000 in student loans now with the interest. I own, like . . . a couple guitars and a frying pan. What's to envy?"

He shook his head.

"You don't see it the way I do. Okay, you don't have a lot of security, but you have complete freedom. You aren't beholden to anyone. Your whole life, it didn't matter what your mother or I said; no one could tell you what to do. You had to do it your way. And you did it your way. Sure, you don't have a Lexus and a townhouse and a 401(k), but what little you have . . . it's *yours*."

We were drying the dishes after dinner on my last night when my dad started.

"Oh! Before you leave and I forget."

"What?"

"That story that you sent me. I wanted to tell you how much I enjoyed it."

"Which one?"

"Well, maybe 'enjoy' is the wrong word. I'll say that it had a profound effect on me. The story about you pumping gas in Saskatchewan when you were sixteen. With the young Indian mother, or Native American, I should say, who passes out with her baby in the junked car."

"You liked that?"

"You got it exactly right. Every detail. The Indians hanging out at the store, the boredom of a Saskatchewan summer. And the sort of overarching hopelessness of the whole thing. Even the dust! It brought me right back there. Not an entirely pleasant journey. But it moved me. That you can do that in just a couple of pages . . . well, it's really good. I'm glad to see you're writing again."

I put the plate I had been drying down on the counter.

"Dad, my life, since I got my stupid, stupid master's degree, has been characterized by a near total lack of writing. I wrote that when I was nineteen. You remember that winter, when I mailed you a bunch of writing? And then I kept calling you to see if you had read it? I mailed it to you twice."

It was a depressing memory—folding up the computer paper with the string of holes along the sides and mailing it off to him a second time, fearing that he would continue to ignore me but still unable to not send it.

"That story was in there?"

"Yeah, Dad. I mean, thanks, I'm glad you liked it. But . . . goddamn. For you to just ignore me like that, that was incredibly painful. You couldn't have read it then?"

He gave me a look.

"You know . . . I was a real bastard back then."

That week, we'd talked about his dead sister, his alcoholic parents, and his disappointing son. But when I brought to light that connection he'd missed, well, that look on my father's face, it was the saddest I'd seen him the entire time.

I kept running through the winter, buoyed by Izgi's encouragement. Only after six months of sobriety could I see how small my life built around inebriation had been. Still, I'd found little to put in its place. Running gave my empty life some purpose, a sense of momentum. I had no idea where I was headed, but I was sure I was making progress toward it. When I was stressed, just thinking about running calmed me.

Running was available everywhere, in unlimited supply, and it was totally free. No partner necessary, no special equipment, and no training—you just started doing it, and then you were doing it. Running was an inverted drunk—you felt like hell first, and then you felt great. Your suffering had meaning, and it actually made you a better person.

Izgi bought me a pair of real running shoes. My feet felt better, but my legs still ached without end. I complained enough that Izgi made up funny songs about my legs to make me laugh. My nipples looked like they had been hit with a belt sander from getting chafed by my sweaty T-shirts. Izgi bought me a couple of slippery, synthetic-fabric shirts and threw my sweat-drenched laundry in with hers without complaint. I loved running in the clothes Izgi had given me, thinking about her while I ran, about how she cared for me, and how I cared for her.

My roommate Esteban was in the kitchen one day, heating up food in his bathrobe while I was getting ready, tying my shoes, filling my water bottle. Our kitchen was small, and he'd gotten large enough that it was tricky to fit us both in there at once. What to do about Esteban disappearing into his body? He rarely left the apartment now. I had no idea how he paid his rent. The heavier he got, the sadder I felt for him, and the more I despised him for giving up.

"Health kick, huh?" he said, throwing some leftover Chinese food in the microwave.

"I don't know about health *kick*. Health shuffle, maybe."

He guffawed. Always in such a good mood. Condescend to him all I wanted, he had still figured out something I hadn't.

"How far do you run?"

"I don't really know. I run as far as I can. When I can't run anymore, I turn around and start walking home. Then after a little while, I can run again. Then walk and run home."

He shook his head.

"Well, make sure you bring a Metrocard with you. Hell, I'd even bring $20 for cab fare in case you need to bail out."

"Not a bad idea."

"I should be your coach," he said, tucking a long oily strand of black hair behind his ear, then stirring his General Tso's chicken in its Styrofoam container.

I slipped into my room on my way to the door. I quietly unzipped the pocket in my water bottle sleeve and took out the Metrocard and $20 bill I had been running with. Esteban was right, you had to have a bailout . . . if you wanted to be like Esteban. I had lived my whole life without a safety net; I wasn't about to start relying on one now that I was sober. I forced myself out the door, down the stairs, and out into the cold.

I had put off going to see a doctor about my legs because I feared they'd tell me to stop running. Finally, the pain got so bad that I made an appointment with a sports doctor who accepted my Medicaid.

Dr. Sofia was an Italian immigrant, short, with a brown ponytail. She was a runner and listened attentively as I described my situation. She inspected my legs and tested my reflexes. She led me through a series of motions to see how my body moved. Then Dr. Sofia sat down and started writing in my file.

"Is it, like . . . stress fractures?" I said. "You can get those from running, right?"

She looked up at me as if she had forgotten I was there.

"No. You're fine."

"But it hurts all the time. Not a little bit. A lot."

The doctor pointed at the chair, and I sat down.

"So, you have been a drunk for a very long time. And then one day you decide 'I am going to be a runner.' Correct?"

"I guess."

"This is great. Good for you! But your body, it's not ready. Sitting on a bar stool, it's not great exercise for legs, you see."

I nodded, feeling like an idiot. I knew what was coming.

"You're going to tell me I have to stop running."

She smiled.

"No. Keep going."

"But it hurts *so much*. I'm not, like, damaging anything?"

"No. Your bones are weak from not doing anything with impact. You are actually doing a good thing. Making the bones stronger. Undoing damage."

"Is there anything I can do for the pain?"

"Ibuprofen."

"Yeah, that's not really cutting it."

"Vicodin is excellent for pain."

"Okay."

"Percocet is even better for pain than Vicodin. Morphine even better than Percocet. But listen to this. You like running. Or running is important to you now, yes?"

I nodded.

"When you are a teenager, you start to drink alcohol. You get sick, headache, hangover. You feel pain, but you keep going, yes?"

I nodded again, flushing.

"So now you like running. You feel pain, but you keep going. Drink lots of water; maybe take some Aleve. You must warm up before, and you must stretch after you run. If you don't stretch, this will cause you problems. After some months, the pain will stop. But you don't need Vicodin. You know how to do this."

Did I? Doing the least I could get away with had been my identity for a long time now. It was easier than confronting my two greatest fears, trying and failing. But every time I went running, I tried and I failed. I tried to run the entire route I had planned without walking, and I failed. I tried to sprint every other block on the way back home along the Williamsburg waterfront till I got to North 14th. I failed. I tried to beat a double-decker tour bus down Broadway to Izgi's. I failed, even with a bunch of tourists cheering me on. But somehow, trying and failing hadn't had any negative consequences. In fact, by trying and failing over and over again, I had actually made a lot of progress. I had rarely met my running goals, but I had gotten closer and closer to meeting them before I failed. When it seemed sure that I would hit the mark the next time, I made more ambitious goals so I could keep failing, keep striving, keep moving forward. My smartass doctor was right—I had endured a lot of pain in order to keep drinking. I'd assumed a lifetime of drinking made me a bad fit for athletic activity. Had it actually tempered me to be a distance runner?

I laced my shoes up the next day and went back out. Could I keep running through the pain? I could. Could I run longer? I could. Could I run longer still? I could. One day, I realized that the aching in my bones was gone. I began to gain confidence. My runs grew of their own volition, from five laborious miles, just out and back, to regular half marathons.

I planned a long run for my birthday—seventeen miles on February 17, over five bridges in three different boroughs. It went wrong. I got lost; I ran out of water; I ran out of food. Finally, I was so faint with hunger that I ate a pizza crust out of a trash can. I was chilled to the bone by the time I got home, shaking so hard I could hardly get my key in the lock.

I couldn't wait for my frying pan of chicken and vegetables to cook, so I worked my way through half a quart of peanut butter while it cooked. The peanut butter tasted good so I spooned another quarter jar over the chicken and veggies and then, fuck it, some honey too. I ate the entire mess right out of the frying pan, four large chicken breasts and mounds of sticky-sweet vegetables, probably thousands of calories. I collapsed into bed. My alarm went off a couple of hours later, and I awoke with a moan. Time to go to work, where I would be on my feet for five or six hours.

I rechecked the route the next day after almost twelve hours of sleep. I'd calculated the mileage wrong. I'd run at least twenty-one miles.

As soon as it started to warm up, I resumed biking to and from work. One night, my bike broke. It was a newish bike, a fancier mountain bike that my trainer Tracy had given me for a song because she rarely used it. Approaching the Williamsburg Bridge on an empty Delancey Street, even pedaling as fast as I could, I wasn't feeling any resistance. Had something gone wrong with the gears? No, I'd just had it tuned up. Had I forgotten how the shifter worked? Nope, it was definitely in top gear. I glanced up. I was *blazing* down the empty street. It wasn't that the bike was broken; my body was fixed. Now, my body's top speed was greater than that of my bike. When I hit the incline to the top of the Williamsburg Bridge, I didn't downshift, just leaned forward. Could I reach the top in the highest gear? As my thighs began to burn, I felt a weird sensation at the base of my skull, like 'shrooms were just coming on, an old, almost forgotten sensation . . . Oh yeah, *pleasure*. By the time I reached the crest of the bridge, I was flying.

My body started to change. One day, while I was shaving, something caught my eye in the mirror as I turned my head. Was that an ab I saw, momentarily interrupting the vast white expanse of indistinguishable meat I called my stomach? I twisted my body to the left and right, craning my neck, staring out of the corner of my eye, but I was unable to replicate the exact conditions that had provoked the first sighting and therefore unable to confirm my hypothetical ab's existence. It would be like the Loch Ness Monster, I decided: a fleeting glimpse of a convex shape, only slightly more than a ripple that, though I would spend haunted years looking for it, would never reappear to confirm the existence of life below. But I was wrong: it came back several times, then decided to stay and even brought along a friend. I had two abs between my burgeoning chest and my deflating beer gut. I recalled the sensation when I was detoxing that half of my body was trying to eat the other half. Could it be that the good half had won?

I found a new New York in the city I had long dreamed of leaving. My circuit had been pretty limited: the clubs where my bands had played, the bars I'd been fired from but still drank in for free, the Greenpoint bars in stumbling distance of my apartment. But now I ran through the huge swathes of New York I had avoided—the Financial District, Midtown, the Upper East Side. They were fine, nothing to be afraid of (as long as you were moving through them quickly). And I ran through the hidden eddies of the city, Woodside and deepest Bushwick, Dyker Heights and Astoria. There were stories everywhere: a four-inch gold-lamé heel hooked into a chainlink fence like the erotically crooked neck of a heron, low places that stunk of human sweat, sebum, and excrement, and, in the night in the middle of the 'hood, huge fragrant wafts of fresh baked bread and powdered sugar, as if you were running through the middle of a giant donut. A marathon wouldn't be long enough, I decided, so I signed up for an ultramarathon in Long Island in early May.

In April, I went to Turkey with Izgi to meet her family, a big step for both of us and something that would have been impossible for me just a year earlier. Our first jetlagged day, she brought me to an ancient tower overlooking the city, and we climbed to the top. Holding Izgi's hand and looking out over Istanbul, that great nexus of humanity, Europeans and Africans and Asians and Arabs, living and struggling and dreaming and dying as they had for thousands of years, I had an epiphany about my own life. I was but one person among millions, among billions. If I never did anything with my life, if I never accomplished Some Great Thing to avenge my mother and make my father love me or fear me or just notice me, Some Great Thing to set myself apart from that threshing sea of humanity, it didn't matter. If I could just treat this good woman by my side right and keep myself inching forward as a human being, that would be enough.

Ten days after we returned, I rose so early it was still dark and drove out to the start of the Greenbelt 50K—thirty-two miles of trail in central Long Island. It wasn't just smaller than or different from the Staten Island Half Marathon; it was almost nothing: a small cluster of runners lit by headlights in the gray mist in a nondescript parking lot for a quick briefing, then shuffling off toward the trees when the race director said, "Okay . . . go."

By the time we reached the woods, the pack had thinned out so much that it was just me, slipping and sliding on a wet, sandy single-track trail in my battered running shoes. The woods reminded me of the woods behind our house in Canada. Was this what my sober life was to be, me wandering alone into the abyss of my memory? I felt a pang of fear: What if I couldn't? Relax, I told myself. You have your water bottle and your iPod. Just listen to the music, keep an eye on the markings, and run, one step after the next, until you can't anymore. They'll send someone in to find you when you fall apart.

People passed me, but I didn't fall apart. I focused on my feet; I focused on the music; I focused on Izgi. I ran alone for a long time. Then I started passing people. Izgi caught me at the last aid station, wolfing down ice-cold watermelon. She had taken the train down to Staten Island.

"Mishka, you are almost done!" She looked stunned. "You have only five miles left!"

I'd already run more than a marathon? I was tired, and I was ready to be done, but I wasn't dying. I could do this.

After less than a year of sobriety and only nine months of running, I completed my first ultramarathon. Izgi was there to take my picture as I ran across the finish line. I'd never even run a marathon, but I was learning that you had to dream big.

We stuffed ourselves after the race, then I folded my tired legs into my little car. We talked and laughed the entire drive home, blinking in the spring sunshine. While I had been running, the clouds had lifted.

CHAPTER 10

Longest Day

Alcohol is an excellent aggregator. When you are drinking to excess, every problem, great and small, seems to fall under the same umbrella. I can't keep a job because I'm a drunk. I'm out of shape because I'm a drunk. I am depressed because I'm a drunk. I have a short fuse because I'm a drunk. My apartment is an indoor slum, a buffet of filth, because I'm a drunk. I can't be counted on for basic social niceties, like saying good-bye or responding to emails or sending a note when your father dies or not mortally wounding your liquor cabinet and stealing the expired Vicodin from your bathroom and pissing my jeans on your couch, should you foolishly allow me to crash at your house for a night, because I'm a drunk.

When you stop drinking, those collected problems scatter. Getting sober is like knocking a jar of your sister's tiny colored glass beads off the arm of the couch. The instant the jar shatters, the beads flee like they have been imprisoned. Sure, you can clean up a big clump of them pretty quickly, but for the rest of your life, you will be finding them between the seat cushions, under the couch, stuck to your feet, sometimes even carrying them into bed with you.

Things went south with Izgi. There was no screaming, no throwing of dishes, no infidelity. There were just fewer shared laughs, fewer shared smiles, fewer shared looks, fewer connections. We talked about it. Izgi and I were each hard-pressed to find something the other had done wrong. Neither of us even raised our voices. Still, there was a shared unease, a mounting sense that, time and again, we were out of sync.

One Friday, that spring, we fought. Our first fight, a big fight, a sad fight. On Saturday, we had the best day we'd ever had together. On Sunday, I packed up the few clothes that I had kept in a bin at Izgi's Soho apartment—the Mishka Box, she had called it—while we both held back tears. Then I drove back to Brooklyn. The least dramatic good-bye I could remember—no threats, no concerned neighbors, no cops. Still, it hurt like hell.

That's how life goes sometimes: don't do anything wrong, do everything right, fail anyway. It was the first breakup I'd ever gone through without the solace of that tireless listener, that bottomless well of comfort, that sympathetic devil: alcohol. It was rough. Izgi was at the center of my new life. But I wasn't a drinker, so I didn't drink. I was a runner, so I ran. I ran as I had before, in the shoes Izgi had bought for me, wearing the shirts Izgi had bought for me. But now I put on sunglasses before long runs so people couldn't tell I was crying.

I ran the North Face trail marathon through the wet Virginia heat only a month after my first ultramarathon. Two weeks after that, a 50K in Montreal, wincing with each step. Two weeks after that, I got in my car at 4:15 a.m. after my shift at Beauty Bar and drove up past Ithaca for the Finger Lakes 50K, a gorgeous single-track trail through quiet forests into broad, sunny cow pastures, the sky exploding blue overhead. Another 50K a month later. Then another two weeks after that. And various local 10K races scattered throughout the summer so I would qualify for the New York marathon the next year. Longer than my punishing first run less than a year earlier, 10K races now seemed so short they hardly even registered in my head. I'd nap on the couch at Beauty Bar for forty-five minutes after closing, bike up to Central Park to race, then bike home and collapse after twenty-four hours on my feet.

I made every mistake possible. I drank too much water, I didn't drink enough water, I drank too much Coke at an aid station and gave myself heartburn. I didn't eat enough, I ate too much, I didn't eat steadily over the course of the day, I wolfed down M&Ms at an aid station and barfed. I got blisters on my heels, I got blisters on the sides of my feet, I got blisters between my toes. My toenails turned black and fell off, grew back, and fell off again. My chubby thighs chafed, my balls chafed, my butt cheeks chafed, my nipples, my underarms, *everything* chafed. I got terrible gas one race and thought I could stealthily squeak it out, a little here and a little there. When the song on my iPod ended, I could hear other runners laughing at me as I farted audibly with each step, like I had a duck in one shoe and a frog in the other. Little by little, though, I started to figure it out.

"My body is a monster driven insane," I heard Nick Cave sing for the first time when I was fifteen. For years I had let my body run wild. Now, like a jittery, wild mustang, it needed to be broken. It needed to be exhausted, punished even, then dominated and mastered. It had to learn to go when I told it to, faster, faster. It turned where I wanted—the long way home, not the short way—and only stopped when I was ready. It had to serve me. But then, as with a horse, I had to care for it.

My counselor had been carping on about all kinds of self-stuff. Self-care. Self-love. What was next, self-fellatio? The problem with America wasn't that we didn't love ourselves enough, it's that we loved ourselves too much. Still, I knew what he was getting at: if you showed a little care and cleaned your kitchen once in a while, you inevitably hated your apartment less. And maybe even felt a little better about your life.

It wouldn't be capitulating to treat my body like my other mode of transportation, my car. Don't waste time, energy, or money on frivolities—car washes and bumper protectors and new floor mats. Just the bare minimum: check the fluids regularly, keep it fueled, and do the necessary maintenance. And if I intended to race the old, high-mileage shitheap, well, I needed to be vigilant about caring for it. I even came up with some rules for running.

Never get hungry. Whenever you're offered food, take it—not a lot, just a little—and keep moving. If you waited till you got hungry, then it was too late. You'd either gorge and get sick to your stomach or feel nauseated and continue not to eat, making the nausea worse. Calorie shortage manifested mentally before it did physically. Depressed? Having a rough day? Ready to quit running forever? Eat something, and watch your worldview swing around. But what goes up, must come down. If you ate a handful of Skittles, you would rocket up, then come crashing down. If you drank a Red Bull before the race, you'd be crawling by the end. I ate white foods—oatmeal, bagels, bananas, cubed potatoes, potato chips—as they padded your stomach, were easy to digest, and were quickly converted into sustained energy. Caffeine was fine, but only for the last quarter. Sugar was only for the last gasp.

Never get thirsty. Every time you thought "Should I drink?" you should drink. Every time you didn't think about drinking, you should drink. Peeing took valuable time, but it took less time than dealing with a muscle cramp. Drink water, warm not cold, and *water*, not soda or juice or any kind of fancy fuel. You could drink that, too, but you had to drink water. And salt. Mix an untasteable amount in your water, or steal a couple of packets from your local McDonald's and rub some on your gums at the aid station. Like it was the good old days and that salt was pure, flaky cocaine.

Never get lost. Each race was long enough without tacking on bonus miles. Never turn down help. A cookie or a chip or a smear of Vaseline or even a hug might keep you going. Never tough it out. That minor chafing or hot spot or little grain of sand in your shoe at mile four might end your race at mile twenty-four. Never give yourself an out. If you said you'd run halfway and then evaluate it, you'd drop at the half. If you said you'd see how you felt, you'd drop when it got dark or when it got cold or just when you got tired. When you lined up at each race, you had to tell yourself that if you bled from every pore, if your feet broke off and you had to run on your splintering shinbones, if monkeys flew out of the sky with AK-47s that shot ninja swords, you were still finishing that race.

Never, ever give up. To be a runner, you had to listen to your body, and you had to ignore your body. Can't run anymore? Walk till you can run again. The race ain't over. Can't walk anymore? Stand till you can walk again. The race ain't over. Can't stand anymore? Sit down, lay down, vomit in the grass, cry and curse God and tear out your hair. Then stand up again. The race ain't over. The race ain't over. The race ain't over.

─

I had blown off seeing the therapist once I'd hit the six-month mark and had my exit interview with Project Link. But I forced myself to start going again. "Be your own father," the narrator in *Invisible Man* had said. I started with a new counselor, Chris.

Chris didn't do anything. Each time I came in and sat down, he asked me how I was doing. Fancy, expensive PhD hanging on the wall, just to be able to ask me how I'm doing?

We talked about the band. We talked about running. We talked about my job. I felt bad because we never talked about how Chris was doing.

"We can talk about me next week," Chris said with a grin as I was leaving.

I showed up in a snit one day and questioned aloud why I was even there. It was one thing to say you were an alcoholic in a bar. The solution there was to have another drink. Saying it in a doctor's office was much scarier—the solution there was to never drink again. I'd been careful not to cross that line and cop to the "A word" with Chris.

At my worst, it was still debatable whether I was an alcoholic. I knew from the Twelve Steps that alcoholics were supposed to be powerless before alcohol. I'd never been powerless. Or at least I hadn't consistently been powerless. I had turned drinks down sometimes, or only had one or two, and had sometimes gone days or even weeks without drinking. It wasn't war all the time. I'd always known people who drank more than me, people who were worse drunks than I was, people in deeper trouble. And I had stopped without rehab or AA. Alcoholics weren't able to do that.

"You keep asking me about my life, and I've kept bouncing it back to you," Chris said. "You really want to know about my life?"

"If you're going to tell me how you're an alcoholic and AA saved your life, then start crying and try to hug me, I *will* punch you, Chris."

"Relax. Nobody's punching anybody. I'm gonna tell you about a friend of mine. Guy I grew up with in Stuytown. Ernesto."

I perked up. I loved hearing about the carnage of others' lives.

"This guy Ernesto, we went to school together. Pretty good ball player, point guard. I could get around him sometimes, and I could shut him down sometimes because I worked harder than anybody out there. You know, short kid disease. But when he committed and really drove to the hoop, he was unstoppable. Ernesto didn't drink every single night or always get shitfaced. But if he could, he would. He didn't black out every single time, but if there was nothing standing in the way, he did. Bad shit didn't happen every single time he blacked out, but sometimes it did."

"I know plenty of guys like that." Big deal.

"We went to different schools but sort of kept up, you know, pickup games in the summer. And we both wound up back in the city after school. Ernesto didn't always drink in the morning, but sometimes he did. I think he wanted to more than he did. He just . . . seemed to have a hard time being happy without alcohol. With it, he was the king of the world, you know, life of the party, girls hanging all over him. Still, any given day, at any given time, he would rather be drinking."

I rolled my eyes. "And then one day he woke up, and he was dead. Moral: don't drink. The end. Very sad, Chris."

"Nah, he's still alive. Doing fine."

"So now he's a custodian and you're a doctor. I saw that After-school Special, too."

"Am I telling this story or are you?"

"Sorry. I'll let you finish."

"No, it's cool; you want to be the doctor, you can be the doctor. So, Dr. Shubaly, do you think Ernesto is an alcoholic?"

I shrugged. "Sure. Yeah, he's a fucking alcoholic."

Chris nodded but didn't say anything.

"So what happened to Ernesto? What's the moral? You're a shrink; there's gotta be a moral."

"No moral, Mishka. There is no Ernesto."

I flushed.

"Aw, fuck off, man."

"I can't diagnose you, Mishka. You're the only one who can make that call."

I suddenly felt very small and very scared.

"Okay. Fine. So I'm a fucking alcoholic. Is that what you want to hear?"

"I don't care either way. You want to take it back? I won't tell anyone."

"No. Fine. I'm a fucking alcoholic. The worst thing is true."

"Mishka, this isn't bad news. Or even news. From what you've told me, you've been an alcoholic for a long time. What's changed is that now you're facing it. You're climbing out."

I hated Chris. I hated him for getting paid to listen to me bitch and complain. I hated the way he spoke, his carefully calibrated mix of "street" and the bullshit lexicon of "steps" and "progress" and "self-care." I hated the careful little traps he laid that I blustered right into. And I hated him for being right.

Biking home, I felt mad and sad and scared. But after a couple of hours, I felt better. Not just better than I had when I had left the session, better than I had felt before the session. When the thing you fear most in the world finally happens, it sucks. But at long last, the fear is gone. The Worst Thing Imaginable has occurred, and you're still here: you've survived it. The dread-filled wait is over, and you can finally get down to the grim business of living the rest of your life.

＝

When we were dating, Izgi had complained several times that my apartment smelled funny. It embarrassed me, as I had noticed it too. I cleaned and cleaned, opened all the windows to air the rooms out, to no avail. Finally, I'd mentioned it to Esteban, and the smell had gone away. When it came back, I mentioned it again. Again, it went away.

The third time, I'd had enough. I waited till I was sure Esteban wasn't at home, then slipped the lock on his door. Bracing, I flipped the light switch.

I had never been clean, but what I saw was worse than anything I could remember. Esteban's room was pure filth and despair. The walls were gray with dust and lint halfway to the ceiling, pocked with greasy handprints. Clothes strewn everywhere, not just dirty but blackened and stiff. Desiccated Chinese food shellacked to aluminum takeout containers. Gay porn magazines, ads for sex clubs, flyers for gay escorts. An imploding couch heaped with so much trash it was impossible to sit on. A fax machine, the phone off the hook, on a collapsing bookshelf. There was a tiny cleared path leading to a defeated-looking chair, one corner propped up with a phonebook, in front of an ancient dusty terminal.

His poker station. Esteban had mentioned several times that he had been playing Internet poker, I thought just to kill time. But apparently, it wasn't just time the poker had been killing. There were three Tropicana bottles next to his computer, all filled with piss. A fourth one, closest to the chair, was half full. Our bathroom worked perfectly. Esteban had been pissing into bottles so he wouldn't miss his poker blinds. He hadn't even bothered to throw the full bottles away.

I turned off the light and locked the door, dialing my landlord even as the door was swinging shut. No more.

It turned out that Esteban was behind on rent as well. Still, it took two months to get him out and then two days for a cleaning lady to make his room livable. I talked my landlord into letting me rent the whole place. Jens, who had played drums for COME ON twelve years earlier, had just broken up with his live-in girlfriend, so he moved in. With my drinking half and my depressing room-mate gone, I felt like a malign spirit had been exorcised.

One day at counseling Chris asked me what I'd been reading.

"I'm reading *The Dark Knight Returns*. You know, the Batman graphic novel that came out in the late eighties?"

"I remember that era of Batman well. When they had that poll to see if Robin should die? I lost friends over that."

"I thought it was such bullshit when Robin died. But now I know that he had to die. Is that the difference between a man and a boy? Men know that Robin had to die?"

Chris shrugged.

"That was after *Dark Knight* anyway. I haven't read it since I was in seventh grade. Man, it's pretty great. Batman's old and fucked up and weak, sort of courting disaster every time he even leaves his house."

"Fantastic premise."

"Do you remember the story?"

Chris cocked his head. Motherfucker was a library of noncommittal gestures.

"It's been a long time for me too," he said.

"I thought I remembered it all but I was surprised at how much I had forgotten. Harvey Dent—Two-Face—they've surgically repaired his face, and he's gone through all kinds of annoying ther-apy so they've pronounced him cured and set him free."

"I guess even Frank Miller values talk therapy."

"Aha, but he's *not* better. That's the thing. As soon as he's re-leased, all these horrible crimes start happening, crimes that could only be the work of Two-Face. Batman hunts him down and cor-ners him in this abandoned warehouse. Always gotta be an aban-doned warehouse, you know?"

"Right."

"But it's kind of a touching scene. These two old men who have known each other twenty-five, thirty years . . . they've been in each other's lives for longer than they haven't.

"They're fighting in and out of the shadows. Great inking there. There's this twinning thing going on. Batman puts on a mask that gives him freedom. Two-Face's face is his mask, and it imprisons him. They've each been transformed by trauma—Batman by the murder of his parents, Two-Face by getting acid thrown in his face. Batman keeps his duality secret; Two-Face celebrates it. And so on."

"I should reread it."

"After fighting for a while, Batman reaches out to Two-Face. He's like, 'Harvey, why are you doing this? You were cured. They set you free. They even fixed your face! You've wanted to be free of Two-Face since he appeared. You had that opportunity, and you threw it away. Why couldn't you let yourself be free?'

"And Harvey says, 'Batman, are you crazy? I'm fucking de-formed.' And he steps out of the shadows. His face? Totally nor-mal. Handsome, even. Pretty depressing."

Chris nodded.

"So what's the point of the story?"

"I don't know. No one is ever cured? Naw, it's Frank Miller, so it has to be darker, more cinematic than that. How about 'the scars of the soul run deeper than scars of the flesh?'"

"Why did you choose that story to relate to me?"

"Oof. I guess I feel like old Harvey Dent sometimes."

"Keep going."

"Like, standing on the street, people just see some jerk waiting for the bus. But I carry all this shit around in my head. All the people I've hurt, disappointing my family, all my failures . . . "

"Other people just see a man waiting for the bus, not a jerk."

"You know what I mean."

"Maybe they even see a good guy. He's in good shape, color in his face, decent haircut. Even shaves sometimes. He could be anything."

"But in my head . . . "

"So how could Two-Face transform back into Harvey Dent?"

"More annoying talk therapy?"

"Sounds like Harvey's already been through a lot—let's not subject him to something so terrible as that."

"I don't know. Isn't it almost time to wrap up?"

"Nah, we've got a few minutes left."

"Chris, you didn't even look at the clock! You always wrap it up at quarter till and it's 2:55! What if I'm late for something?"

"Tell me one thing Harvey can do to not turn back into Two-Face. Then you can go."

"Okay, shit. Let's see. He can make a list of things that Two-Face does—committing crimes themed with duality or incorporating the number two, deciding the fates of his foes with a coin toss—and a list of things that Harvey does—pursuing justice, reinforcing good, punishing evil. Then he can focus on doing the Harvey things, reward himself for doing those things, and, you know, not capture his foes and torture and terrify them. Good?"

Chris gave a half smile and pointed to the door.

On the bike ride home, I flip-flopped. I believed in Chris. He'd helped me see that my relationship with Izgi had been not a failure but a success—a normal, adult relationship that had run its course. And he was right, that was true. It had been rough between us for a minute, but now Izgi helped me, and I helped her;

we supported each other, and we would stay friends for life. Chris was a good guy.

But Chris was also manipulating me. Blatantly, right in front of my face. He had recognized how hardheaded I was, so he didn't feed me new age wisdom; he forced me to volunteer it for myself—the only way I would accept it. Positive reinforcement would never help Harvey Dent. Two-Face would always undo the honest DA obsessed with justice. More importantly, without Two-Face, Harvey Dent wouldn't exist, would never have existed.

Had Harvey Dent never been disfigured, had Two-Face never appeared, readers would never have known Harvey's name. He would have lived and died outside the frame—a nobody. If Two-Face disappeared, the man Harvey Dent would only be important because he was No Longer Two-Face, or At Least Not Right Now. And bad guys only disappeared for one reason: to come roaring back in the next episode.

Chris had tried to use the parable of Harvey Dent and Two-Face to show me that changing my inside world would change the outside world. Maybe that was true. But his parable made me realize something else, that my disfigurement—my drinking, my *alcoholism*—was the only thing that made me special. Without it, I was nothing, not even worth naming, just another of the anonymous masses, or not worth drawing at all.

≡

I kept my head down at races, alienated even from myself. Still, I made new friends. It was impossible not to out on the trails, running side by side with strangers for miles. The runners I met made me look like a short-timer, a rank amateur. Johnny Rocket was a shit-talking mason from Jersey who did almost no training between his fifty- and one-hundred-mile races. Joe Reynolds was a dirty old man with a white mustache like a scrub brush; he streamed pervy jokes and unforgivable puns while casually racking up lots of 50K finishes, even the occasional fifty-miler. His wife, Christine, hosted the Finger Lakes 50s race. She was as sweet as Joe was salty, and she ran with a beatific grin on her face, only marginally wider after a couple of postrace beers than it had been at mile forty-nine.

A long, lean brunette always encouraged me as she blew past, even though she was perpetually racing a longer distance than I. After our third race together, I finally asked her name: Zsuzsanna Carlson. She had a small face with deep, expressive eyes and a little button nose that, combined with her bouncing ponytail, called to mind a bunny rabbit. Her legs required a completely different metaphor. They were the legs of a statue magically sprung to life—shiny, polished granite in constant, impossible motion, thrashing tirelessly up a narrow rocky split in the side of a mountain. Her favorite races ground up one tear-inducing rock face and plunged down another in the beautiful but brutal mountains of Virginia: the Massanutten Mountain Trail fifty-miler, the Hellgate 100K, the Grindstone hundred-miler. Zsuzsanna talked about running 66.6 miles up the side of a mountain in the middle of the night in the dead of winter with the kind of open desire most women reserve for dark chocolate.

I ran with Republicans, I ran with Mormons, I ran with born-again Christians. Conversation—with anyone, about anything—was the only antidote for the boredom, doubt, and pain that came late in a race.

I ran with a bubbly librarian, Cherie Yanek, who ground out competitive finishes at some barbaric hundred-milers, hosted a 50K race at Burning Man, and ran dressed as a pink flamingo whenever the opportunity presented itself. If you had told me before I started running that I would become friends with an Italian American personal trainer from New Jersey with six-pack abs who listened to dance music and dressed, daily, in a track suit and a visor, I would have told you the notion defied logic, that it violated laws of physics, that it defeated ironclad mathematical truths, that it was impossible a thousand times over. Yet Jerome Scaturro—a black belt and Ironman several times over—became not just a buddy or an acquaintance but a trusted friend.

I made no mention of my past incarnations: the Wannabe Writer, the Soused Songwriter. I was a night manager at a bar. I played bass in a band called Freshkills. I happened to not drink. But it turned out I wasn't the only one with secrets.

One by one, my running buddies opened up. Zsuzsanna had been a hardcore alcoholic—straight vodka, from a plastic bottle. She'd been sober for fourteen years when we met. Despite suffering from asthma since she was a child, Melissa O'Reilly dreamed of running Badwater, the 135-mile race across Death Valley in the heat of summer. Steroids in her asthma medication had weakened her bones, so she kept getting stress fractures. But as soon as each new injury healed, she was back running again. A race director I met had sixteen years sober and had run ultras of all distances, including a 144-mile self-supported run. Bob Bodkin had been diagnosed with sarcoidosis—granules in his lungs—which he treated by running the Grand Canyon, rim to rim to rim, then the Oil Creek hundred-miler a week later. I got wind of David Clark, a 320-pound alcoholic who had lost 150 pounds in eighteen months by running. For the fifth anniversary of his sobriety, he ran Leadville, a grueling high-altitude hundred-miler through the Rockies. Like me, these people had used running not as a means of escape, but of transformation.

When I'd lined up for the first time at the Staten Island Half Marathon, I had stared at my feet and thought, I am not like you. When I lined up at another backwoods ultra, where first prize was a carved log or a painted rock, I shook hands, I looked at faces, I looked into people's eyes. Sure, they were runners, but they were also alcoholics and junkies and sex addicts and anorexics and diabetics, survivors of domestic abuse, morbid obesity, cancer, incest. You had to be a little bit crazy to run more than thirty miles for fun. These freaks—these damaged, wounded, frightened, hopeful people straining to get better, to be better, to overcome, to truly live before they died—they were my people.

When I showed up for my shift at Beauty Bar a little after 10:30 one night, I hung around outside for a minute instead of going straight in. It was nice out, and I wasn't eager to blow another night in a bar. True, I would be working, not drinking, but tonight, that only felt worse. This was my ex-world, but I hadn't been allowed to leave it behind.

I sat down on the doorman's stool for a minute to rest my tired legs. A woman down the block squawked something unintelligible. I made out one word: "phone." A skinny young guy sprinted down the street in front of us. A thought went through my head: he is not running for the bus.

And then: I bet I can catch him.

I leapt off the doorman's stool in front of Beauty Bar and dug in hard, sprinting with everything I had.

The kid flew up the block, then down the steps into the Third Avenue subway station. He was thin and lithe, a sprinter, and he was moving fast. I had never been fast, even as a kid. At our sixth-grade track meet, Chuong had won every single distance. I wasn't even fast enough to compete, not by a long shot. I certainly hadn't gotten any faster in the last twenty-plus years. At thirty-three, it took a lot of work to get my 215 pounds moving at all. But most fast people aren't fast for long. This kid probably wasn't even a runner. I was. I could run all night if I had to. As long as I didn't lose sight of him, he was mine.

I was still accelerating when I hit the staircase down to the subway. *Shit.* I sent some hapless tourist sprawling as I skidded down the steps but somehow managed to stay on my feet. If the kid hopped the turnstile and made it onto a train, I was screwed.

But as I skittered off the steps into the station, I saw him disappearing up the staircase on the other side. I dashed across the station, then sprinted up the stairs, three at a time, and followed him south across 14th Street, dodging oncoming traffic.

I hollered, "Stop, thief!" and "Stop him!" and "Call the cops!" My helpful fellow New Yorkers did nothing.

But eighteen months previous, I wouldn't have done anything either. I certainly couldn't have given chase. I probably wouldn't have even been able to stand up. I'd passed out at Beauty Bar my last two visits there before I quit drinking: once from snorting Opana in the bathroom, once from simply being so drunk that even snorting chalky lines of crushed Adderall hadn't revived me. The only reason I hadn't gotten thrown out on my ass was that Zack, who'd barbacked there for ten years, had vouched for me.

If I had been a conscious witness to the grab-n-go, I'd have told myself that the kid needed the phone more than she did, that this was a more equitable distribution of wealth—trickle-down economics at work! And if it wasn't? Hey, not my fucking problem.

After crossing 14th Street, the thief ducked left on 13th and sprinted down the block toward Second Ave. My jeans were wet and sticky, clinging to my legs, my quads already burning, but I was rapidly closing the distance between us. I started yelling at his back, perspiration already soaking through his T-shirt: "I can run all night long, motherfucker. Drop the phone! You hear me gaining on you? *You hear me gaining on you?* I *will* run you down!"

I was disappointed that no one joined in to help. So many people had tried to help me in the past, just a stranger in trouble. As I lay wasted on the sidewalk outside Luna Lounge or Motor City, people had offered me change or tried to buy me food because they thought I was homeless. A professor had followed me out of class after I had shown up with fourteen stitches in my hand, bought me dinner, then given me quiet hell for the way I was living. A bartender in his fifties came over the bar when I was getting stomped by about six guys on St. Patty's Day, broke the fight up, chased them out, and let me drink for free the rest of the night. A stranger helped Allison get me up four flights of stairs one night. Strangers woke me up on buses and subways so I wouldn't get robbed or miss my stop. I had been helped into cabs by at least half the city.

And the cab drivers, man . . . Several cabbies turned the meter off halfway through the ride or just waved off my attempts to pay them entirely: "Ah, you're having a rough enough time as it is, buddy. This one's on me."

When I stood covered in blood outside Mike's Papaya one morning at sunrise, a big, white bandage covering fresh stitches in a wound on my arm, a cab cut across two lanes of traffic to scoop me up. I marveled aloud that the cabbie had stopped at all.

"The blood, it's not good, but in the face, I see you are a good man," he said, grinning.

The night after Jacob had died, I cried all the way from Bedford and North 5th in Brooklyn up to 107th and Amsterdam in Morningside Heights. The taxi driver silently handed me Kleenex after Kleenex through the plastic divider. He didn't even turn the meter on till we were on the FDR, which was good as I didn't have enough to pay the full fare, just a $20 Jens had stuffed in my hand. That driver never spoke a word to me. I can't recall ever seeing his face, but I will never forget him or his kindness.

Screaming at this kid as I chased him down the street, I realized that for once I wasn't the one in need of help. I was *helping someone else*.

The thief whipped desperately across Second Ave, weaving through honking cars. I was right on his heels and closing fast. He was done.

When we reached the other side of the avenue, he whirled around, his chest heaving from exertion, his face a mask of exhaustion and bewilderment: Where did this guy come from? And why can't I get rid of him?

In high-pitched moments of drama, I never, ever say the right thing. But this time, I did.

"Dude," I said, looking him dead in the eye, "give me the phone, and you walk away. Or we fucking go to war."

I had at least fifty pounds on him. His face twisted with anger. I had ruined his night. It felt great.

He reached in his pocket and withdrew the latest iPhone, released only that week. He tossed it to me. I caught it and slipped it into my pocket. I pointed in his face—*I got you*—and walked away without another word.

By the time I got back to Beauty Bar, a small crowd had assembled outside.

"Aw, man, he got away," the doorman said when he saw me approaching, empty-handed.

"Nope."

I pulled out the phone and held it high. People cheered. Mike Stewart, the bar owner, gave me a high five.

"I just came outside a minute ago to yell at you for not keeping an eye on things," he said, grinning.

I felt good. I had done a good thing, done it without even thinking about it. It hadn't come out of the Big Book or a sermon or even a session with Chris. Something decent inside me had woken up and acted without any prompting, without anything holding it back.

A group of people clustered around one panicked girl walked toward the bar from the Third Avenue subway stop. As I watched, she hit a button on the cell phone in her hand and held it to her ear. The iPhone rang in my hand. She looked up in shock. Her eyes met mine, and a look of recognition flashed over her face. Her face lit up.

"My phone! You got it back!" She threw her arms around me. "Oh my God, you're a hero!"

Well, no. But there was no denying that I was something more than I had been before.

＝

That August, less than a year into my running life, I met my shadow self. I was driving up for the Green Lakes Endurance Run in Fayetteville, New York. I talked to Johnny Rocket to see if he wanted to go in on a campsite or ride up together. He wasn't going, but he hooked me up with another runner who was: Luis Ramirez.

Luis stood up from the little campfire he had going when I pulled in, and we shook hands. We talked while he prepared his food for the next day. He was broad; I was tall. I was pale; he was dark. He was clean-cut; I was shaggy. I was soft from years in bars and on the road. He was ripped from years in the Marine Corps. I was Canadian American; English my first language and French my second. He was Dominican American; Spanish his first language and English his second. He was a proud father and a super-dad. I had no children and intended to continue that hot streak. He listened to "anything"—meaning dance music, hip-hop, or Latin music. I listened to "anything"—meaning rock, soul, country, punk, or indie rock. We had so little in common that we appeared to exist in opposition.

I had a good race. My left knee started to hurt running down the hills, but I still ran my best 50K time of 5:24. It didn't bring me any joy. On my best day, I was still only in the middle of the pack. And a 50K wasn't even a real ultramarathon. At thirty-two miles, it was just a prolapsed marathon. My father had run marathons, high-altitude marathons; he'd even run Pike's Peak. In his prime, my dad could have easily run a 50K. As fast as I'd run today, Dad still probably would have beaten me.

Luis was running the 100K distance. I knew I wasn't ready, but, God, was I envious: sixty-two miles, a real ultramarathon, a race that was impossible to diminish. But the day got really hot, and Luis fell apart late in the afternoon. He threw up, then hallucinated, and, after hugging a tree for a couple of minutes because he couldn't stand on his own, decided his best bet was to drop.

If we had bonded around the campfire the night before, it was nothing compared to after the race. We had taken our bodies to the limits, alone and together, and we were exhausted and giddy. We told filthy jokes and more than one dark story from our pasts. Luis was disappointed that he'd been forced to drop, so I did my best to buck him up.

"Luis, this shit that we set out to do . . . not everyone does it, you know?"

"I know. I just had my mind set on doing it and not giving up. When I say I'm going to do something, I do it."

"That's great. I wish more people lived that way. But . . . man, it's different with ultrarunning. Biting off more than you can chew, that's sort of the point. You don't go out there to win."

"I didn't want to win," Luis said, staring into the fire. "I just wanted to finish."

"Luis, you can't think that way. You don't go out there to finish, you go out there to get beaten. You finish a run, that means you played it safe. You could have killed the 50K. Shit, as fast as I ran it, I should have been doing something longer.

"You go out there to leave everything you have on the trail. You find something bigger than you, you throw everything you have at it, and *maybe* you come out on top. If you only fight dudes you know you're going to beat, you're not a fighter; you're a bully. If you only fight dudes you know may beat you, well, that's how a fighter becomes a champion.

"The finish line, it's not the finish line. The external distance is just a distraction, an exercise. The goal is to cover new terrain in here."

I tapped two fingers against my temple.

"If you fall short, you don't cross that arbitrary line, it doesn't mean that you suck. It just means that you have ambition, that you try to do big, heroic things. That's what matters. A DNF should be a badge of honor. It means your dreams are boundless. Ultrarunning is the opposite of real life, Luis: when you fail, you win."

He looked up at me.

"That was fucking deep, man. You should be a motivational speaker."

"Sorry. I got worked up."

He grinned.

"So what race are we doing next?"

I whooped, and we high-fived. Luis howled and pounded on his chest like a great ape.

"You got me fired up, man! I'm ready to run *now*," he said.

"Have a blast. I'll keep the fire going till you get back."

Driving home the next day, the words I had heard myself say echoed in my head. I talked a good game. Did I believe any of it? My mantra at the end of my drinking career had been simple: *fuck it*. It had been brutally difficult to overcome that nihilist bent. If I wanted to erase it fully, I needed to overwrite it. I needed a new code to live by, but in early sobriety I'd had nothing to write in its place.

I had read through the Twelve Steps several times and figured out quickly that they weren't going to work for me. But after eighteen months of sobriety, I'd accrued some wisdom on my own:

Alcohol can't make it better; it can only make it worse. As bad as I felt, as sad, lonely, depressed, or angry as I got, drinking was only a palliative that would magnify the problem down the line. I had done exhaustive field research on that subject. I could not let myself forget it.

Make it watertight. Addiction was like water—it would find any hole, any crack, a pinprick even—and it would get through. If I wasn't going to drink unless I saw a bald eagle, I would convince myself at happy hour that the sparrow I'd seen at fifty yards was a bald eagle at two hundred, and then, "Bartender! Let me get one of everything!" "I will try not to drink today" had failure written into it. Nothing but *nothing* could make me drink.

Make a list. It was impossible for me to even take a shower without writing it on a list. Each morning, the things I had to get done swarmed like a cloud of gnats around my head. When I wrote them down, the cloud disappeared. Even if I had more to do than I could get done that day, the tasks appeared manageable. And at the end of the day, crossing items off the list? That was a powerful high.

Do the worst thing first. Every year, I worried about doing my taxes from January 1 to midnight on April 15, when I finally mailed them off. It never took me more than forty minutes. Go through the list you've made, pick the thing you dread the most, then bite the fucking bullet and get it done. Putting it off and living in dread always takes more energy than cleaning the damn cat litter or whatever it is you have to do.

Harness the wolves. Avoiding temptation was a farce. There was beer in the deli downstairs, a liquor store across the street, and rubbing alcohol in the bathroom. Hiding from the wolves only showed them—and me—that I feared them. Alcoholism didn't have me, I had it, and I was the boss. When the wolves approached, stiff-legged and snarling, I held my fucking ground. When I yearned for a drink I had loved, I called to mind a brutal hangover and the consequences my days-long drunks had brought on. Then I showed the wolves I wasn't afraid: I poured drinks at the bar, counting out the liquor glugging into the glass, and I poured beers, the foam frothing over the backs of my hands. And then I slipped cords around the wolves' necks: alcohol had made me weak, but alcoholism had made me strong. Wolves were wild animals, and they could never be trusted, but if I was vigilant, I could harness their strength, make them serve me instead of destroying me.

Escape is no escape. Some nights, trucks would grumble by on the BQE, the apartment would tremble, the closet door would swing open, and I'd turn back into a little kid, hiding under my blankets, heart racing, terrified something was coming to get me. Controlling my breathing did nothing. Trying to steer my mind elsewhere just spurred on the most horrific visions— flayed bodies crawling up my comforter, children with gnashing mouths instead of eyes. Finally, one night, I dragged myself out of bed, shaking with fear and anger at myself, pulled the closet door open, stepped inside, then closed it behind me. "Let's do this, then," I said. Nothing happened. Then my heart slowed. Then I got bored, climbed back into my bed, and slept. Escape only bred a need to escape. When you felt bad, you didn't try to evade it—you went as deep into it as you could. And then you came out the other side.

Try every day. Staying sober alone wouldn't cure me. It wouldn't fix the eyes that saw only ways for things to go bad, wouldn't correct the mind that sought out negatives and magnified them, wouldn't cut the endless loop of death-and-failure pornography churning round in my head. Just staying sober wouldn't give me the big life I had dreamed of as a kid. Bukowski had "DON'T TRY" engraved on his tombstone. Well, fuck you, Chuck. I would try every day. It didn't matter at what. Try at everything, try at anything. I had let that little muscle atrophy, the trying muscle, and I needed to build it back up. Little things, like not jerking off for a day or doing more than fifty push-ups in a row, and bigger things, like trying as hard as I had to make my relationship with Izgi succeed, and even bigger things, the biggest.

That last one, that was it. It was true, what I had told Luis. You had to dream big. You had to try. Luis and I signed up for our first fifty-mile race together, only four weeks away: Virgil Crest, a rugged ramble over hilly, single-track trail, with over ten thousand feet of elevation change, including up and down a ski hill twice. We talked to other runners who had done it, picked their brains about the course, and compared training strategies. It wouldn't be easy, but it wasn't impossible. My father had never run fifty miles. I would.

I'd had some pain on the side of my left knee running down the hills at Green Lakes, but it went away after a couple of days. Two weeks later, at the Groundhog Fall 50K in Pennsylvania, my knee got so bad that I had to walk the last five miles. It was bizarre. I could charge up the hills, but the minute I tried to descend, I felt stabbing pain about an inch to the left of my knee, like someone was knifing the air next to my leg. That couldn't be good. Nerve damage? The phantom pain throbbed through the night. The next day, I couldn't put any weight on my left knee without it buckling. I picked up a brace at Duane Reade and forced myself to rest.

Two days before the Virgil Crest fifty-miler, I got jumped by three guys at Beauty Bar. I managed to land correctly when we hit the concrete—on top of them—and didn't further injure my knee. Still, two miles into Virgil Crest, I could no longer run. Luis stuck with me, determined not to leave me behind.

Fifteen miles into the race, I couldn't walk. Luis hadn't dressed for the weather so I handed him my black long-sleeve shirt, one that Izgi had given me. I dropped out, the first time I'd had to do so. My first DNF ever. I was crushed. It was clear that I wouldn't be running again for a while. I had the cold, shitty winter ahead of me. It felt like alcohol was tenting its fingers in anticipation, waiting for me to come crawling back.

≡

For a few days after the race, it was hard to walk. There was no question: I had to stop running completely. I missed several expensive races I'd signed up for. With running, my anti-alcohol, out of my life, I had lots of time to reflect on why I had found a home in alcohol. Closing down the back bar by myself one night, I caught a whiff of Jameson as I was wiping down the necks of the bottles. It was more than some exotic perfume; it was like the scent of a girl's hair mixed with her sweat, like a rabbit's trail to a hound, like blood to a shark. I could pop the speed pourer out of the top and take one huge, incandescent swallow from the bottle. Who would know? It's not like I had to worry about Izgi leaving me now. I was alone and angry. If I couldn't run, why not drink?

My cravings for alcohol were unexpected and intense, like a visit from a succubus. Different drinks appeared before me in succulent, pornographic detail. A frosty Sol longneck, a voluptuous lime crammed rudely into its top; a salty dog, grapefruit juice gaily pink like a child's dress, salt on the rim sparkling like rock candy; an unadorned measure of scotch in a highball, honey from enchanted bees swirling around a single ice cube.

As I'd promised myself I would, for every drink I conjured, I recalled an equal and opposite hangover. There was a direct line between that alluring first drink, the retching hell the next morning, and the half life I'd lived. I could not let myself forget vomiting off the side of an escalator in the DC train station, the spatter getting louder and louder as the escalator carried me higher and higher; laying on the bathroom tiles in Allison's apartment, freezing and sweating, then frantically pulling my boxers down and sitting on the toilet, liquid shit splattering the bowl and my bare ass, then, as the smell hit me, vomiting onto my belly and crotch; hunching over a stranger's toilet, expelling undigested alcohol, then chewed-up food, then bile as my stomach, my esophagus, and my throat convulsed in staccato rhythm like some terrible engine run dry of lubricants and tearing itself apart. What would come up next? A kidney? My testicles? Little bits of my soul? An old rubber boot?

When I slept, I was plagued by dreams of the drughole. There was a space between the pipe that heated my room and the plywood loft I'd built for my bed. Whenever I'd gotten too fond of a drug, I threw it down this hole—the drughole—so it was no longer accessible, though not lost forever. The thought of digging through the dust- and lint-covered cardboard boxes—one actually labeled "DEPRESSING EX-GIRLFRIEND HELL"—under my loft was enough of a deterrent that I wasn't about to go in there after them. (Eventually, of course, I had moved the dead amps and broken guitars and boxes of unlabeled crap and, yes, snorted the contents of every baggie, vial, or little twist of plastic I found under there.)

Now that I couldn't run, the drughole occupied increasing psychic space in my idle, depressed dreams. One night, I dreamed I stretched its narrow, splintery plywood opening like taffy and crawled into that rabbit hole, which was, of course, cavernous and filled with many wonders. There were Vicodin the size of cheeseburgers, Opana the size of ottomans . . . it was heaven. One rolled toward me, and I tackled it, then fell to the ground with it, gnawing on the corner like a rat.

I awoke with a lingering, mournful sadness, as if I'd been dreaming about the first girl I'd ever loved. I knew I was slipping.

For those who suffer from it, "depression" has ceased to be an accurate word for the malaise. It calls to mind the unhappy-faced blob with a dark cloud over it from that Zoloft commercial, which is distant in essence from the quietly writhing despondency I know. David Foster Wallace, who in the end learned more about depression than he could bear, called it "a black hole with teeth." That's pretty dead-on. But this concept—an absence so severe it manifests as a malign presence—is hardly new or limited to Wallace. It appears in *The Neverending Story* as "The Nothing," an all-consuming void of darkness. And in *Spirited Away*, it's No Face, a monstrous shadow that, once invited into a home, devours everything it encounters. Falling into this hole is not just feeling blue or bummed out. It's nihil and nadir. It's acedia.

Searching for the perfect word for this rotting sadness, I came upon the concept of acedia. In Christian theology, it's an antecedent to sloth, the least sexy of the seven deadly sins. Thomas Aquinas winnowed it down for me: acedia is sorrow so complete that the flesh prevails completely over the spirit. You don't just turn your back on the world; you turn your back on God. You don't care, and you don't care that you don't care.

Still, there was one more layer to this black hole in my head. It's a French word, originating from *oublier*—to forget—and literally meaning "the forgotten place": the oubliette. The oubliette was a specific kind of dungeon created in the Middle Ages, one where the only entrance was a hole high in the ceiling. There was no way out. The hapless captive was tossed in, the door was closed, and the prisoner was left, alone with his sin or perceived sin, to go insane and slowly wither away and die. It was a life sentence, solitary confinement, *and* a death sentence. The oubliette was called "the forgotten place" because it was reserved for prisoners so low that their captors wished to forget them. That for me was the final element: it's a man- and God-forsaken black hole with teeth where not only are you staring into nothingness, not only is it slowly consuming you, not only does no one seem to know or care, but if they ever did find out, *they would try with all their might to forget you.*

When I was young and fell down this well, I'd try to comfort myself by imagining some outrageous good fortune: winning the lottery or saving the life of some modern-day princess or just stumbling on a trunk of cartoony jewels like Scrooge McDuck's. As a teenager, I would conjure up the next Girl Who Is Going to Save Me and hold her face out toward the darkness like a candle. As I got older, my concept of escape matured. At the end of my drinking days, my reliable pick-me-up was envisioning my suicide.

I would ensure that my death wasn't the frightful mess my life had been. In the fantasy I finally settled on, I'd pawn a couple of guitars and buy a scrip of Opana, some speed, and a tarp. I'd snort the speed and go through all my shit—my books, my scribbled-in notebooks, my cassette tapes, all that crap. I'm hideously disorganized and still have boxes I haven't unpacked from three or four moves ago. I'd go through all of that shit, throw out everything I could, and organize my entire house, then clean it, a thorough top-to-bottom scrubbing like I was moving out and absolutely had to get the security deposit back. I'm a slob, and people have been cleaning up after me my entire life. No more!

When the place was totally clean and everything had been dealt with, I'd lay the tarp on my mattress and lay a blanket my mother made when I was a kid down on top of it. That way, when I was discovered, there wouldn't be any mess to clean up—they could just gather the tarp up by the corners and lug my body off to Potter's Field. I'd cut up three pills of Opana into one long, thick serpent of a line. Then I'd swallow all the remaining pills and quickly snort the line. The shit I snorted would knock me out before my stomach could get upset and I could vomit. It would also prevent a last-second change of plans. I'd just drift away like Lily Bart in *The House of Mirth*. Comforting, isn't it?

There were no angels. Survival came down to me. Drag myself out of that hole, or topple headlong into it, it was my call, and mine alone.

I'd been humbled in so many ways. Getting so out of control I'd had to quit drinking forever. Being shamed by the doctor at the STD clinic. Forcing myself to apologize, not to one friend or a couple of friends, but to lots of people, even a few I didn't really know. Going to therapy—therapy!—and admitting I was an alcoholic. I had subjected myself to humiliation after humiliation, and each had come with a reward, or at least an alleviation of pressure. What was one more?

I forced myself to ask Chris to refer me to the staff psychiatrist. Dr. Beeder was a small woman with straight brown hair and owlish glasses. I didn't want to be medicated into idiotic bliss, I told her, but my relationship with suicide didn't strike me as normal. It slipped unnoticed into my head. I'd only realize I'd been planning to die when Freshkills booked a decent gig, and I'd think, Okay, I'll wait until after that.

She wrote me a scrip for something she said wouldn't change who I was. "You'll still be you, just maybe ten to fifteen percent better. Ironically, it may make you feel more like yourself."

I hesitated for a minute outside the pharmacy. Really? Antidepressants? Shit, I'd taken every drug I could think of to *not* feel like myself. Why be such a pussy about taking something to feel like myself? It worked. Like she said, not a lot, but a little. Enough.

I went back to Sofia, the sports doctor who had coached me through my shin splints. After listening to me describe my current symptoms, she spoke.

"I told you to stretch. Did you stretch?"

I looked at my feet. Of course I hadn't.

"So here we are," she said.

There was nothing wrong with my knee, she said, but I had acute iliotibial band syndrome.

"Sounds tropical," I said. "Is it fatal?"

She swatted me, then explained. In ITBS, the long band of muscle that extends from your hip down to just below your knee becomes so tight that it rubs painfully on the bony protrusions of your knee. Rest and physical therapy should take care of it, but, Dr. Sofia warned, it might bother me for the rest of my life.

I found a physical therapist in my neighborhood, Eva, a redhead with cutting blue eyes who had run for the Polish national team. Two weeks into physical therapy, my left leg stopped hurting. With Eva's tentative permission, I went out for a short run. It was miraculous! I was cured! I wanted to throw down my knee brace and burst into song. Then I felt a familiar pain outside my right knee. By the time I got home, I could hardly walk. The next day, Eva began treating my right leg.

For the next six weeks, I went to physical therapy four times a week. It was painful and time-consuming and hardly encouraging. I stretched daily and spent many a night lying in bed with a bag of frozen peas strapped to my leg, wondering if Izgi missed me, wondering if Allison ever missed me, wondering if anyone ever missed me. Eva dug her sharp elbow deeper and deeper into the flesh of my right thigh, but still I couldn't run for more than a few blocks at a time.

I'd signed up to run the NYC marathon for Luis's charity, but when the race rolled around, I'd run less than ten miles total in the preceding two months. Eva stopped just short of absolutely forbidding it.

"You shouldn't do it," she said. "I'm telling you not to do it. But I know you. So if you do it, do not run. If you feel pain, you must stop. If you don't stop, you're going to undo all the work we've done here."

The morning of the marathon, I allowed myself to run over the Verrazano Bridge and then forced myself to walk. People were cheering but also kinda looking at me like, "What's your problem, man? Run!"

By the time we got to Manhattan, I was in the back of the pack with the absolute beginners, a seventy-year-old Buddhist with a long white beard and a guy with one leg. The last ten miles, my leg was in agony. But I finished . . . behind Meredith Vieira, Jared from Subway, and the Chilean Miner, who had been able to do more training underground than I had above. I did beat Al Roker. Big whoop.

I redoubled my efforts at rehabilitating my stubborn leg. I did a series of painful stretches daily and iced my leg so long and so frequently that I gave myself frost burn. Most importantly, I took three weeks of total rest. When the oubliette came for me, I closed my eyes and imagined myself running through a moist, verdant tunnel of foliage with Luis, both of us laughing at some filthy joke.

Slowly and carefully, I began to run again. One mile. One and a half miles. Two miles. Three and a half miles. Five miles. Eight miles.

I went down to Mexico in January to stay with my uncle Albert, the same uncle who had invoked my mother's wrath by slipping me a couple of rum-and-Cokes at a family reunion when I was nine. Albert used to work all year long in northern Canada so he could go on an epic bender each winter in Mexico. The previous year, he had bottomed out, and the town where he had run amok became the town where he had gotten sober.

I slept on the floor in his tiny casita on an air mattress. He went to his meetings, and I ran. One day on, one day off, stretching my IT band hard several times a day. I didn't know what I was running from. I didn't know what I was training for. I didn't even know who I was. I didn't know why running was good for me, but I knew it was good for me, so I ran.

I had let myself get out of shape, and building my endurance back up in the blazing Mexican sunshine exhausted me. Nightly, I plunged to the bottom of an ocean of sleep.

One night, I dreamed that I had returned to our family home in Canada. I lived in a cave under a bridge with my mother and father and my four brothers. We dressed only in leather made from the skins of animals we had hunted or trapped. But our living, our way of life, our reason to exist was the enormous marlin that swam in the river under the bridge. My brothers and I fed our family by leaping onto the backs of these giant sailfish, twenty or thirty feet long, wrangling them toward the shore like marine cowboys, then slitting their throats with our wooden-handled scimitars, butchering them, and smoking the flesh. It was, at once, infinitely strange and infinitely familiar. My people had lived this way since the beginning of our history. Our purpose was narrow—we had been created to eat the marlin, as the marlin had been created to feed us—but we fulfilled that purpose to perfection. I was where I was supposed to be, doing what I was supposed to do. For the first time in my life, I belonged. There was so much love radiating from my heart that my chest felt hot. I was truly happy.

I awoke from the dream with a succinct epiphany, the reason why my father and I couldn't get along: he had been the first person to disappoint me and the first person to express disappointment in me.

Dreams were meaningless, just the brain idling, I told myself. As emotionally stirring as my dream had been, it was just the detritus in my head: part coward's fantasy of being macho, part white boy's fantasy of being "Indian," part modern urbanite fantasy of returning to savage nature, 100 percent pure jumbled fiction. But I'd encountered many truths in fiction, perhaps more than in any other genre or even in my real life. *The first to disappoint me; the first to be disappointed in me.* Was my pickled brain even capable of manufacturing such a tidy, fortune cookie explanation? It was like a Möbius strip cut out of a page of *One Hundred Years of Solitude*, shorter than a joke, denser than a black hole.

This couldn't be the incantation that would cleave the heavy chains apart, spring the rusty old locks open, could it? There was something to it, more than just poetry. Was it even true? I had worshipped my dad, been fascinated with the hair growing out of his face, the smell of his pipe, his sweat. How had he disappointed me? Maybe by allowing himself to be henpecked, always evading my mother with jokes or just kowtowing when she was mad? No, there was something before that. A big disappointment, maybe the biggest. He didn't like me.

There was no question that I had been a disappointment to him. I had disappointed my father in ways great and small. If I had been one thing to him, over the arc of each day and over the arc of my wasted life, I had been a disappointment. I saw only one way to undo that.

Dad loved my running. His running years were behind him— he'd already had a knee replaced—but he loved hearing about my running, loved talking about running, and wanted a detailed report after each new race. In the same way that seeking revenge on my father had hurt us both, running was a way for us to both root for me. Each new accomplishment of mine felt like a joint victory.

I hit the dusty cobblestones that morning with new fire. I banged out ten miles before Albert crawled out of bed. After his breakfast, my lunch, I went out and ran another six.

I ratcheted up my weekly mileage, pushing the length and pace of my runs. I had never trained this diligently or consistently. Had I ever applied myself to anything with this much focus? From the time I awoke until I fell asleep, I had one thing on my mind: fifty miles.

CHAPTER 11

Darkest Night

M y whole life, I'd been a lightning rod for trouble. But when I got back from Mexico, good things sought me out with the same urgency trouble had.

I was driving home from Costco with a carload of groceries in January 2011 when my phone chimed. At a red light, I fished it out of my pocket and clicked it on to check the email that had come in.

When the stoplight turned green, I was still staring at my phone, reading and rereading the short email, dumbfounded. The car behind me honked. I looked up, pulled through the intersection, then pulled over to read the email one more time.

> hi mishka, is that you? if it is you call me, if it not you i'm
> sorry wrong person heheheh or call me talk to u latter bye

Chuong.

He had left a New Mexico number. I called it instantly, without thinking. The phone rang several times, and then someone picked up.

"Hello?"

The voice was distant and muffled. It could have been anyone. What was I supposed to say? If it was him, he wouldn't recognize my voice right away.

"Chuong?" I said.

"*Brother*," he said.

Chuong had been in Albuquerque this entire time. How many times had I been through there on tour? Five? Six? After the first time, I hadn't even tried to look him up in the phone book. Had I given up hope of finding him? Or was it because I was wasted and hungover and depressed and had no idea how to deal with finding him? No matter. He had found me.

Chuong's English hadn't improved dramatically in the twenty years since I'd seen him, and his voice was indistinct. He ran his own landscaping business. He had a wife and a sixteen-year-old son. "How is Mom?" he asked, then "How is Dad?" He sounded stunned when I told him that our family had flown apart. How could he not know of the biggest thing in my life? But he had been gone such an incredibly long time.

He was sorry for running away, he had missed me, he had missed all of us. He had tried again and again over the years to find us, hundreds of calls to information, but it had been hopeless. He couldn't wait to see me again, for me to meet his wife, meet his son.

I told him I was broke, but I promised that I'd find some way to come and visit him. That would be great, he said; we would drink lots of Heinekens, lots and lots. Hoo boy.

When we were saying good-bye, he said, "Tell Mom that I am okay and have a son." He had always loved her, and she had always loved him. Then he said, "Please tell you dad I say I'm sorry." He sounded sad. It was sinking in now, the divorce and all the sadness and pain that had followed. In his mind, we had been one big happy family this entire time.

One night in mid-March, I drove out to rural New Jersey for Ultrafest, an ultrarunning event with races of fifty kilometers, fifty miles, and a hundred miles run on the same loop course. When I got to the event home base—an open field behind a small church—Johnny Rocket grabbed me before I could set up my tent, the same tent my mother had given me when I was seventeen for Simon's Rock graduation.

"We got a tent all set up for you, man. Don't worry. Yo, Christine, I'm putting Mishka in your tent, okay?"

Christine Reynolds laughed her great throaty, honeyed laugh somewhere off in the dark. Sure, that tent was just set up as her changing station for when she ran the hundred-miler the next day, so I was welcome to it now. I quickly loaded my gear in, unrolled my sleeping bag, and lay down. It was windy, and the tent rustled and flapped loudly, but I forbade myself from changing positions for fear of tossing and turning all night.

The hundred-mile race started at 4 a.m., so all my buddies rattled my tent and heckled me as they ran past. Had I slept at all? I felt like I'd just hallucinated all night long. I willed myself to take more sleep, but my heart was already hammering. I dragged myself out of my sleeping bag and began getting dressed. No way could I run fifty miles today. I felt ill prepared to run five.

When I stepped outside, the night was pure black, as dark as it had been when I'd pulled in. My stomach felt like a plastic grocery bag full of live eels. It was hopeless. I would fall apart. I would fail.

The darkness was still untainted when we clustered at the starting line, each runner just a voice behind a blinding headlamp, familiar or unfamiliar. Too cold. Too early. Too lonely. Rick McNulty, who ran the New Jersey Trail Series, gave us his usual spiel: The course was well marked but pay attention. Use the port-o-potties provided, as this was a bridle path through a residential neighborhood. Don't litter. Stay warm. Have fun. And . . . *go.*

We ran through the wet grass up a sloping incline into some trees. I could see my feet and the ground immediately in front of me, maybe the back of the next runner, and that was it. As we ran, the pack dispersed. Lonely as it had been at the start, it got lonelier.

The morning grayed as the sun began to approach the horizon. The air filled with mist. I saw figures weaving through the trees toward us. They looked like aliens. Then, one after another, they called out to me.

Zsuzsanna. Christine. Johnny Rocket. Luis. All running the hundred-miler. They high-fived me, they hugged me, they slapped my ass. No way I could run the fifty miles, but I couldn't drop yet. Wait till the sun comes all the way up, see what the course looks like, see how my knee holds up.

I fell into step with a stranger, and we talked for a while. We shed layers as the sun climbed in the sky. I stopped to stretch my IT band at an aid station, and the other guy left me behind. I struck out alone. The scenery . . . there was none. It was banal, nowheres-ville New Jersey, brown and gray, post-snow and pre-green. My exposed skin was too cold, my torso too hot, my legs leaden and half-asleep. But I got a boost each time I encountered a running buddy I'd made over the last year. Christine gave me a huge smile and a thumbs-up. Luis slapped me five and danced by, jamming out to his iPod. Zsuzsanna hugged me without breaking stride. I got a quick sniff of her conditioner before she was bounding away down the bridle path. The miles ticked by.

Every race, someone commented that I was too big to run. They'd said the same thing to my dad. It didn't matter. We ran. My feet hurt, often for days after a race. Had his feet hurt like that?

Thirteen miles down now. The ascent of Pike's Peak was thirteen miles. My father had run it twice. Yeah, but that was thirteen miles at high altitude, thirteen miles with more than a mile of vertical gain. Thirteen flat miles in New Jersey was nothing.

My mother had never been a runner, or at least I had never seen her run. She had always been an avid hiker, so I had asked her once, as a little kid, why she didn't run like Dad. She explained to me that I had been such a big baby that giving birth to me had damaged her bladder. If she tried to run now, well, she leaked a little bit. That was my mom, answering honestly every question her kids asked, even if what she told them blew their fucking minds. And that was me, a ruiner before I even left the womb.

A marathon down. Had Tatyana ever run a marathon? I couldn't remember. She'd run something—a marathon or half marathon— but that was before I could differentiate between the two. Back then, 13.1 and 26.2 had both extended well into the realm of impossible numbers.

The farthest my father had ever raced had been 26.2 miles. Less than a mile from the finish of the Russian River Marathon in California, he'd blacked out cold and come to with road rash on his face and a medic standing over him, but he'd finished a marathon in Colorado. I still remembered the long-sleeve T-shirt from one of Dad's races, designed to look like hands pulling a button-down shirt open to reveal the race name underneath it, like Superman revealing the emblematic *S* under his shirt, as though finishing that race had made you a superhero. That was my dad.

Thirty-four miles. The furthest I'd ever run. Dad had run thirty miles one time, maybe thirty plus. He couldn't recall exactly how many, but every time we talked about that run, it got longer, stretching to thirty-two miles then thirty-four then thirty-six. That was my dad, always retreating into the distance.

Running a fifty-miler in under twelve hours qualified you to apply for a hundred-mile race. I'd soaked up that information somewhere and stored it in a dark corner of my mind, shielded from hope. If I kept this pace up, I would beat twelve hours. I would beat eleven hours. Shit, I would beat ten hours.

Thirty-seven miles. Further than I'd ever run. Further than he'd ever run. No questioning it. Each step was a new personal best. The sun was all the way up now, had been for a while. It made the water in the creek sparkle. Then the snow sparkled. Then little rocks in the bridle path sparkled. Then the whole path was spar-kling and breathing and moving, like I was running on the back of some great jeweled serpent.

I had heard someone say that 90 percent of running an ultra-marathon is mental, and the other 10 percent is mental. Old joke. Big laugh. It had just scared me. My brain was always trying to eat me alive. As a kid, terrified of the dark, I had insisted my parents tie my closet door shut. But then the monsters were under the bed. "If you don't believe in them, they don't exist," my mother had said, her final word before she stalked out, exasperated with me. Great, so what you're saying, Mom, is that if I believe in them, they *do* exist. I'd learned to fall asleep fully covered with blankets, drenched with sweat, sucking air in through just the tiniest gap. Well, I wasn't a kid anymore. I had thirteen more miles to run so, Brain, if you don't have anything positive to contribute, shut the fuck up.

Everything was breathing and moving and sparkling, the sky not just a faraway thing or a tinted absence but an enormous sky-blue air mattress, inflating and deflating, its surface a rough but soft texture, like velvet. I had never been more alert.

A mental game, then. How much could I remember from my life, from my first memory till now? No, stupid idea; that would be torture, sick as I was of sorting through my life. My dad's life, then; how much could I recall? I waded back through his life, before us, before Mom, before college, before high school, before school . . . What was the earliest thing I knew about him, as a child, a boy, a baby?

When it came to me, my right leg buckled. My body canted to the right. I kicked the back of my right leg with my left foot and almost sprawled into the dirt. Adrenaline hit me instantly. Seconds earlier, I had thought I couldn't be more alert. Now I almost had X-ray vision, my heartbeat a drumroll.

A decade earlier, during my kamikaze yearlong tour, I had stopped off at my father's house en route to a show—LA, maybe. He had been traveling for work, so he left me the key. It was an opportunity to get a good night's sleep in a clean bed, wake early, take a shower, then leave feeling rested and recharged, with plenty of time to make the drive.

My father's house was full of wine. I opened a bottle as soon as I walked in, one of the big ones, a cheap one he wouldn't miss. I took it in the shower with me and sucked on the bottle thirstily, the cool wine so luxurious in the steaming shower. I dried off. Friends in San Francisco had given me some pills, so I ate them and went to my father's computer. Nobody home—I could get as loose as I liked and jerk myself into oblivion.

One hour? Several hours? I tried to make it last as long as I could.

Hands shaking, I cleared the Internet history, then closed the browser. I took a long, parched pull from the wine, killing it, then put the empty bottle on the desk and glanced at the computer. There, on the desktop, was a file labeled "Annulment."

It would be wrong to read it. It wasn't intended for me. My father had read a letter I'd accidentally left on the printer when I was sixteen, and that had been incredibly violating. I wanted so badly to read it. But I had to be better than him. I could not allow myself to do it.

I put both hands on the desk and pushed the rolling chair back, away from the computer. I let my head fall back. Whoah, I was fucked up. My head lolled to the left.

One filing cabinet drawer was slightly open. One folder peeked out. I had to close one eye to read the label. "Annulment." It could not have been any clearer—I was meant to read it.

I worked my way through the thin, stapled document, concentrating hard to keep my eyes from crossing. It was shit I'd already read in the email he'd sent me, supposedly explaining why their marriage was invalid. I chafed at his insincerity, his fake humility, how he sounded so blameless and put-upon. Some mean-spirited stuff about Mom, about them smoking pot together once, but none of the earth-shattering revelations I had hoped for.

I'd had a rough time of it with women. Even if it was mostly my fault, it had left me bitter. But the way Dad talked about Mom suggested a rancor deeper than anything I'd felt. Even after he had bailed on her, had bailed on all of us, had successfully made his escape, to still hate her like she had been his jailer . . . it scared me, and it made me incredibly sad.

It had been a mistake to read the annulment, in part because it was the wrong thing to do, but mostly because it was a waste of time. Our family and the tragedy of our family were unexceptional, mundane, almost impossibly so. Christ, had my father just wanted a younger wife and a convertible sports car? Could he be that shallow, that mercenary? There was nothing in his writing to justify the great tearing apart, no explanation. Then I found it.

My father had been molested by his mother until he was fourteen.

⸺

That was the memory, suddenly issuing forth in the middle of the sunlit bridle path, that had buckled my knee. The earliest thing I knew about my father's life was that he had been horribly, horribly betrayed. I hadn't known what to do with the information, had secreted it away in a corner of my brain I never used, concealed it from myself. I'd been searching and searching for a key to understand how my father could abandon us. I couldn't find that key because I'd been carrying it, hidden, in my head for almost ten years.

It explained everything. My father, the most powerful man in my world, a helpless child, stripped of all power, used by the very one charged with his protection. What had it done to him? The sound of my feet in the dirt was suddenly thunderous, my breathing like an approaching hurricane. It was all there. The relentless compulsion to please. The avoidance of confrontation. The unerring conviction that he was both special and persecuted. The poisonous guilt he carried. His emotional alienation. His vacillation between arrogance and self-loathing. His debilitating resentment. All things I'd intuitively learned from him.

We weren't just from different generations or different experiences. We were from different worlds. Turning his back on us was an appalling thing. There was no justification for it. But here, finally, was an explanation. A way to understand it. And, maybe, a way to finally forgive him.

———

I crossed the finish line at a dead sprint. The muscles in my legs twitched and protested when I tried to brake. I circled and slowed. Ah, fuck it. I flopped down on the cold, wet grass.

"Heartbreaker," Rick called out to me. "You came so close to breaking nine hours!" He looked down at his laptop for the exact time.

"Nine hours and twenty seconds. Not too bad. Faster bathroom breaks next time."

I lay flat on my back, sucking air too hard to even laugh. Rick had no idea who I really was. Or at least who I had been. For Rick, it was twenty seconds too slow. It was also two hours, fifty-nine minutes, and forty seconds faster than I had dared to hope to run it. This was an accomplishment not even I could diminish. There was no denying it. I was one of those top-tier wackjobs. I was an ultrarunner.

Once I caught my breath, I wobbled into the church we were using as our home base. I dug my phone out of my bag and made a call to my old nemesis.

"Well, you can't be finished yet," my dad said when he picked up.

"Dad. I did it."

"Congratulations, my son!"

"Nine hours and twenty seconds."

"*Wow.* That is fast! Jesus, that's like two 4:30 marathons back-to-back. Mishka, that's really incredible."

"Thanks, Dad."

"I am so proud of you, Mishka. All the changes you've made, and now this . . ."

"Thanks, Dad."

He hesitated.

"You know, Mishka . . ." and his voice softened, "it's not a competition."

He was right. The competition was over. We had both lost: lost years and years of our relationship. If there was a competition now, we were competing together—against time, against circumstances, against distance, against the burden of our convoluted history, against the ineffable distance between fathers and sons—to try to love one another.

"I know it's not a competition, Dad."

I could hear him smiling through the phone before he spoke.

"But *I* never ran fifty miles."

My legs were crying in pain. My neck was cinched in spasm. My face was chapped and aching from hours of exposure to the winter wind. My right IT band felt like a piece of red-hot wire buried in the side of my leg. I felt absolutely hollowed out, both physically and emotionally drained. But I grinned so hard my cheeks started to cramp and my eyes flooded.

"I know, Dad. I know."

When I got home, I went to the diner near my house and ate a bacon cheeseburger and fries. Then I ordered a steak and eggs and cleaned those plates too. I crawled into bed, but I was in so much pain I couldn't sleep. After a couple of hours, I got up and ate a quart of yogurt with blueberries. A couple of hours later, I ate another, even licking my bowl clean. I woke up after a full night's sleep, ate four fried eggs with toast, then went back down for another eight hours of sleep.

When I finally dragged myself out of bed, I felt battered but satisfied. I had found something bigger than me, something that scared me. I had worked diligently, and then I had been brave. I had taken my licks, and I had won. I didn't have to explain how difficult it had been to my father, because he understood—we both did—that I had finally done something worthwhile.

Did that race change me, or had I been changing for a while? My whole life, I had been terrified of being alone. It was monsters under the bed as a kid. In my twenties, it was the Snuffleupagus of Despair, an emptiness that threatened to consume me the minute I was left on my own. A night of solitude had felt monstrous toward the end of my drinking days, and I would do anything to evade it—drink, drugs, escapist sex, anything. Shortly after my first fifty-miler, I was suddenly alright when left to my own devices. Sure, I looked forward to band practice with Zack and my old friends in Freshkills, and I missed my buddies at Beauty Bar after a couple of days off. But I wasn't lonely or lost and had no trouble filling my days. It wasn't just that I didn't crave alcohol anymore (though I didn't). I was no longer afraid. It struck me as funny: I had run enough that there was no longer anything to escape.

Still, I had a few things to confront. Turning a person into your drug, that was a low, evil thing, and I couldn't just let it slip by unaddressed. I tracked down some of the women who'd had the misfortune to be involved with me during my lazy, years-long spiral down. Apologizing to them was even less satisfying than apologizing to my band mates—they were even more generous than my pals.

"Mishka, I forgave you even in the moment. You told me the first night we met that you were a mess. And, boy, you delivered on that! But you were never unkind."

"You were fun, and that's all I was looking for at that time. I mean, not a whole lot going on at the end of the night. But you were snuggly, and you usually made up for it in the morning."

"Um. Did we ever actually . . . you know? I can't remember, I was so drunk that night."

"Mishka, you were so drunk that you probably don't remember this . . . but I picked *you* up, not the other way around. It's sweet of you to think of me, but there's no apology necessary. I got what I wanted out of it, you know?"

"Dude, shut up. I should apologize to *you*."

More than one woman sat and listened to my entire apology . . . and then not only refused the apology itself but rejected the entire narrative I'd dwelt on of how I had traumatized her, made her hate me, ruined her life. I had been a blip on the radar, or my sins had been eclipsed by those of the men before and after me, or they even had fond memories of me as this sad, funny whirlwind of cheap liquor and shitty coke. It was maddening.

I brought it up with Aaron over lunch one day. He listened patiently, a smile playing over his lips.

"What?" I finally said. "I can see you thinking, and that makes me nervous. Spit it out, man."

Aaron grinned.

"I'm sorry, man, I don't mean to make light of it. But it's been really interesting to watch it play out."

"Glad you're entertained. I should have brought a tip bucket."

"See, that's just it. You probably get all kinds of props for the big life change you've gone through."

"Manopause has been very good to me."

"I don't intend to diminish your accomplishment. It's a big deal. Kudos."

"Yes, golf clap. Cut to the mind-blowing epiphany."

"Well, that's just it. There is none. You haven't changed."

I snorted.

"Okay, you've changed a little bit. Coherent longer, unconscious less. Less of a liability, but also less fun. But you're the same person. Intelligent. Abrasive. Loyal to the death. The same asshole we've come to know and love. The biggest difference is probably . . .

there were days when we had band practice where you were so depressed, you couldn't even lift your head. Couldn't make eye contact. I haven't seen that happen once since you quit."

"This is such bullshit! What about that time I punched you in the neck in Dayton?"

He shrugged.

"I had that coming to me. And that night is memorable not because it was typical but because it was atypical."

"But all the drunken bullshit, I mean, passing out on the street . . . "

Aaron waved a hand.

"Sure, it was a hassle sometimes. But you were far from the worst person in our crew. It was just part of the package with you. And you made up for it—if you said you were going to help me move furniture at 9 a.m., you were there and ready to work at 8:59, if stinking of whiskey. We didn't hate you, you did. The day after you'd had a big night, we'd always get these self-lacerating apologies, apologies incommensurate with the sins of the night before."

"Thanks, I guess. But I'm pretty sure it was rougher for the women."

"What makes you so sure? You were convinced that you were a scourge on your friends, and that's been credibly debunked. Not to be too reductive here . . . but women are people, too, man. They have needs and desires and issues and personal agency. If they were unhappy with how you were treating them, they were free to leave. And many of them did! The one-night stands and hookups . . . hey, women have been fighting for forty years for the right to act as sleazy as men. Who's to say they didn't get exactly what they wanted?

"All of your trespasses fall neatly under the umbrella of 'normal human shittiness.' You never hit a woman. You never menaced a woman. I've never even known you to lie to a chick to get her into bed. You were always just like 'Yo! I'm a train wreck!' and sometimes it worked. Cheating on Allie, well, that sucks, but here's news for you: you're not the first guy to cheat, drunk or sober.

"I understand your desire to apologize. It's as noble as it is misguided. You need to realize that the drunk you were in your head and the drunk you were in the world . . . well, there's a wild disparity there. Hate to break it to you, but you're not a monster. And you never were."

Nearly twenty years of cravenness, trouble, and woe. I'd been sure it had all been my fault. Now I could find no one to agree with me. Shannon had forgiven me quickly and admitted that her instability had rivaled my own. Riley and I had each torn at the other. Speck I certainly owed a real apology to, but both she and Riley had gotten married and moved on with their lives—to contact them now would just dredge up unhappy memories. Though I had apologized to Oksana during our entire fling, I did it once more, sober. She confessed to fabricating her entire tragic history—the dead father, the dead brother, the dead lover, the cancer-stricken mother—then tried to lure me back into bed. Shilpa would agree enthusiastically with every bad thing I might say about myself, but she'd lied and manipulated and made false accusations the entire time I'd known her, to say nothing of the physical abuse I'd endured. When she'd tried to file a spurious lawsuit for over $1 million, well, that had dried up any desire to make things right with her. Allison . . . God, I owed her a long, elegiac apology, a litany of apologies, a never-ending stream of them. She deserved not a letter or a phone call or a painful, awkward lunch but something epic—a monument of apology. Somehow, I couldn't bring myself to make even the smallest gesture toward her, not because she wouldn't forgive me but because she would.

Aaron's theory, it was a total cop-out. I didn't want to be pardoned. I didn't want to skate on a technicality. I needed the world to hear my grand apology, then punish me, excoriate me for my sins, and give me absolution. All the shit I'd done, all the nights I'd wasted, all the night's I'd *been* wasted . . . I wanted blood to flow. Surely there was someone I had wronged badly, someone who had not moved on or forgotten about it, someone who felt compelled to receive my mea culpa with the same urgency I felt compelled to give it?

At the same time, Aaron had a point. There was one person I had abused above all others, a person who had elicited ornate cruelty from me, a person who had lived with my foot on his throat for years: me. And if that was true, how to apologize, how to forgive?

Dave Blum, my editor from the *New York Press*, emailed me. He had taken a job working for Amazon and wanted to talk to me about a writing opportunity. We met up for breakfast at the Noho Star, a café in downtown Manhattan. Amazon was launching this new platform publishing exclusive content for Kindles, and he wanted me to write for it. I had read about the Kindle. It struck me as just another expensive fad, a way for those burdened with surplus money to alleviate the strain.

"You could make some serious money," he said.

My writing wouldn't be printed at all; nor would it be available on a website. There was no flat payment for the work, not even fifty or a hundred bucks. I would get paid only for sales of my work, seventy percent of the gross.

"Dave," I said, "don't take this the wrong way . . . but this is the worst fucking idea I've ever heard in my entire life. It'll never work. I don't know a single person who has one of those *nerd pads*. There's so much free writing available that nobody's going to pay to read something. And if it does work, it won't work for me. Why would people buy something of mine? My mom would buy it, that's it. Besides, I'm sober now. I don't have any more stories."

"You don't have *one* story left?" Dave said.

I couldn't think of a single thing. In nearly two years, I hadn't blacked out anywhere strange; I hadn't done any weird new drugs; I hadn't been involved in any rock 'n' roll depravity on the road. For the first time in seventeen years, my life was stable, verging on boring.

"Well . . . I did get shipwrecked that one time," I offered.

Dave smacked himself in the forehead.

"Mishka, you asshole! That's the story."

≡

I had written the story of the shipwreck shortly after it happened. It had sat on my hard drive for nearly ten years. If I had ever had a writing career, it was over. But if this story made five hundred bucks, well, it was five hundred bucks I didn't have before and five hundred bucks I sorely needed. I spent a weekend giving it a spit-polish, then emailed it to Dave.

Shipwrecked published in April. I refused to let myself hope. Five hundred dollars. I would try to make five hundred dollars. Still, I emailed every single person I knew. Nothing happened. God fucking damn it, nothing ever happened.

Then *Shipwrecked* started to creep up in the rankings. Then it crept up further. A week after publication, it hit number one. And stayed there.

After three weeks, it finally dropped to number seven. Then it roared right back up to number one and stayed there.

≡

By my rough calculations, I was owed a decent chunk of money. Right, I'd believe it when I got the check. Best to play it safe. Or safe-ish. I mean, it would be more than five hundred bucks, right? I booked a trip out to Albuquerque to see Chuong.

As soon as I stepped outside the airport, a sporty little white car whipped up, tinted windows, bass thumping. I couldn't see into the car. This couldn't be Chuong, could it? The driver's side door swung open and a dark head popped out.

"Sup, bro?"

Chuong.

He ran over and gave me an awkward little one-arm hug, holding his cigarette away from me. In sixth grade, we'd been almost exactly the same height. He hadn't grown an inch since then. He felt like a strong child in my arms.

I threw my bag awkwardly in the trunk, then tried to get into the front seat. It was pulled all the way forward. No way I'd fit in there.

"Oh, shit. Hold on," Chuong said. He fiddled with a lever, and the seat slowly slid all the way back. We waited another long, awkward minute while he reclined it almost all the way back.

"Long time. Sorry."

Finally, I was able to squeeze myself into the tiny car. I did up my seat belt, and we zoomed off.

I looked at Chuong. His skin was much darker, from the sun, and grayer, from the cigarettes. He was careful when he spoke, but I could tell that most of his teeth were gone. There were bags under his eyes, wrinkles under the bags. Ah, I couldn't have looked much better. Chuong looked at me.

"So, wassup, bro," Chuong said and smiled. "How you been?"

How do you catch someone up on twenty years of sorrow and trouble?

"Chuong, my brother," I said, "I been great. Lots to tell you, but I'm great."

We loaded up a couple of cars with everyone Chuong knew— his wife, Helen, his mother-in-law, his brothers-in-law, various friends and relatives and friends of relatives—and headed to the restaurant where his brother, Chin, worked. Chin had left Vietnam after Chuong, but they'd arrived in the US around the same time, because Chin hadn't gotten stuck in the refugee camp. He had been placed with a family in Albuquerque.

Chin had been prim and proper, clever but too clean-cut and rule abiding for Chuong and me. Though he was my age, whenever he had visited us in Los Alamos, Chuong and I had treated him less like an equal as much as an annoying kid sister. He must have gone to college instead of dropping out in eighth grade like Chuong —maybe he owned the restaurant?

It was a Japanese hibachi-style restaurant, a big deal in a small city like Albuquerque. The place was packed when we walked in. The hostess looked panicked as our party grew and grew as Chuong's frail mother-in-law was helped through the door and his boys finished their cigarettes and trickled in. No way were we getting a table.

Chuong grabbed my arm and pulled me past the hostess.

"Don't worry 'bout her, bro."

He tugged me through the crowded restaurant to the best table in the house, a huge grill with ten or twelve chairs around it. A tall Asian dude wearing chef's whites stood behind the grill, wiping a spatula on his apron. His arms were cut with muscle, covered with tattoos. He was grinning from ear to ear.

"Sup, bro."

"Chin? Holy shit, man. You grew!"

We shook hands. His hand was nearly as big as mine and hard, like rebar in a leather glove.

"Look at you! You're a monster. Chuong, is this why you're so small? Chin ate all the food?"

"Our dad, he's tall," Chin said. "Chuong, he a bad boy, smoke too many cigarettes."

I remembered that. Chuong had started smoking when he was eight.

"But your arms. You a gym rat?"

"Nah," he said, fist bumping with the guys in Chuong's family. "I had to go away a couple of times. Not a lot to do there, you know what I mean?" He winked at me.

Polite little Chin in prison? Multiple times? It really had been an eternity.

As soon as we sat down, the show began; a constant stream of dirty jokes, flying food, and sake bombs. Chin was a hell of a cook, a consummate showman, even a good dancer. And, man, he and Chuong could really throw them back.

We didn't know how to talk to each other or what to talk about, so we just remembered things out loud. Remember Mom driving us to the movie theater, blasting Guns N' Roses in the back of the Ford Aerostar? Remember when we found those old *Penthouse* magazines? Remember when you gave me fish sauce and told me it was Vietnamese beer?

The busboy kept giving me looks. Was I doing something wrong? He said something to Chin in Vietnamese.

"Bro, this guy says he knows you."

I looked at him. Dark skin, much darker than the other Vietnamese, even Chuong, with his farmer's tan. Stocky, with kinky black hair, clearly Vietnamese but somehow less Vietnamese than Chuong or Chin. Holy shit.

Chuong had had a friend from the refugee camp, a boy named Lum who lived in a group home in Albuquerque. He was "Amer-Asian," my mom had told me, a word I only knew from a Clash record, the son of an American GI and a Vietnamese woman. I hadn't gotten it then, but I understood now: an African American soldier and a Vietnamese prostitute. And Lum, a child neither of them wanted.

"Lum?" I said and stood up.

Lum threw his head back and laughed. Chin clapped him on the back. Lum dumped his bus tub on the edge of the table and gave me a quick, strong hug.

"You roll deep with the Vietnamese, bro," Chin said, nodding. "You need anything—*anything*—you let us know."

Beers had been arriving at our table steadily since we'd sat down. By the time we tucked into the food—ridiculous fare, scallops and shrimp and lobster tails, mounds and mounds of it, more than we could eat, more than twice our number could eat—there was nearly a case of Heineken sitting open next to Chuong.

"Chuong, you gonna drink all those?"

"Help yourself, bro. Mi casa . . . it's your house, too, man."

"I'm fine, thanks. But I mean . . . are you going to drink all these?"

I had drunk a case of beer in one night many times. But I weighed twice what Chuong did.

"Respect," he said and thumped his chest. "In Vietnam, somebody help you, when they walk ina restaurant, you send one drink, say thanks for help me. When I come to Albuquerque, I am the only Vietnamese speaking English."

He waved an arm at the span of the restaurant. "I get *all* these motherfuckers jobs."

Then he fixed me with his watery eyes.

"And you teaching me speak English," he said.

He raised his Heineken. I grabbed my glass of water and clinked it against his beer bottle. We drank.

Helen drove us back to the house after dinner. Chuong was pretty lit. We sat in the kitchen and talked. He showed me pictures of his family, Chin's boys, Chase and Chandler, and his son, Charles. All boys, he said, all *Ch* names, like him and Chin. I wanted to explain to him that it was a little ironic for a Vietnamese boy to be named Charlie, but I thought better of it.

It was hot in the kitchen, so Chuong unbuttoned his shirt. I saw ink.

"You have tattoos? Let me see."

"No," he said, pulling his shirt closed.

"Chuong, he shy," Helen said. She reached down and grabbed his lapels and spread his shirt. Chuong didn't resist, just rolled his head to glare drunkenly up at her.

He had one tattoo. A shaky outline that covered his entire torso, a star inside it. A handmade poke-and-stick tattoo. He had taught me how to do them when we were kids, a sewing needle stuck in the eraser of a pencil, thread wrapped around it to hold the ink. It was the outline of Vietnam, with a star for Saigon, his hometown.

"Where did you get this done?"

Chuong hadn't said anything about going to prison, but this looked an awful lot like a prison tattoo.

"Right here." He pointed to the floor, indicating his kitchen. "My buddy, we copy from Vietnamese menu. One night only."

"Chuong, he very drunk," Helen said. "So, so drunk like crazy. Take long time." She petted his hair, rubbed his neck.

"Chuong, when you found me . . . when we talked for the first time . . . how did you feel? What did you do?" I said.

He shrugged.

"I feel . . . good. I feel happy. Here," he said, gesturing at his chest with pursed fingers, "in my soul."

"Oh, Chuong," Helen said, smiling gaily, shaking her head. "Chuong cry. He cry and cry and cry!"

My whole life, I'd felt like an alien, exiled in America. I'd thought of myself, romantically, as a wild orphan, a lost boy. But I had never been lost—I had been hiding. Chuong was the lost boy; he had been all along. He had been trying desperately to be found, to find his way.

⸺

One day an envelope from Amazon came in the mail. I weighed it in my hand—had to be the check. I recalled the feeling I'd had, when I got my acceptance letter from Simon's Rock, that my whole life was about to change. Christ, almost twenty years ago. I brought the envelope upstairs and carefully slit it open in the kitchen. I read the numbers on the check. I read the numbers again. Then I put it back in the envelope. I took it out again. I read the numbers again.

I brought the check with me to work that night. When Mike Stewart showed up, I asked him if I could talk to him outside for a second.

"Of course, man. After you," he said, pointing to the door.

I felt like shit for what I was about to do. Mike had been a friend for a long time, long enough to know that he should have never hired me in the first place. But he had, and he had become one of the pillars in my new life.

"What's up, man?" he said when we were outside.

"Shit, man. I feel like I'm breaking up with you! I need to quit."

Mike nodded.

"I understand. This bar, it's a way station. It's not a career, it's just a gig. You do it till you get something else happening, and then you move on. I'm always glad when that happens. Can I ask why you're quitting?"

I withdrew the check from my pocket and handed it to him. It was the biggest check I'd ever seen in my life—more than $9,000. And that was just for my first month of sales.

Mike's face lit up. His jaw dropped, and he looked at me, then whooped.

"Holy shit, dude! I'll quit, too!"

Mike wasn't big on hugs, but he shook my hand for a long time that night.

≡

My trips to visit my father had become more frequent, twice a year or more if I could squeeze it in. Each visit was a little less treacherous, a little less fragile, even occasionally approaching something I would call fun. I was curious about my father's life, and I asked him if he would let me interview him on tape. To my surprise, he agreed, so we sat down one day, my iPhone between us on the dining room table, recording the conversation.

"Should we just dive right into it, Dad?"

He snorted.

"Is there any other way to do it?"

"Okay. I guess . . . when did you realize that you had to leave the marriage?"

"Well . . . I can't just give you a time and a date, you know? I've got to go a ways back. I always felt stressed and strained. When we were living in Los Alamos, there were two occasions when I blacked out. In one situation, I'd had maybe two glasses of wine. I biked to my friend's place, and I got off my motorcycle. Then I woke up on his couch.

"But the second time, I was stone sober. I woke up in an ambulance headed to the hospital in Los Alamos, strapped to a gurney, getting pumped full of antianxiety drugs 'cause I was convinced I was dying."

I hadn't remembered this. As my father spoke, I recalled it happening and little snippets of information filtering down to us kids from my mother. But it wasn't something I had carried around in my head while I was taking cruel measure of my father.

"When we moved to New Hampshire, I stopped blacking out, but it wasn't unusual for me to have 'brownouts.' I'd be driving into work, then wake up on the highway going sixty or seventy miles an hour with no idea where I was. Sometimes I'd overshot my office by forty-five minutes.

"I figured, I have to do something, I can't keep on going this way. At your mother's urging, I went to see a psychiatrist who specialized in work-related stress. The second meeting, the shrink said, 'Your problem isn't work. Your problem is your home relationship.' I went ballistic. I was ready to walk out of there. After I calmed down, she said, 'I think you just proved my point.' I wouldn't accept it. I just couldn't accept it. Then, for whatever reason, you guys all decided you wanted to move back to Canada."

"Dad, I don't . . . I don't remember this at all. I mean, the way I remember it, you sought out a job in Vancouver because you were so unhappy in your job in New Hampshire."

"I was unhappy, but by this time I was beginning to realize that it wasn't the job. You always have disagreements with your bosses and so on but, working with this psychiatrist, I began to realize what the problem was. The problem was that *I didn't want to be there.* I didn't want to be a husband. I didn't want to be a father. I didn't want to have to do all these things that my father kept telling me I needed to do. And I didn't want to always feel guilty about doing something for myself."

It jumped out at me that my father was speaking as though his father had been present: "my father kept telling me . . . " When we moved to New Hampshire, his father had been dead for more than ten years.

"You guys just hated it in New Hampshire. You hated the people, you hated the kids; it was such an awful place to live. I had a really good job. I was making lots of money. The housing market had gone way down. I didn't want to move. But the way it was put to me was, 'We all want to move back to Canada.' Alright, so . . . that's what I have to do.

"Recruiters had always been wanting me to move, and one of them was from Vancouver. So I moved to Vancouver, which was the worst job situation I have ever been in, bar none."

My dad realized that he'd been talking a lot. He looked at me, waiting for me to say something. I couldn't speak. It was starting to come back to me. We had mounted an extended campaign to move back to Canada. Mom & the Kids vs. Dad, the way it had always been. Finally, he had capitulated. I had forgotten this completely. Or wiped it from my memory.

"Uh . . . just keep going, Dad," I finally got out.

"Okay, so . . . I was in Vancouver working with this guy, and I couldn't believe how crooked he was. It was unbelievably bad. I was kind of ready for the police to burst in at any moment and haul us all off to jail . . . because I was complicit in some of this stuff. Even with that bullshit, I'd had no problems in Vancouver—no brownouts, no blackouts, nothing.

"To answer your original question, I realized my marriage to your mother was over during that second visit with the psychiatrist. But I didn't accept it till a lot later. You guys came up to Vancouver for a visit in April."

I remembered that trip. We stayed not at my father's apartment but in a hotel room. Freddie Mercury had just died, and his farewell concert had been the only thing on TV, an endless loop. I had been miserable.

"Ten minutes, fifteen minutes after you guys arrived, I was like, okay, the shrink was right. This is the problem. The family is the problem. And if I don't do something, I'll be dead by my own hand in a year. That's when I accepted that I had to do something about it."

Unloading the silverware from the dishwasher once, I had grabbed a heavy, sharp knife by the blade. I realized what I had done and loosened my grip without letting go completely, and as the knife slid out of my hand, it cut deep into the pads of my fingers. To finally hear my father say how much he hadn't wanted us, how much he hadn't wanted me . . . it was exquisitely painful.

"Even after that trip, I wrote some of these really loving love letters to your mother—this was after you guys had been there—trying to convince myself. But in the morning, when I read them . . . well, I couldn't send them, because I knew that it wasn't true. I mean, I say I accepted it, but, really, I vacillated wildly. It was an incredibly dark time for me, walking around Vancouver alone, worried I was losing my mind.

"Because to me, I was an absolute *failure* if I got divorced. Everything my dad had drilled into my head said that getting divorced would be admitting that I had completely failed in my role. But I was convinced I was going to be dead soon if I didn't."

"Were you able to make a distinction between being a husband and being a father?"

"At that time . . . no, I don't think I could distinguish. Mishka, realize that in our family there was Elaine and the kids . . . and then there was Murray."

"As I've gotten older, that's become clearer to me. And Dad . . . I'm sorry."

"Well, it wasn't anything that you did. Apparently, from talking to various different counselors, this is pretty standard: the mother builds a wall by, you know, having the kids have dinner first, and then Dad has dinner by himself. Each time, there were good reasons for it, but the aggregate result . . . Listen, Elaine's family situation was pretty dysfunctional as well. Her father was an alcoholic, like mine. I don't hold a grudge against her. She did what she thought was right, you know, what she had been programmed to do. As did I."

"I try to put myself in your shoes, you know, putting in a long day's work to provide for your family, fighting your way through traffic, then walking in the door to a family that is united against you. That would be incredibly hard for me."

"It's interesting—a year or so after we broke the news, I was up in Boulder, talking with Tatyana. She said, 'Dad, you should have done it *years* before. It just wrecked everybody for you to stick around that long!'

"But, Mishka, let me tell you, it was the most difficult thing I had ever done in my life. That's why, as much as the Simon's Rock shooting had an impact on you, I couldn't be there for you. I was thankful that you'd survived, but I was just completely burned out. That whole period is a blank in my memory.

"When I told your mom I wanted a divorce, she laughed at me because she said she didn't think I had the guts to do it. You remember our old dog, Princess? Well, Princess came over and put her nose and one paw on my foot, like she was trying to comfort me. So I remember little things like that. But that's it."

"When I found out about the divorce, I went and got a roll of quarters . . . because I thought you had to have a roll of quarters in your hand to punch somebody out. And then when we got to the airport and I saw you . . . I couldn't. 'Cause you were my dad, you know? I felt like a total failure because I couldn't do it."

He looked at me with sympathy and shrugged.

"Looking back, even shortly after I'd left, there were many things that happened where I should have just bailed. But it took *all* of those things for me to get my courage up to admit that I was a total fucking failure. Which is really what it was. For me, I had to admit that I was a complete failure as a man because I could not do this husband-father thing.

"When I wrote up the thing for the annulment, I had a really difficult time with it. The priest said to me, 'Don't you think you're coming down just a little too hard on yourself?' And my reaction was, 'Well, no, of course not. I'm a complete failure. I have completely failed.'"

"There's no such thing as being too hard on yourself."

He nodded.

"But as soon as I said that to the priest, I was like, oh shit. It *wasn't* just me. Because all along, everyone—myself included—was convinced it was just me. It was always my fault. Even if someone was laying a guilt trip on me, it was my fault because I allowed them to do that. That process helped me realize that, though I had made mistakes and I had certainly done things wrong, that I hadn't done every single thing wrong."

"If you had it to do over, what would you do differently? Are you able to articulate specifically what you would have wanted? I mean . . . did you ever want to have children?"

"Nope. No. I never saw myself as having children. I never saw myself as being married. I saw myself as a hermit scientist. If I had to do it over again, would I do something differently? Yeah, there's one pivotal thing that I would have done differently. When Elaine showed up at my door and said she was going to move in with me, I would have said no."

I had to hand it to him. He had picked the right decision to undo. Undoing his marriage to my mother erased her, erased me, erased all of us. One discrete correction, and we all disappeared.

"Letting Elaine move in was a mistake. I should have said no. But I couldn't because I felt guilty. I wasn't ready to get married. I wasn't ready to settle down. It wasn't part of my picture. I'd had it drilled into me that when you get married and have a family, you don't count anymore. My father would say, 'You're not better than the rest of them because you're smarter. You're *less* than the rest of them.'"

"Wow. Dad, that's . . . totally counterintuitive."

"I know. But as far as he was concerned, it was my responsibility to take care of others. Anyone, but especially my family."

"It strikes me as bizarrely ironic that, from a young age and then very much so as I got older, I told myself, I'm going to be totally different from my dad. I'm not going to do what he did. I'm going to do my own thing. Instead, I'm *very much* like you—the guilt, holing up and tinkering with my guitars late at night like a mad scientist, going on long runs alone . . . "

"And you're doing all the things I wish I had done."

"All the shit I felt would be a colossal disappointment to you."

"Mishka, I *always* wanted to be a musician. So many of the good scientists I knew were musicians, whether it was a flute or a piano or a guitar. I wanted to do that! But I chose a different path. No, to be honest, I feel like I had a different path chosen for me. When you grow up in an alcoholic family . . . my mother was a champion at guilt. It took me a long time to realize how easily manipulated I was. And I didn't have the courage or faith in my own convictions to say no."

"You weren't incredibly supportive."

"No, I wasn't. You have to understand, I had it drilled into my head from a very young age that you had to support your family. That was job number one, and there was no job number two. I'll say it, Mishka: I was wrong. I wanted you to do something more practical. Or at least have something to fall back on. Because, shit, it's hard to make it as a musician or a writer! And I'll admit it, I didn't think you could do it. And I'll say it again, Mishka: I was wrong."

His arms were crossed, as they were always crossed. I noticed it, and he noticed me notice it.

"I'm sorry. I know that this is kind of a . . . closed position. But if I let my arms hang down, I just feel like a chimpanzee. So I'm like, fuck it, you know? I'm comfortable this way."

"It's cool, Dad. I know. That's like the default Dad position. We can leave it here, if you want."

"No, let's keep going."

"You sure? I feel like I've dragged you through a lot."

"It's not fun, but look at it from my point of view. It's important for you to know some of this. For the first time since the divorce, you've asked me for my side of the story.

"It's been tough for you guys. I know that. I remember one time—this was in Pleasanton when I was living with Lis—Tatyana came to the door. She'd been there earlier that day, and she'd gone away to do something, and then she'd come back. I looked out 'cause there was this little side window and . . . I saw her just standing there, frozen, not knowing what to do. She didn't know whether she could just walk in or whether she had to ring the bell. And I thought, How bad are things that she doesn't feel she can just walk into her Dad's house?

"So I know it's been hard for you guys. But—and it's taken me a long time to be able to say this—it's been tough for me too. Very tough. The hardest thing I've been through in my life. All of it has been tough, from long before the divorce up until, oh, maybe a couple of years ago. I'll even say this: thank you for asking me about it. It's a great relief to be able to tell it. And Mishka, even if I remember it wrong, this is how I remember it.

"People misremember things. One thing that bothers me . . . a couple years before Marilyn died, I went up there to visit her, and we went through our old report cards from school."

"She had *your* report cards? I don't think I have my grade school report cards. Hell, I don't have any of the fancy degrees I haven't paid for."

"Oh yeah, Marilyn kept all that stuff. It was really curious to go through them. When I was a kid, I was the golden boy. My parents put a lot of pressure on me. I had to be at the top of the class. There was no question about that. And then the reason I was at the top of the class was because I was their little genius. It wasn't easy pulling down those grades because life on the farm was hard. From the day school let out, I worked from dawn to dark, sometimes later. But I remember being the smart one—getting the grades, getting the awards, getting the praise. And Marilyn hated me for it.

"She remembered being told all through her school career— and she believed all through her life—that I made way better marks than she did. When she found our report cards, her marks were better than mine. Not once or twice or in one subject. Consistently, across the board, Marilyn got higher marks than I did.

"We looked at those report cards, and she said, 'That can't be! Somebody must have changed them.' She could not accept what she was seeing because she had had it drummed into her that she was second-class. And she wasn't. She was better than I was."

My father had wound up a rocket scientist. His sister, who was smarter than he was, became a farmer. I didn't doubt that if we compared my report cards to Tatyana's, we would have found that she outpaced me as Marilyn had outpaced my dad.

"You look like you're fading so we can wrap it up. But there's one last thing I want to share with you on the subject of misremembering. You talk a lot about the foreclosure."

"Yeah. I mean, Dad, that was probably the biggest thing in my life. Bigger than the shooting, bigger than the divorce. To have the bank trick you guys into missing a payment and then take our home away from us, kick us when we were down . . . it's so fucked up. It made me hate everything: you, Mom, myself, banks, money, capitalism, America, God. Yeah, it was big then, and it's only gotten bigger."

Dad shook his head.

"Mishka, there was no foreclosure."

"What are you talking about?"

"I'm not sure if it's something your mother told you or just something you pieced together in your head. Yes, they advised us to run late on a payment. Yes, they formally initiated foreclosure proceedings, but that was something they had to do in order to get us out of the mortgage. Think about it, Mishka. I was in Vancouver. Tatyana was in Colorado. You were at Simon's Rock. And you all hated New Hampshire. We had to get rid of the house.

"The bank didn't steal our home away from us, Mishka. They were very fair to us. In fact, they did us a favor. They took it off our hands."

———

I felt physically exhausted when I finally turned off the recorder on my phone. We had gone deeper than I would have ever hoped, deeper than I had been prepared for. He had volunteered answers to questions I would never have dared ask him. Because he wanted to work things out.

I lay around the house in a stupor for the rest of the day, my mind unable to parse what had just taken place. Shortly after dinner, my dad and Theresa retired, so I went into my room and crawled into bed. Instantly, I was wired, my mind working furiously, like I was on acid. After a while, I got out of bed, put in my earbuds, and listened to the interview with my father.

It was no big deal, just my father and me talking. Then I noticed we had the same vocal tics—"I mean" and "you know." Then my skin crawled like I was hearing some soothsayer's prophecy about my life, recorded long before I was born.

Like me, he had resented his father's attempts to steer his life. Like me, he had been terrified of failure. Like me, he had lied to himself, assured himself that the truth wasn't true. Like me, he had woken up, halfway through his life, trapped in a nightmare borne out of his weakness. Like me, it had taken him a long time to work up the courage to surrender. Like me, when he finally accepted he had failed, he had brutally excoriated himself.

And his revelations . . . yes, we had petitioned at great length to leave New Hampshire. I had forgotten that entirely, but it rapidly filtered back to me. Yes, he had cared about us. I remembered hugs and pony rides on his knee and games in the public pool and my dad screaming his fool head off for us at our soccer games. In telling my dad to fuck off, that I was going to do my own thing, I hadn't disappointed him at all. Rather, I had done exactly what I needed to do, exactly what he wished he had done, and I had given him every reason to be proud of me.

The Letter that I'd clung to as proof of my father's infidelity, the unaddressed, unsigned one my mother had found in the back of a book he'd been reading, was probably a love letter he had forced himself to write *to her* because he couldn't deal with the reality that his marriage had failed. The foreclosure—lasting proof that we were persecuted and doomed and that the world was out to destroy us, the betrayal around which I'd built my entire persona—not only had it never taken place, but the bank had been fair, generous even, in helping my parents dispose of a property neither of them wanted. Even the trivial detail of Princess comforting him when he broke the news to my mother . . . I'd imagined that Princess had hated him, and I'd even conscripted her death into my war against him. But Princess had loved him, and reluctantly but genuinely, he had allowed himself to love her. She had probably crawled into his La-Z-Boy recliner to die because she missed him.

I'd built a life in response to my father's infidelity, to the evil in his heart, and to the bank's bloodthirsty theft of our home. I had been wrong, and I had been wrong, and I had been wrong.

⸺

Luis enlisted my help to tackle the Vermont 100, one of the original hundred-milers, a race more than twenty years old. It was a hardcore race in every respect: hillier, hotter, and much more psychologically demanding. His goal was to "buckle": to complete the race in less than twenty-four hours, thereby earning a silver belt buckle. It was only his second hundred-miler, and he'd run his first in 27:33. Buckling meant knocking almost four hours off his flat-course hundred-mile time . . . and doing so on a mountainous course with over 28,000 feet of elevation change. My job was to run the last thirty miles through the night with him and get him in on time.

Luis rolled into the Camp Ten Bear aid station at mile seventy shortly before 8 p.m. He was shirtless and slick with sweat, but he looked great. He was some kind of specific female fantasy—voluptuously chiseled physique, broad, easy smile, just poetry in motion. He was grinning and moving well and howled my name when he saw me. He gave me a quick high five, then yelled over his shoulder as he passed, "You ready? I want to be out of here in ten minutes."

He got weighed by a volunteer and briefly inspected by a medic. He was on time, but just barely. No way was he going to buckle. I was already prepping my consolation speech to him: in a race this long, a finish is a win, and so on. My goal was just to get him across the finish line, no matter how long it took. That would have to be enough.

Having passed his physical, Luis flopped down on a cot while I tended to his needs. His hydration pack had to be filled with ice; he wanted some peanut-butter-and-jelly sandwiches and some Coke and some of the big Medjool dates I had brought for us. His feet were bothering him in several places, and I could see blisters deep under his calluses. Not good. A volunteer fumbled with moleskin and a damp roll of thin tape.

A clueless volunteer had derailed his 100K attempt at Green Lakes, we had figured out later. The dude had pumped Luis full of salt on an empty stomach when he was already dehydrated. Not this time.

"You know what," I said, "I have some better tape here."

I pulled a roll of thick, waterproof fabric tape out of my bag and waved the volunteer away. I pulled off the tiny piece of tape the volunteer had used. No way that would hold on to a wet, spongy foot for another thirty miles. I dried Luis's sweaty foot on my shirt and went to work on his left big toe. Two minutes later, we were on the move.

"Okay, we're going to talk shop for a minute and then we're going to talk about anything but running, alright?" Luis was in good spirits, but I could tell he was already in pain. "We've got eight hours left. If we can cover four miles an hour, I can break twenty-four hours. So that's what we're going to do."

It sounded doable. I'd run thirty-two miles in less than five and half hours. You can almost walk four miles in an hour. But that's on flat pavement. The last thirty miles of the Vermont 100 were supposed to be the toughest of the race. Vermont had hills as steep and sustained as any I'd seen around the country. Throw in a couple of chatty stops at aid stations and a couple of bathroom breaks, and it'd be easy to go over our allotted eight hours.

Luis already had seventy miles under his belt, and he had two blisters coming up deep under his calluses. We'd have to push his body to its limit to break twenty-four hours. Anything and everything could go wrong in thirty miles. One small problem, and we wouldn't make it. He might not finish at all. Hell, we might end the night in the ER.

He started shivering. The guy never brings enough clothes. I pulled a shirt out of my bag, the same black shirt from Izgi that I had passed off to Luis at Virgil Crest when he'd had to leave me behind. The significance wasn't lost on him. He nodded at me with a grin and then pulled it over his head.

We ran down a dirt road for a little while. He wanted to know how my day had been. While he was out running seventy miles in the hot sun, had I been able to find a nice, quiet place to work? Had I gotten enough to eat? How had I slept?

An arrow pointing to the left on a yellow pie plate tacked to a post directed us off the road and onto an inclined jeep trail. We hiked up the muddy, rocky ruts in silence broken only by the labored sounds of our breathing. Luis was lagging behind. I couldn't imagine how he was feeling.

It was beginning to get dark. Once we reached the top of the hill, we stopped so I could pull my headlight out of my bag. Luis was already wearing his, and he reached up to switch it on.

"Fuck."

He pulled the headlight off, flipping the switch several more times.

"Dude, it's not fucking working."

I flipped on my headlight and handed it to him. He put it on without a word, and we began to run.

The terrain was a narrow, rocky, and root-ridden trail through the woods. Occasionally, it was wide enough for us to run side by side, but more often than not, we had to run single file. The headlight was bright and showed the trail in high relief: golf-ball-sized rocks, thick roots protruding from the ground, tiny, steeply angled ravines in the earth—all perfect hazards on which to catch a toe and go face first into the dirt or, worse, roll an ankle and do enough damage that you'd be immobilized. Luis and I had done a fun run with our pal Jerome in which the two of them, running side by side, hit an ice patch. Luis was fine, but Jerome broke his ankle badly, had to be carried a mile out, and couldn't walk for six weeks.

The light was so bright that, after illuminating the path for Luis, it made my path behind him seem that much darker. I tried watching the shining path in front of him to memorize it when I went over it. That didn't work. I tried not looking at the illuminated spot in front of him, just staring at the blackness behind him so my eyes would adjust to the dark. That didn't work either. Finally, I realized that the only way to do it was to run in front of him, zigzagging back and forth so my own shadow wouldn't block out the hazards of the terrain in front of me.

We wove our way through the woods, following the glow sticks that hung from the trees every hundred yards or so, like we were on some mystical quest. It was a beautiful night, the moon high and full, its light glinting off the dew on leaves as we ran past. As the night wore on, I did everything I could to distract Luis, telling him the worst, most offensive jokes I could remember, unfolding debauched stories from my life on the road, singing Elvis songs, doing everything I could to take his mind off his pain and exhaustion. Mostly he suffered in silence and just kept moving relentlessly forward.

Twelve miles from the finish, we were incredibly still on schedule. At the final weigh-in, we saw a man of probably fifty sitting at a picnic table. He looked hollowed out, a total zombie. I knew that he, like Luis, was trying to buckle. He looked finished.

"Dad," his daughter waved a cell phone at him, "I just got a text from Mom. She said no way can you beat twenty-four hours."

He looked dazed, unable to respond.

"Hey, Dad," I said, catching his eye, "I think you can do it."

"Yeah," he said. "Yeah," he turned to his daughter, "you tell Mom to stuff it." He wobbled to his feet and stumbled off with his pacer. Luis wolfed down some fruit and some more Coke, and then we were moving again.

We passed UltraDad, he passed us, we passed him, he passed us. Step by step, Luis started to fall apart. I put my arm through his to help him up the hills. At one point, his head dropped to my shoulder. He had fallen asleep but somehow kept walking.

Luis was such a good man. He'd served his country without complaint. He was a good friend, a good son, a good father. I hope to never find myself in a foxhole, but if I do, I want Luis by my side. It amazed me that he wanted to be friends with me, a low-rent, druggy, drunken, useless piece of shit.

My friend asleep on my shoulder, I looked back at all the petty failures in my life. At every fork in the road, I had taken the coward's path. I had lied to my friends. I had stolen. I had cheated. I had made excuses. I had deceived. I had hurt people who cared about me. A long list of people would never speak to me again. In no way was it remarkable that my father and Tatyana had walked away from me. Time after time, I had defaulted to anger and pain and let weakness dictate my choices. Amazingly, against common sense, against the burden of evidence that I was unsalvageable, my mother and Tashina had never given up on me. I had rewarded their unwavering faith with disappointment after disappointment. It was all darkness, impenetrable.

The night had gone on too long. Luis was exhausted. We'd never make it. I should just let him sleep by the side of the road. Then I could run off into the bushes to cry about what a fucking failure I had been.

No.

I'd duped myself before, duped myself for most of my life. No more. Yeah, I had been that bad man. But I forced myself to do an inventory of my current life: I'm a good roommate. I'm a good friend. I'm a good brother. I'm a good son. I had even been a good boyfriend to Izgi. Was it possible that now I too was a good man? It seemed impossible, but the facts were plain. But if I was a good man, I had sure as shit better get out of my own head and focus on the task at hand: getting my friend in on time.

"Lou," I said softly, waking him up. He groaned and lifted his head from my shoulder.

"Oh my God, I am so tired."

Again, we began to run. Again, we passed UltraDad and his pacer.

"This is it," I said. "Late-night blood pact, one of my specialties. Everyone gets in under twenty-four. We're committing now. All of us."

The other runners grunted their assent. UltraDad looked like he was about to fall over. No way he was going to make it.

Finally, we made the final aid station: an unmanned picnic table with only water.

"This is it, Lou," I said. "Two point two miles. Now you empty the tank, bro. You're going to run a couple of miles for your daughter, Lou. Run it in for Isabella."

I headed out first, into the darkness. Every time we came to a flat or a downhill, I called back to Luis: "We've got a decline coming up. Open it up now!" Suddenly, there were glow sticks in empty gallon jugs on the ground on either side of us: lights placed by the race organizers to light the last stretch. As we whipped through the glowing gates, I allowed hope to bubble up. Were we actually going to make it?

I ran down a soft, pine-needle-padded trail, the makeshift green lanterns on either side of me blurring into each other. Then I saw it—a huge wooden arch in an open field, with "FINISH LINE" in glowing red neon at the top. I hauled ass out of the woods and ran around to the other side of the finish line and started calling for Luis to bring it in, come on home, baby.

I'd gotten a ways ahead of him and couldn't see or hear any sign of him. I heard the officials muttering about the time. God, it would be such a heartbreaker if he didn't make it. Then I saw a light bobbing through the trees, like some will-o'-the-wisp. I screamed Luis's name as loud as I could.

I was answered by a long, desperate, wordless howl, pained and joyous at the same time, a wail from the bottom of the well of human endurance. Luis burst out of the trees, running hard, and flew across the finish line to wild cheers and applause, then toppled to the ground, groaning and laughing.

"We did it," he said. "Mishka, gimme a hug."

I looked at the clock: 23:55. He had started at 4 a.m., traveled one hundred miles, and made it home at the moment of darkest night. He had done it; we had done it. Then, incredibly, Luis sprang back to his feet.

"We gotta get Dad in!" He sprinted off into the woods from which he'd just emerged, calling, "Dad! Dad!" like a lost child.

Minutes passed. They felt like months. It was a valiant effort by Luis, but no way was UltraDad gonna make it in. Then, blinking through the trees, I saw Luis's headlight and another dimmer light. Oh God, it was going to be close. No way could they get in before the twenty-four-hour cutoff. Wobbling but running hard, UltraDad emerged from the woods and unsteadily crossed the finish line. I immediately looked at the clock: 23:57:58. UltraDad had made it. He had beat twenty-four hours by just two minutes and two seconds. John Lacroix, UltraDad, was the last person to buckle.

I helped Luis up to our campsite by a tiny dugout. While he cleaned himself up in his tent with baby wipes, I stripped off all my clothes and dove into the freezing water. When I surfaced, the sun was just coming up, its glorious pink-orange creeping up into the cold sky, still shot through with stars. We had taken a journey through the darkness and emerged, whole but transformed, on the other side.

CHAPTER 12

The New Life

After *Shipwrecked* had finally fallen out of the top ten, Dave Blum invited me to lunch so we could talk about my next Kindle Single. The next one? I hadn't had any ideas for the first one. Still, I couldn't turn down a free lunch, even if it meant braving the wasteland of Midtown.

Dave brought me to a *nice* restaurant, you know, with the cloth napkins and two forks and no decimal points on the menu. I had foolishly assumed "lunch" meant the corner deli, so I'd thrown on my cutoff jeans, a T-shirt with the sleeves ripped off, and Vans with no socks. I'd worked at Beauty Bar the night before our lunch, so I hadn't gotten to sleep till 6 a.m. I was so short on sleep, my eyes felt like they had been carved into my head. As the suits rolled in with their gelled hair and silk ties, I felt like a real dirt bag. God, it never changed. I shrank into the booth and quietly unfolded a couple of half-baked ideas I'd thought up for stories.

Dave turned his nose up at all of them.

"What you need to write," he said, "is how you went from being this shitfaced, drug-abusing gutter-dweller to a sober ultrarunner. I even have a title for it. It will be called 'The Long Run.'"

I pushed back gently.

"Dave, are you kidding me? Nobody wants to read about how I fucked my life up and the grim process of unfucking it up. It was like eating a bucket of sand."

"Trust me," Dave said.

After the years I spent buying drugs and working off Craig's List and buying drugs off Craig's List, nothing gets my hackles up faster than those two words. But Dave knew he was the only person who could get away with speaking them to me. In my darkest hour, writing for Dave at the *New York Press* had been a strand of spider's silk in hell, a slender, glistening, translucent thread of hope that I might not die filthy and anonymous in Greenpoint after all.

I slunk back to Brooklyn after lunch, leery of the task I'd been burdened with. I did not want to go back into that hole. But I did trust Dave, so I went home and "got out the big shovel," as he'd said. I dug deep and laid the wreckage of my life out on the page. It was liberating, like coming out of the closet. And it was dark and humiliating and ugly. Best-case scenario, I only allowed myself to hope that *The Long Run* would do half as well as *Shipwrecked* because I was convinced that *Shipwrecked* had been a fluke. Moreover, I worried that *The Long Run* was so depraved that it would destroy my fledgling writing career, which had ironically only begun to thrive once I'd given up on it for good.

Two days after its publication in late October 2011, *The Long Run* leapfrogged stories by Stephen King and Dean Koontz to hit number one. It sold more than 65,000 copies in less than six months. It only dropped out of the top ten in February, when my next number one pushed it out.

Each day brought fan mail. Not just from other runners, drunks, and ex-drunks, but also from Republicans, schoolteachers, Christians, and a fourteen-year-old Mormon. One kid did a PowerPoint presentation for his high school English class with slide titles that still crack me up: "Mishka Goes to College"; "Mishka Travels"; "Mishka Gets Checked for AIDS"; "Cough

Syrup." *The Long Run* established me as a writer, and it was the genesis of this book.

It turned out Dave was right, again: people did want to read about that long aggregation of mistakes I call my life. The very thing I thought would scare them off—the darkness—drew them in droves. I had been wrong; I had been so, so wrong. When I had been in pain, hating myself, feeling utterly alone, that was when I had been the least alone. Thousands, hundreds of thousands, millions of other people had been feeling alone at the same time. We had been alone together.

Now six years sober, my life has changed so much that I hardly recognize it. I still live in the same creaky, rundown apartment by the BQE that trembles every time a truck goes by. My ride still provokes looks of pity and horror every time I gas up. I'm still wearing the same jeans and a lot of the same T-shirts. I still need a haircut. But everything is different. My life has pivoted on its axis so that instead of staring down at the ground, I can see the sky.

I haven't had a boss in four years. I don't have to wear a polo shirt with the company logo stitched onto it. I don't have to wear a blazer. I don't have to wear pants if I don't want to, and so I rarely do. I moved to New York City with $300 to become a writer and a musician, and just seventeen hellish years later, what do you know, I kinda did it. I have a couch. I have ice cube trays. I have health insurance. *Health insurance.*

I am still an alcoholic. What that means, in medical terms, is that there is a shiny black scorpion with a long, armored, serpentine tail coiled around my spine at the base of my neck. Its pincers reach through gaps in my vertebrae to gently but firmly grasp my spinal cord. Its reticulated tail lovingly circles my spine, cradling each wildly curved bone, its terminus hovering expectantly over that braid of nerve endings, a bulb pregnant with poison, then a thick, cruelly curved spike.

This spiny black abomination is not some rare tropical parasite that wormed its way inside me. It's not a hive of nanobots implanted by an elite squadron of secret UN commandos. It's not a malign interplanetary virus injected into me by some universe-hopping alien scientist. Cell by cell, molecule by molecule, atom by atom, I built this monstrosity, one little bad decision after another. It's a devil of my own creation, blood of my blood, flesh of my flesh, my mistakes incarnate.

The scorpion is sleeping. Life is pretty sweet right now. But when I get a whiff of Jameson or gasoline or I get too angry or tired or depressed, it twitches uneasily in its slumber, its tail writhing minutely, its pincers digging ever so slightly into my spinal cord. I live in fear of what will happen if that evil little fucker ever wakes up.

The Jameson thing, I get. The common wisdom is that I will be an alcoholic for the rest of my life. The rustling of the scorpion in its arachnid dreams when alcohol vapor hits my sinuses is a purely chemical reaction. But this vile crustacean/arthropod/dinosaur/demon stirs for other things too: pornography, video games, eBay, Facebook . . . even a fucking Snickers bar. The price of freedom is eternal vigilance, as the saying goes.

But when I run under the blazing hot sun until I'm exhausted or find a smelly dog on the street in Mexico and scratch that tickle spot that makes its leg skritch and it sheds all over the clean shirt I just put on, or when I make my sister's kids laugh in the backseat of the car by singing bathroom songs, good, healthy blood runs over this sleeping scorpion, softening its armor, turning its thick, black shell to walnut, then rich, racehorse brown, then liver, and finally pink, slowly eroding and dissolving it, absorbing its minerals and proteins back into my body. I will stay vigilant, and I will prevail.

One hard truth I stumbled upon is this: *I drank because I wanted to drink*. Every single drink, every single drug I took, I took because I made the decision to get fucked up, and fuck the consequences. I was sad and angry and lonely, and a little alcohol made me feel better. It took me a long time to figure out that a lot of alcohol made me feel worse. Whoops.

I know that ultrarunning is not entirely the opposite of abusing drugs and alcohol. I used to run around all night, go to sleep at dawn, and sleep like the dead all day. Now I'm up at dawn, run around all day, and sleep like the dead all night. The girls I've dated since I've been sober haven't understood why I'm drawn to running long distances, just as, in the past, my girlfriends didn't understand my marathon benders. Now, as then, I spend a lot of time walking funny. And when you treat your body as a science experiment, whether with ultrarunning or ultradrinking, you spend a lot of time sleeping and a lot of time in pain.

But if I am addicted to exercise, it has been by far the dreariest, most painful, least thrilling addiction I have ever experienced. I never had to goad myself to take a drink or a pill; it was always a reward for good behavior. "Wow, you've been awake for six hours without getting fucked up! You deserve a treat. But best not to eat a whole Opana—we're getting low, and that shit is expensive. A quarter pill will do the job with the correct method of delivery—life is too short to swallow anything you can snort!"

No, having spent most of my life as an addict, I have a decent understanding of addiction, and I am not addicted to running. I *hate* running. It's never gotten easy for me. The last mile is not the hardest mile. The hardest mile is the *first* mile. What's harder than the first mile? Lacing up your goddamn running shoes before you even leave the house. Finally getting moving after a dry ocean of irritable procrastination is dispiriting—I'm sore or crampy or just tired, my legs feel wooden, my feet clumsily scuff the ground. I'm a big guy, and it takes me a long time to warm up, six or eight miles. After I get warmed up, it's okay, but only for a minute. Then I want to stop, I want to slow down, I want to walk, I want to take the shorter route, I want to turn around and grab a cab and go right home.

Running is hard. *It's supposed to be hard.* Running keeps you honest. There is no short way to run a mile; there is no easy way to run a marathon. You can't force it. If you are out of shape, you can't just go out and run twenty miles today and be back in shape—you'll injure yourself and wind up worse than you were before. If a bully is picking on you at school, it takes only instantaneous courage to throw a punch, take your lumps, and get him off your back. If you find yourself twenty pounds overweight in the spring, it takes will-power to lose weight. But if you're a sedentary person, in order to run a marathon, you must change everything. You must do what you don't want to do and give up what you *do* want to do. You must repeat that, over and over again, whether you fail or you succeed, for a very long time. You must tear down the faulty life you've built, the faulty person you've become, and rebuild everything from the ground up. It takes not just courage and planning and hard work but patience and determination and an ability to quietly suffer a lit-tle each day for a long time without giving up. It's worth it.

I don't run as frantically as I used to. I don't need to. I still bang out the occasional marathon on my own, but I don't feel a desire to compete against others. Nor do I feel compelled to run a faster marathon or run further than I have before. I don't desire to be su-perhuman. I never did. I wanted to become human. I have.

Running hasn't solved every problem in my life. It hasn't made me a perfect man. I feel like I felt after that first half marathon and that first ultramarathon and that first fifty-miler: I can't believe how far I've come, and I know I still have a long way to go.

⸻

When I was seventeen, I made the decision to believe in Heaven. Not the oppressive, puffy-overwhite-clouds-and-smug-angels-with-harps-annoying-you-to-fucking-death Heaven but a more cluttered, relaxed, God-free zone where you would just be reunited with everything and everyone you had ever lost. The childhood dog you loved, the grandfather who died when you were only six, your dead junkie friends, and your quiet neighbor who suddenly succumbed to lung cancer though he had never smoked a day in his life. Also the green corduroy hat you wore hitchhiking across country and left in a Burger King bathroom, and that 1969 Gibson Les Paul Goldtop you pawned for coke, and your old friend Charlie, the stuffed toy dog you had as a baby, which you managed to hang on to till you were thirty-two, though it was disgusting and gray and had been for years, thoroughly saturated as it was with your saliva from years of oral adoration as an infant, till you left it in the trunk of a Kia you rented on a trip to Cleveland that the Hertz desk clerk Shenikwa never found, though you called and called and called. In my Heaven, every single thing you have lost will be restored to you.

I've found some of that Heaven without having to die. Since I stopped drinking and started running in 2009, the things I had lost—the most meaningful things in my life—have flowed back to me almost effortlessly. My relationship with my mother has never been threatened, and Tashina and I have always stuck by each other in our loner, hardheaded way. But when Chuong and Helen drove out to California and I got to see him hug my mother, well, that was a singular happiness. My mother gave him back his Vietnamese-English dictionary, which she had held on to for him all these years. "I knew you'd be back," she said with a smile when she produced it and put it in his hands. He never finished eighth grade, but his stepdaughter is in medical school, and his son is in dental school. "Never do drugs, never go to jail. I did good, Mom?" he said to her. Yes, Chuong, you did good. We're planning a trip to Vietnam together so I can finally meet his mother.

Tatyana and I didn't speak for seven years after she kicked me out of her house, coincidentally the same amount of time I didn't speak to my father. Even before that, it hadn't been unusual for Tatyana and me to go a year without speaking.

Tatyana and her husband Bill welcomed me back into their lives unconditionally. I wanted to be forgiven, and they wanted to forgive me. But that wasn't enough. When their dream home came up for sale, they let me loan them money, money that was just lying around because, never having had it, I had no idea what to do with it. The "Redneck Ranch" is gorgeous. It's a sprawling five-bedroom house on over an acre, as was our old house in New Hampshire, but as perfect as that home was flawed. Tatyana and I get along better now than we ever have in our lives, even before the divorce. We talk or text almost every day and haven't argued once since our rapprochement. It's odd, in your mid-thirties, to find a best friend who knows you inside and out, a best friend you have known your entire life.

I spend as much time at the Redneck Ranch as I can. As unpopular as I was with my family, I am infinitely popular with Tatyana's four kids. Tatyana's dogs love me so well that, the last time I visited, they cried and tackled me the minute I got out of the truck. It was pitch-black, the middle of the night. But they knew my smell.

Karma, a chubby chocolate Lab, is happiest when she finds me sprawled out on my sister's couch, exhausted from a long run. Harley is content to lick every salty surface he can find. My legs, arms, shoulders, tummy. But Karma crawls on top of me—this is a sixty-pound dog—carefully spreads her entire body over me in order to immobilize me as completely as possible. Then she roughly polishes my face, in disgusting detail, with her tongue, trying to force it into my ear canals, up my sinuses, and through my clamped lips into my mouth. Yuck.

There's a curious blurring that goes on when I'm at my sister's house. Harley is a shaggy black mutt, adopted from the shelter. My old dog, Katie, was a black mutt from the shelter. Zeke, Tatyana's old dog, was a retriever; Karma is a retriever. Karma's eyes are amber, almost yellow, like our old dog Princess's eyes. Karma growls like a friendly Wookie when she's happy and wags her tail so hard her hind legs skitter across the floor. Zeke did the exact same things. The black fur on Harley's belly is riddled with white hairs, like Katie's. Karma sheds horribly, like Katie did, great tufts of brown hair drifting off of her every time you scratch her back.

One afternoon when Bill was at work and the kids were at school and Tatyana was running errands, Karma sat in front of me, her tail thumping the floor, laughter bouncing around in her eyes. Then she rolled onto her side and stretched out, waiting for me to pat her. I went down on one knee and obliged. Then both knees. Then I got on all fours, and instead of petting her, I just put my head into her fur and inhaled. She smelled exactly like Katie, my dear old dog, now long dead. I kept my face in her fur and kept breathing in her smell, that good, musty smell of a friendly old dog. I closed my eyes. It was Katie under my hands, under my nose. God, Katie, I have missed you so much. I kept my eyes closed.

This blurring happens with people too. When I'm there, no one is capable of calling my nephew Mika and me by our correct names. I gave my mother shit for it until the day I called Mika by my name. At school, Mika insists that people call him by his birth name, Mikhail. At school, I insisted people call me by my nickname instead of my birth name, Mikhail. We are both named after Michael, my grandfather, a man neither of us knew. When Mika was a baby, he couldn't say my name, so he called me Minna. When his younger brother Kai was a baby, he couldn't say Mika's name, so he called him Minna. The mother of my father, Murray, was named Minnie. The beloved dog of Bill's childhood was named Murray. The confusion really stacks up sometimes.

Once, when I was visiting for Mika's eleventh birthday party, it got to be too much. We were sitting at the dinner table, a simple pine table my dad built before we left Canada, the same table we had gathered around each night for dinner before my family flew apart. I sat in my spot, and the other kids sat in their spots. We were sitting in the same chairs we had always sat in, chairs that were always in need of new felt on the feet, chairs that had always been creaky from the kids leaning back. There was a black dog,

Harley, and a brown dog, Karma, just like there used to be a black dog, Katie, and a brown dog, Zeke. There was a mom there across from me, where my mom used to sit. There was a dad at the head of the table, sitting in the special chair, the only one that had arms, where my dad used to sit. We were eating, talking, horsing around, and laughing. The mom loved the dad, and the dad loved the mom, and the only thing the parents loved more than each other were the children. I felt so good, sitting there at the table with my family. I was supposed to drive to LA after dinner to catch a flight home. The thought of leaving made me so sad that I had to run upstairs and cry. Not a dignified cry either, like you're supposed to have when you're an adult and a tear just drips out of the outside corner of your eye, and that's it. An ugly cry where your face looks shitty, and the tears mix with snot, and you can't get any air into your lungs, and you feel again like a helpless infant. I wasn't ready to go. I never am.

———

In 2012 Simon's Rock invited me to speak at the twentieth anniversary of the shooting, a perfect 180 from trying to kick me out five days before graduation. For the first time, I finally reached out to Galen's father, Greg Gibson. I sent him the piece I intended to read at the memorial and expressed my hope that the anniversary would not bring him any new sadnesses. His response took my breath away:

> After Galen's murder, I thought we would always suffer the damage of this catastrophe, and that the kids, being young and strong, would grow past it. More and more now, I see I was wrong. We were old and tempered and already formed. We suffered, grieved, and got on with our lives. It was the kids, unformed, who were most profoundly affected by this terrible demonstration of the fact that we cannot control what happens in this world. So, in fact, this anniversary doesn't bring any new sadnesses to us. We've just got the old, familiar, almost comfort-

able ones. But I sense it is you, the young ones, for whom the new sadnesses must continually come.

The father of a murdered son, a man I had felt so sorry for that just thinking about his plight racked me with poisonous guilt and shame and anger and grief . . . well, he had been feeling sorry for *us*. How many miles will I have to run before I can equal him, in his integrity and strength and grace?

———

When I was sixteen, I swore to rescue my mother, get revenge on my father, and make some mark on the world. Wonder of wonders, I was able to make good on my arrogant, adolescent vows . . . just not in the manner I'd envisioned.

In June 2013, exactly twenty years after I swore through angry tears, at our final, sodden, tragic yard sale in the driveway of our house in New Hampshire, that I would restore my mother, I bought her a little house in California. I chose it because it was only eight miles away from Tatyana's house in Fallbrook, so my mom would be able to spoil the rotten kids rottener. It's technically located just over the line in the neighboring town of Rainbow— somewhere over the rainbow, if you will, fitting for the house I'd dreamed of for so long. It's a tiny, brick three-bedroom on half an acre, perched so high on a hillside that you often wake up in a cloud. Every penny of the money I put down on it came from writing. I resist naming cars and guitars because I understand now that things are just things, but I had to name the house: Sweet Revenge.

My dad drove the eight hours down from Sutter Creek with a load of tools in his Volvo to help with the renovations. We worked together in the blazing hot sun, ten days in a row, fourteen-hour days, like we had when he helped me build out the Brooklyn loft ten years earlier. We worked side by side for a while, then branched off to do separate jobs after a couple of days. He took the opportunity to listen to his iPod and was rocking out to Guns N' Roses while he hung sheetrock with his shirt off, occasionally stopping to wipe the sweat from his face and fist-pump or howl tunelessly along with the lyrics, the gray hair of a grandfather and the heart of a teenager.

Working in the kitchen, I found a newspaper clipping in a drawer: some 1950s housewife perched atop a column of brick-work. So what? I'd been working for twelve hours, still had hours to go, and there was no end in sight. I skimmed the article. The woman had spent three years building a house and was still only halfway done. Looking again, I realized it was the house I was standing in.

I read the whole article now, my heart thumping. The house I had bought for my mother was built by Carol Coast, a mother of three, just like my mother. Carol Coast was a sculptor who had been experimenting with the local clay. When she realized the soil was the right consistency for brick, she designed a house, then built it herself—pouring each of the bricks *by hand*, then laying them herself.

I walked through the gently curving hallway at the center of the house, running my hand over the bricks, Carol's bricks. How much work had she put into it? Hundreds of hours, at the very least. Thousands of hours?

The fireplace was her crowning achievement, with bricks of many sizes that she had tinted different colors, according to the ar-ticle. I'm more careful about swearing oaths now than I was when I was sixteen (as they can be a real pain in the ass to fulfill), but I swore that one day I would peel the decades' worth of paint off of Carol's fireplace and restore it to its original beauty.

It was perfect: the house had been designed and built for my mother by another mother, an artist, a nurturer, and one hell of a hard worker, a woman who had toiled patiently, year after year, building her life one brick at a time. Just like my mom.

My mom came by one afternoon after most of the renovations were done, and I gave her the tour. She had been in China teaching

English to preschoolers while I was in the process of buying it, so she had never seen it. We had never even really talked about it. She seemed happy, but then she always does.

"So . . . what do you think, you old bag of bones? You like it? Do you love me now?" I said to her after the grand tour.

"Oh, my darling boy, of course I love you! And I loved you just the same when you didn't have a penny to your name."

"But you like the house? You deserve a home of your own. And I will fight to my dying breath to ensure that no one ever takes this one away from you."

My mom put her arms around me and looked in my eyes. It's a much different gesture now than it used to be because I am over a foot taller than her. Since the day of the last yard sale, I had dreamed of this moment.

"Mishka, you are a sweet boy. But I'm just a young woman of sixty-six! I can't be tied down to a house now. I have lots of things I want to do before I get old. I want to travel! I'm not ready to settle down."

A friend of mine once asked me how you know what a woman is thinking. I replied, "Just *ask* her," and marveled silently at my own brilliance. I had never asked my mom if she *wanted* a house. In many ways, my life has unfolded like some ancient Chinese curse: may you be forced to understand the wisdom of the advice you have given. Yes, my mom was rescued, but not by me. It was very sad that dark day of the last yard sale when she collapsed in our driveway and I had to carry her into the house. But the very next day, she rescued herself, and she hasn't needed rescuing since. If anything, it was she who saved me over and over in my life, more times than I can count, almost every single day.

⸺

I got my revenge on my father. I froze him out of my life for long enough—seven years—that he cracked before I did and asked me if I would try again. I wasn't bluffing when I bid him a final farewell at twenty. Reaching out to him only to have him ignore me and let me down again and again was more painful than having no relationship with him at all. I didn't shut him out to hurt him. I was convinced that he didn't care at all, that I was just something he could cross off his job list. I alienated him to save myself from pain. But yes, I had been perversely delighted to hear how it had hurt him. I had sworn that I would hurt him, and I had succeeded . . . but winning that vendetta had damaged me a thousand times worse than it did him.

It's taken us many years to sort things out, but we've done a lot of work. It was devastating to hear that the cruel things I'd suspected for years were true, that he had never wanted to get married or have children and that, when he divorced our mother, he wanted to divorce all of us, that entire life. And it was an incredible relief to find out that what I'd felt to be true actually was true, that I hadn't just been crazy.

"It's weird, Dad," I said to him on his back porch one evening, "you not wanting to get married and not wanting to have children and not wanting to have a family . . . and I feel now not just that you're happy in your marriage to Theresa but that you're proud of us—"

"Oh, I am."

"And, you know, that you love us."

"Mishka, I did from the day that you were born. I remember building this cradle for Tatyana before she was born. Working frantically, last minute, to build a cradle that swung just right. I was there when she was born, and I remember thinking, Oh Jesus, she looks like hell, 'cause when babies are born, they don't look so great. And then I saw her later and got to hold her for the first time, and I was like, holy shit. That was it—I was in love with that kid. I would have done anything for her. And it was the exact same way with you."

It's funny, you know, I'm a big tough man, got the tattoos, can run all day, and I will fight anyone, even if I know I will lose (especially if I know I will lose). But hearing my old man tell me he loves me sure fucks me up.

It took me a while to believe him, but now I know it's true. He ignored my writing when I was younger, but now he can't wait to read every new piece. He bugs me to finish a story while I'm writing it, then bugs me to send it to him while I'm editing it. When I send it to him, he dives right in . . . and then takes a while to get through it because it's painful for him to read about the hard times I endured before my transformation.

The way I see it, parents have two responsibilities. They have to care for you until you reach reproductive age—you know, propagation of the species and all that. And parents have to ensure that their kids come out a little less fucked up than they did. Not a lot, just a little. My father did both of these things. He made mistakes, but he loved us, in his way, and I've spent most of my life vilifying him.

My father never terrified me, never oppressed me, never brutalized me, never tortured me, never degraded me. All the shit he endured—ostracism, teasing, alienation, his mother picking BBs out of his ass with a butcher knife, for God's sake—it stopped with him. He took it, and he absorbed it, and he *never* made us feel it. He is a relic from the age of corporal punishment, and as a kid he saw a lot. A friend's father broke a two-by-four over his kid's back. At school, you were disciplined by having your knuckles rapped. Not with a ruler, with a yardstick, and the teacher buried that thing deep in the sensitive flesh of the fingers, breaking the skin on each one. "Getting your ass kicked" didn't mean losing your soccer game. If you showed up late for dinner, your father told you to turn around and touch your toes, and then he kicked you in the ass as hard as he could, lifting you off your feet, sending you sprawling. None of that came down to us kids. My father never hit me. He never lifted a hand as if he were going to hit me. He never even verbally threatened to hit me. Not once. For all the drinking and drugging his parents did, I have never once seen my father drunk.

The childhood that made him who he is was a barbaric one. He went to great lengths to make sure that none of us got even a taste of what he endured.

My father made some really big, shitty, painful mistakes. So have I. I know what it's like to realize suddenly in the middle of your life that, out of weakness, you have gone down the wrong path. I built my adult personality around the foreclosure and The Letter, proof of my father's infidelity. I'm struck now by how comparatively generous the bank in New Hampshire was, and I'm touched by my father's hopeless but sincere gesture of trying to write love letters to the wife he knew he had to leave. I protested aloud for fifteen years that I didn't need him, that I hated him, that my father was irrelevant. I only proved that I need him, that I love him, and that my father is incredibly important to me. Even in my early sobriety, when I told myself there were no angels, I was surrounded by them. I have treated women brutally, and more often than not, my angels were women: Allison; Izgi; Tracy Helsing, who did more to make me quit drinking than anyone who told me to quit drinking; Sofia, the doctor who kept me running; Eva, the physical therapist who got me running again; Zsuzsanna, who taught me everything she could about running; my sisters; my mother.

I told my father once that if I had a friend who acted like him, I would no longer have that person as a friend. But you have more than one friend, and if you lose a friend, you can make another. You only have one father. Mine was gone for most of my childhood and all of my early adulthood. Keeping him away, now and forever, would not remedy that hurt.

I have forgiven my father, and I'm trying to forgive myself. It's tricky. You can't just forgive someone once and then it's done. You have to keep forgiving them; you have to *keep them forgiven* from that day forward. I forget sometimes, but, as I've taught myself, you have to try every day.

I guess I made my mark on the world. Thousands of people have read my writing about how I have screwed up and screwed up and screwed up and somehow made it out alive. More than alive— I have flourished, not despite but *because of* my mistakes. I am a one-man mistake industry. And despite my protestations, the story of my life has one word applied to it, over and over again: "inspirational." That I have become not just a success but a sober *inspirational* success strikes me as the greatest irony of my life. But I'll take it.

One good morning, I drag myself out of bed at 7:30 a.m. It's late in my father's house, and I have been waking slowly to the sounds of my father and his wife talking and laughing together for a while, the cat yowling, their coffee cups scraping on their saucers. I stumble to the bathroom, then out into the living room in my PJs.

"He lives!" my dad says, big grin on his face, same tired joke he's been making since I was a little kid.

Theresa smiles at me from her overstuffed chair, cappuccino in hand, sheepskin slippers on her feet, her ancient Himalayan cat Rosie Belle scowling up at me from her lap. Even I can't begrudge Theresa her sweet spot right next to the wood stove—even on her days off, Theresa works longer and harder than my dad and I put together. She is both Catholic and Republican; yet somehow we've never argued. She's only ever treated me with kindness, kindness I can't fathom.

"You must be sore today," she says. "How are your legs?"

Each month, my father's gym has a stationary bike race: people post their times for completing a computerized "course" to compete for a prize. Each time I visit, I go to the gym with my father and destroy the competition, winning not just my age group but the entire thing, not by seconds but by minutes. And my dad fucking *loves* it. I don't think he called me when I graduated from Simon's Rock, and

I know he didn't call me when I graduated from CU. We weren't even speaking when I got my master's. He never remembers to call me on Christmas, and only sometimes grudgingly calls me on my birthday. But I win a dumb exercise bike race at an old people's gym in a tiny town, and he gets *pumped*: "Hello, can we get someone over here to verify his time? My son has done it again!"

Yesterday, I gutted the thirty-five to fifty-five category by a four minute margin and beat the best time overall by fifty-four seconds. It's a small victory—last year's prize was a pair of wool socks—but I'm not above small victories these days.

In answer to Theresa's question, I bust out five fast, deep squats, to hoots and guffaws from both Theresa and my dad. Even I'm surprised by how I feel. My legs don't feel okay or even good; they feel great, fresh, hungry for more.

We don't go to the gym this morning but linger over oatmeal with raisins and sunflower seeds and a second cup of coffee. It's not enough food, and I'm not satisfied, but then I'm never satisfied. I am the Unsatisfiable Hunger, the Unquenchable Thirst, and I'm pretty well used to it by now.

On the way out to the car, I snag a couple of fresh persimmons from Theresa's tree in the front yard. They look like orange tomatoes, and this early in the season, they're harder than unripe pears. Still, they taste so amazing—like honey and melon and citrus—that it's as if they are made-up, some ancient fruit from before sin.

It was a mistake for my father to marry my mother. The first time he told me that, I hated him for saying it, instantly and for years afterward. I mean, I hated him already, but I hated him with new, specific venom for saying that: "I never should have married your mother." It took me until now—twenty years since he divorced her—to figure out what he meant. He wasn't saying that no one should have married my mother, that she was a vile witch no man could tolerate, that she was an unmarriageable monstrosity who should have been bricked into a high tower with no staircase or buried alive in a tomb so that no man should ever gaze upon her. He was saying that *he* shouldn't have married *her*. Which is probably right. And also, *she* shouldn't have married *him*.

It was a mistake. A big mistake. Out of which came me. And Tatyana. And Tashina—at least the Tashina I know. That epic mistake of my mother and father marrying the exact wrong person created that person I love more than almost anyone on earth, my sister Tashina, as much as it created Tatyana and me. And then Mika. And Brianna. And Koko. And Kai. That's seven people, created by mistake. Seven people *so far*.

If you think about it, my parents *really* blew it. They made their mistake, and the consequences keep getting bigger and broader and deeper, long past the point of no return. Thank God for that. Thank fucking God in Heaven, driving a long, shimmering, silver-white stretch limo with a moon roof and plasma TVs and a hot tub in back full of fat, frolicking, naked little cherubs that my foolish parents fucked up so badly, wed the exact wrong person in error, and then compounded that mistake by making me. I am finally grateful to be here.

We drive out of Sutter Creek, past a strip mall and several big-box stores, past homes that get smaller and further apart, to a tiny airfield with a miniature runway. There is a long open shed there with stalls, like a flea market or a firing range, and a turquoise port-o-potty. We park, and my dad gets out and greets the other old guys there: Leon, in a round, wide-brimmed straw hat, and Ron, in a baseball hat and a silver ponytail. He introduces me.

"You're the writer from New York," Leon says, pumping my hand, "and running all those crazy long marathons! Congratulations on all your success. What a good son you are to come out and visit your dad."

I glance over at my dad to see if he's put Leon up to this, but he's just taking it all in.

"Murray," Ron calls out my dad's name after a quick hand-shake, "you know lots of stuff . . ."

My dad and I both laugh, recognizing a setup if there ever was one. Ron starts quizzing my dad on the minutia of some remote-controlled model-airplane quandary.

My dad knows lots of stuff, lots and lots of stuff. He is an electrical engineer, he's a nuclear physicist, he's a fucking *rocket scientist*, for God's sake. The program he was part of was actually called Star Wars—yes, like the movie—and they sent shit up into outer space and then blew it up with motherfucking *laser beams*. My dad builds superconductors and semiconductors and particle accelerators and duopigatron ion sources. What a duopigatron is, I don't know. But my dad does. My dad is a fucking awesome dude.

He doesn't just *know* stuff; he can fix stuff, and he can build stuff. He can pound a nail all the way in with one stroke of the hammer. He can hang a door in your house *just so*—it'll swing shut on its own if that's what you want, or it'll swing open on its own if that's what you want, or it'll just stay put if that's what you want. He's one of the old breed. My old man is like leather! My old man is like steel! No, he's not like leather or steel because leather dries out and cracks and steel rusts. My dad . . . my dad is like an old, liquor-soaked Christmas fruitcake: he never goes bad; he just gets older and drier and harder and heavier and more potent. My dad will outlive me, he will outlive you, he will outlive all of us.

Like the computer he introduced me to as a small kid, my dad can answer almost any question. And also like that computer, my dad does not know how he works. My father's son is the same way. So be it. He's more good than bad. He knows lots of stuff. Not everything, but then nobody gets to know all the stuff.

Leon launches and then pilots a remote controlled glider, making big lazy loops in the sky with it before landing it roughly on the tarmac to skid on its belly and then bump in the grass. Ron takes his turn, piloting a miniature electric Styrofoam biplane buzzing like a hornet in the sky.

As I sit in the sun, drinking my coffee, it occurs to me that this is the first time I've come out to fly model airplanes with my dad. He's been doing this my entire life, longer than I've been alive. He's been designing and flying his own airplanes since he was sixteen, and this is the first time I've ventured onto his turf, the first time I've engaged with him about this weird hobby that is somehow incredibly important to him. What else don't I know about him? What else haven't we shared?

Behind me, my father has assembled an egregiously large model airplane—at least five feet long, gleaming teal and red and silver. No way can that thing actually fly. And if it can, well, no way it can do much. It's so big and unwieldy, like a tuna with wings. I look at my dad: What is he thinking? He's wearing the gray hoodie that he wears all the time now, a habit I think he picked up after borrowing one of mine. Jesus, we have come a long way. Does that mean we're nearing the end? We've lost so much time. Quick, Dad, don't let the sun go down on you, on us. I still have so much to learn.

Now he's wearing a wide-brimmed straw hat. And he's strapped on one kneepad. Really, Dad? Only one? I try to stanch the feeling, but it's too quick for me: I pity him. It's a loathsome thing, to feel pity for your parents. This will end in his defeat, in our defeat.

He gently places his monstrosity on the ground, secures its tail, then starts the prop. It's loud as hell, like a two-stroke street bike, a little frightening. The silver fiberglass propeller whirls, and I wonder what it would do to my legs if I walked into it. Then he frees the tail and navigates the plane carefully with the remote control along a little concrete strip to the runway.

"Murray, taking off here, left to right," he calls out, but he doesn't need to. It's impossible not to watch the winged chainsaw in front of us. Then he guns the throttle.

The plane hurtles along the runway for a second, gaining speed, then unexpectedly flings itself into the air and rockets straight up. Up, up, up, and it rolls over, once, twice, three times, then climbs further into the sky, four hundred feet, five hundred feet, then slows and slows, till it stops dead in a stall. Fuck. *Dad*.

The plane falls neatly to its left, hurtles groundward, then noses up and careens toward the far end of the runway. A gorgeous, sexy, swooping turn, then back over the tarmac, rolling, climbing, falling, Jesus, flying *upside down*. I smile, gasp, laugh, and keep laughing, amazement bubbling out of me uncontrollably.

Only once do I glance over at my father. He is gone. Utterly still, his face turned to the sky, motionless save for the small twitching movements of his hands on the controls as if he were immersed in a particularly engaging dream. I turn away. My dad's not there. The body next to me, with its chromium knees, the missing prostate, the divots out of the red, veiny nose where the skin cancer has been removed, the improperly mended clavicle from going over the handlebars on his motorcycle, the gray hair, the age spots: it's only a shell. His soul is elsewhere.

This isn't some kitschy old man's hobby. This is astral projection. This is fucking *magic*, dude. My father is up there in the untroubled blue, gleaming in the sunlight, banking, accelerating, pitching, stalling, arcing, then roaring back to life, blazing across the sky.

Dad executes a perfect landing, his plane hitting the tarmac squarely, braking neatly, looping slightly right for a sharp left turn to return to us for refueling. I'm careful to stand behind a metal gate, but that's for my dad's benefit, not mine. If I stood directly in the plane's path, my father could skillfully pilot it around me. And if he wanted me to stand in the middle of the tarmac so he could fly it right into me at full speed, well, I would let him.

He shuts down the motor and looks at me, waiting for my reaction.

"Dad! That was fucking awesome! I had no idea. Those aerials, man . . ."

He chuckles.

"Funnily enough, the hardest thing is flying straight and level. You know, just not making any mistakes."

"No shit, Dad."

He nods his head. Then he looks at me, and he smiles.

Acknowledgments

Thanks to my parents, Elaine Lalonde and Murray Shubaly; my sisters, Tatyana Beath and Tashina Lalonde; my brother-in-law Bill Beath, my stepbrother Jesse Fuchs, my foster brother Chuong Dinh, my not-my-real-Mom-so-she-can't-yell-at-me Theresa Shubaly. Thanks to Byrd Leavell, Ben Adams at PublicAffairs, and David Blum. Thanks to Lawrence Weschler, Lucia Berlin, Sidney Goldfarb, and Alan Ziegler. Thank you, Zachary Lipez. Thank you, Bill Whitten. Thank you, Aaron Lazar. Thanks to James Sparber, Damien Paris, Tim Murray, Karl Myers, Jonathan Rauberts, Erik Nickerson, Michael Dean Damron, Alex Steininger, Charles Kennedy. Thanks to Cynthia Ellis, Caitlin Flanagan, Ellen Twaddell, Tim Kreider, Sarah Bradley, Emily Mah Tippetts, Chris Parris-Lamb, Hilary Jordan, Molly Gaudry, and Jeff Bezos. Thanks to Paul Fuchs, Joe Purdy, JT Habersaat, Rasha Proctor, Greg Chaille, Brian Hennigan, Ben Lebovitz, Ryan McKee, Jennifer Bryant, Tina Lipsky, Natalie Rogers, Bob Bodkin, Mike Doughty, Chris Thomson, John Prine, Cáit O'Riordan, and Mark Lanegan for inspiration. Thanks to Peter and Ginger Sparber, GeGe Kingston, Tim and Charlotte Kent, Jennifer George, Jed Collins and Marseille Markham, Eben Burr, Jessica Roach, Ben Bertocci, Mariko

Suzuki-Bertocci, Kelly Lum, Scott Winland, Chris Sturiano, Ann Beeder, Jenifer Hixson, everyone at The Moth, everyone at Amazon, and everyone I've forgotten.

Music, T-shirts, posters, and tour dates at www.mishkashubaly.com.

Download a free song here:

Mishka Shubaly began drinking at thirteen and college at fifteen. At twenty-two, he received the Dean's Fellowship from the Master's Writing Program at Columbia University. Upon receiving his expensive MFA, he promptly moved into a Toyota minivan to tour the country nonstop as a singer-songwriter. At thirty-two, he got sober and shortly thereafter began publishing a string of best-selling Kindle Singles through Amazon. His third solo album, *Coward's Path*, was released in 2015 by Invisible Hands Music.

Photograph courtesy of Leslie Hassler

PublicAffairs is a publishing house founded in 1997. It is a tribute to the standards, values, and flair of three persons who have served as mentors to countless reporters, writers, editors, and book people of all kinds, including me.

I. F. STONE, proprietor of *I. F. Stone's Weekly*, combined a commitment to the First Amendment with entrepreneurial zeal and reporting skill and became one of the great independent journalists in American history. At the age of eighty, Izzy published *The Trial of Socrates*, which was a national bestseller. He wrote the book after he taught himself ancient Greek.

BENJAMIN C. BRADLEE was for nearly thirty years the charismatic editorial leader of *The Washington Post*. It was Ben who gave the *Post* the range and courage to pursue such historic issues as Watergate. He supported his reporters with a tenacity that made them fearless and it is no accident that so many became authors of influential, best-selling books.

ROBERT L. BERNSTEIN, the chief executive of Random House for more than a quarter century, guided one of the nation's premier publishing houses. Bob was personally responsible for many books of political dissent and argument that challenged tyranny around the globe. He is also the founder and longtime chair of Human Rights Watch, one of the most respected human rights organizations in the world.

. . .

For fifty years, the banner of Public Affairs Press was carried by its owner Morris B. Schnapper, who published Gandhi, Nasser, Toynbee, Truman, and about 1,500 other authors. In 1983, Schnapper was described by *The Washington Post* as "a redoubtable gadfly." His legacy will endure in the books to come.

Peter Osnos, *Founder and Editor-at-Large*